Sleight of Mouth

The Magic of Conversational Belief Change

by

Robert B. Dilts

Dilts Strategy Group

Dilts Strategy Group
P.O. Box 67448
Scotts Valley, California 95067
Phone: +1 (831) 438-8314
E-Mail: info@diltsstrategygroup.com
Homepage: http://www.diltsstrategygroup.com

© Copyright 1999 by Robert Dilts and Dilts Strategy Group. Printed in the United States of America. All rights reserved. This book or parts thereof may not be reproduced in any form without written permission of the Publisher.

Library of Congress Card Number 99-07-44 02
I.S.B.N. 978-947629-02-8

Contents

Dedication	vii
Acknowledgments	viii
Preface	ix

CHAPTER 1 LANGUAGE AND EXPERIENCE — 1

The Magic of Language	2
Language and Neuro-Linguistic Programming	8
Map and Territory	11
Experience	14
How Language Frames Experience	18
The 'Even Though' Reframe	20

CHAPTER 2 FRAMES AND REFRAMING — 21

Frames	22
Shifting Outcomes	26
Reframing	31
Changing Frame Size	35
Context Reframing	39
Content Reframing	41
Reframing Critics and Criticism	44
The Sleight of Mouth Patterns of 'Intention' and 'Redefining'	49
One Word Reframing Exercise	53
Perceiving a Situation from a Different Model of the World by Taking 'Second Position'	56

CHAPTER 3 CHUNKING — 59

Forms of Chunking	60
Chunking Down	63
Chunking Up	66
Chunking Laterally (Finding Analogies)	68
Exercise: Finding Isomorphisms	71
Punctuation and Repunctuation	73

CHAPTER 4 VALUES AND CRITERIA	**77**
The Structure of Meaning	78
Values and Motivation	81
Criteria and Judgment	83
Chaining Values and Criteria by Redefining Them	85
Chunking Down to Define "Criterial Equivalences"	87
Reality Strategies	89
Reality Strategy Exercise	93
Chunking Up to Identify and Utilize Hierarchies of Values and Criteria	98
Hierarchy of Criteria Technique	104
CHAPTER 5 BELIEFS AND EXPECTATIONS	**109**
Beliefs and Belief Systems	110
The Power of Beliefs	113
Limiting Beliefs	116
Transforming Limiting Beliefs	117
Expectations	120
Expectations and the Sleight of Mouth Pattern of Consequences	127
Mapping Key Beliefs and Expectations	131
Assessing Motivation for Change	134
Belief Assessment Sheet	136
Using the 'As If' Frame to Strengthen Beliefs and Expectations	138
'As If' Exercise	140
CHAPTER 6 THE BASIC STRUCTURE OF BELIEFS	**141**
The Linguistic Structure of Beliefs	142
Complex Equivalence	143
Cause-Effect	145
Types of Causes	148
The Influence of Formal Causes	150

iv

Sleight of Mouth and the Structure of Beliefs	154
Values Audit	158
The Values Audit Worksheet	163
Belief Audit	164
Using Counter Examples to Reevaluate Limiting Beliefs	167
Some Verbal Frames for Eliciting Limiting Beliefs Statements	170
Generating Counter Examples	172

CHAPTER 7 INTERNAL STATES AND NATURAL BELIEF CHANGE — 175

The Natural Process of Belief Change	176
The Belief Change Cycle	178
Belief Change and Internal States	184
Recognizing and Influencing Internal States	186
Exercise: Accessing and Anchoring a State	189
Mentoring and Inner Mentors	190
The Belief Cycle Procedure	192
Implementing The Belief Cycle Procedure	195
Belief Chaining	197
The Influence of Non Verbal Communication	202

CHAPTER 8 THOUGHT VIRUSES AND THE META STRUCTURE OF BELIEFS — 205

The Meta Structure of Beliefs	206
Thought Viruses	210
Presuppositions	221
Self Reference	228
The Theory of Logical Types	232
Applying a Belief or Generalization to Itself	234
Meta Frames	240
Logical Levels	243
Changing Logical Levels	250

v

CHAPTER 9 APPLYING THE PATTERNS AS A SYSTEM   253

   Definition and Examples of Sleight of Mouth
      Patterns   254
   The Sleight of Mouth Patterns as a
      System of Interventions   269
   Using Sleight of Mouth as a System of
      Patterns   270
   Creating and Maintaining a 'Thought Virus'
      Using Sleight of Mouth   288
   Sleight of Mouth and the Law of
      Requisite Variety   297
   Reframing and 'Outframing' a Thought Virus
      Using Sleight of Mouth   300
   Practicing Sleight of Mouth   308

CHAPTER 10 CONCLUSION   **315**

AFTERWORD   319
BIBLIOGRAPHY   321
INDEX   325

Dedication

This book is dedicated with affection and respect to:

Richard Bandler
John Grinder
Milton Erickson
and
Gregory Bateson

who taught me the magic of language
and the language of 'magic'.

Acknowledgments

I would like to acknowledge:

Judith DeLozier, Todd Epstein, David Gordon, and Leslie Cameron-Bandler for their input and support at the time I was first evolving the ideas at the basis of Sleight of Mouth.

My children, Andrew and Julia, whose experiences and explanations helped me to understand the natural process of belief change and the 'meta structure' of beliefs.

Ami Sattinger, who (as she has for so many other of my books and projects) helped with the proof reading and editing of this book.

John Wundes who transformed some of the deeper structures underlying Sleight of Mouth into images, so that they could be seen more clearly. John created both the innovative cover picture and the wonderful drawings at the beginning of each chapter.

Preface

This is a book that I have been preparing to write for many years. It is a book about the magic of language, based on the principles and distinctions of Neuro-Linguistic Programming (NLP). I first came in contact with NLP nearly twenty-five years ago while attending a class on linguistics at the University of California at Santa Cruz. The class was being taught by NLP co-founder John Grinder. He and Richard Bandler had just finished the first volume of their groundbreaking work *The Structure of Magic* (1975). In this work, the two men modeled the language patterns and intuitive abilities of three of the world's most effective psychotherapists (Fritz Perls, Virginia Satir and Milton Erickson). This set of patterns (known as the *Meta Model*) allowed a person such as myself, a third year political science major, who had no personal experience with therapy of any type, to ask questions that an experienced therapist might ask.

I was struck by the possibilities of both the Meta Model and the process of modeling. It seemed to me that modeling had important implications in all areas of human endeavor: politics, the arts, management, science, teaching, and so on (see *Modeling With NLP*, Dilts, 1998). It struck me that the methodology of modeling could lead to broad innovations in many other fields involving human communication, reaching far beyond psychotherapy. As a student of political philosophy, my first "modeling project" was to apply the linguistic filters that Grinder and Bandler had used in their analysis of psychotherapists to see what patterns might emerge from studying the Socratic dialogs of Plato (*Plato's Use of the Dialectic in The Republic: A Linguistic Analysis*, 1975; in *Applications of NLP*, Dilts, 1983).

While this study was both fascinating and revealing, I felt that there was more to Socrates' persuasive abilities than the distinctions provided by the Meta Model could explain. The same was true for other verbal distinctions provided by NLP, such as representational system predicates (descriptive words indicating a particular sensory modality: "see", "look," "hear," "sound," "feel," "touch," etc.). These distinctions provided insight, but did not capture all of the dimensions of Socrates' powers to persuade.

As I continued to study the writings and speeches of people who had shaped and influenced the course of human history—people such as Jesus of Nazareth, Karl Marx, Abraham Lincoln, Albert Einstein, Mohandes Gandhi, Martin Luther King, and others—I became convinced that these individuals were using some common, fundamental set of patterns in order to influence the beliefs of those around them. Furthermore, the patterns encoded in their words were still influencing and shaping history, even though these individuals had been dead for many years. *Sleight of Mouth* patterns are my attempt to encode some of the key linguistic mechanisms that these individuals used to effectively persuade others and to influence social beliefs and belief systems.

It was an experience with NLP co-founder Richard Bandler that lead me to consciously recognize and formalize these patterns in 1980. In order to make a teaching point during a seminar, Bandler, who is renowned for his command of language, established a humorous but "paranoid" belief system, and challenged the group to persuade him to change it (see Chapter 9). Despite their best efforts, the group members were unable to make the slightest progress in influencing the seemingly impenetrable belief system Bandler had established (a system based upon what I was later to label "thought viruses").

It was in listening to the various verbal "reframings" that Bandler created spontaneously that I was able to recognize some of the structures he was using. Even though Bandler was applying these patterns "negatively" to make his point, I realized that these were the same structures used by people like Lincoln, Gandhi, Jesus, and others, to promote positive and powerful social change.

In essence, these 'Sleight of Mouth' patterns are made up of verbal categories and distinctions by which key beliefs can be established, shifted or transformed through language. They can be characterized as "verbal reframes" which influence beliefs, and the mental maps from which beliefs have been formed. In the nearly twenty years since their formalization, the Sleight of Mouth patterns have proved to be one of the most powerful sets of distinctions provided by NLP for effective persuasion. Perhaps more than any other distinctions in NLP, these patterns provide a tool for conversational belief change.

There are challenges in teaching these patterns effectively, however, because they are about words, and words are fundamentally abstract. As NLP acknowledges, words are *surface structures* which attempt to represent or express *deeper structures*. In order to truly understand and creatively apply a particular language pattern, we must internalize its 'deeper structure'. Otherwise, we are simply mimicking or "parroting" the examples we have been given. Thus, in learning and practicing Sleight of Mouth, it is important to distinguish genuine *magic* from trivial 'tricks'. The magic of change comes from tapping into something that goes beyond the words themselves.

Until now, the Sleight of Mouth patterns have typically been taught by presenting learners with definitions and a number of verbal examples illustrating the various linguistic structures. Learners are left to intuitively figure out the deeper structure necessary to generate the patterns on their own. While, in some ways, this mirrors the way that we learned our own native language as children, it can also present certain limitations.

For instance, people (especially non-native speakers of English) have experienced the Sleight of Mouth patterns as powerful and useful, but at times they can be somewhat complex and confusing. Even Practitioners of NLP (including those with many years of experience) are not always clear about how these patterns fit together with other NLP distinctions.

Furthermore, the patterns are often presented and used in an adversarial framework; as a tool primarily for argument or debate. This has given them the reputation of being potentially bombastic.

Some of these difficulties simply reflect the historical development of these patterns. I identified and formalized these patterns before I had the opportunity to fully explore the deeper structure of beliefs and belief change, and their relationship to other levels of learning and change. In the time since I first identified the Sleight of Mouth patterns, I have developed a number of belief change techniques, such as Reimprinting, the Failure into Feedback Pattern, the Belief Installation process, the Meta Mirror and Integrating Conflicting Beliefs - See *Changing Belief Systems with NLP* (Dilts, 1990) and *Beliefs: Pathways to Health and Well-Being* (Dilts, Hallbom & Smith, 1990). It has only been in the last several years that I have gained enough insight and understanding about how beliefs are formed and held cognitively and neurologically that I feel able to make the deeper structures underlying Sleight of Mouth sufficiently clear and concise.

The goal of this first volume is to present some of these insights and understandings in order to provide the foundations for using Sleight of Mouth patterns. My purpose in this book is to present the underlying principles and 'deeper structures' upon which the patterns are based. In addition to definitions and examples, I want to provide simple structures by which you can practice and apply each pattern, illustrating how they fit in with other NLP presuppositions, principles, techniques and distinctions.

I have also planned a second volume, subtitled *The Language of Leadership and Social Change*, which will explore and illustrate how these patterns were used by individuals such as Socrates, Jesus, Marx, Lincoln, Gandhi, and others, to establish, influence and transform key beliefs at the foundation of our modern world.

Sleight of Mouth is a fascinating subject. The power and the value of knowing about Sleight of Mouth is that it can help you to say the right words at the right time – without the need for formal techniques or special contexts (such as those typically related to therapy or debate). I hope that you enjoy this journey into the magic of language and conversational belief change.

Robert Dilts
Santa Cruz, California
May, 1999

Chapter 1

Language and Experience

The Magic of Language

Sleight of Mouth has to do with the magic of words and language. Language is one of the key components from which we build our mental models of the world, and can have a tremendous influence on how we perceive and respond to reality. Verbal language is a characteristic that is unique to the human race, and is considered to be one of the major factors that distinguishes humans from other creatures. The great psychiatrist Sigmund Freud, for example, believed that words were the basic instrument of human consciousness and, as such, had special powers. As he put it:

> *Words and magic were in the beginning one and the same thing, and even today words retain much of their magical power. By words one of us can give another the greatest happiness or bring about utter despair; by words the teacher imparts his knowledge to the student; by words the orator sweeps his audience with him and determines its judgments and decisions. Words call forth emotions and are universally the means by which we influence our fellow-creatures.*

Sleight of Mouth patterns come from the study of how language has been, and can be, used to impact people's lives. Consider, for instance, the following examples:

A police officer receives an urgent summons to a local residence to handle a reported incident of domestic violence. The police officer is on alert, because she knows that it is in these types of situations that she is actually in the most physical danger. People, especially violent, angry people, don't want the police interfering in their family affairs. As she approaches the apartment, the police officer hears shouting and screaming coming from inside. A man is yelling loudly, and the officer hears the sound of various objects being broken along with the terrified screams of a woman. Suddenly, a television set comes crashing through the front window, smashing into pieces on the ground in front of her. The police officer rushes to the door and begins to pound on it as hard as she can. She hears an enraged male voice from inside the apartment shouting, "Who in the hell is that!" Eying the pieces of the mangled television set spread over the ground, the police officer blurts out, "Television repairman." There is a moment of dead silence inside the apartment. Finally, the man breaks out in laughter. He opens the door and the police officer is able to make her intervention, avoiding any further violence or physical confrontation. She later reports that those two words were as useful as months of training in hand-to-hand combat.

A young man is hospitalized in the psychiatric ward of a mental facility, suffering from the delusion that he is 'Jesus Christ'. He spends his days unproductively, wandering the ward and preaching to other patients who pay no attention. The psychiatrists and aides have had no success whatsoever in their attempts to persuade the young man to give up his delusion. One day, a new psychiatrist arrives. After observing the patient quietly for some time, he approaches the young man. "I understand that you have experience as a carpenter," he says. "Well . . . yes, I guess I do," replies the patient. The psychiatrist explains to the patient that they are building a new recreation room at the facility and need the help of someone who has the skills of a carpenter. "We could sure use your assistance," says the psychiatrist, "That is, if you are the type of person that likes to help others." Unable to disagree, the patient decides to lend a hand. He becomes drawn into the project, establishing new friendships with other patients and workers who are participating in the construction. The young man begins to develop normal social relations and is eventually able to leave the hospital and find a stable job.

A patient awakens from surgery in the recovery room of the hospital. She is visited by the surgeon, who is to inform her of the results of the operation. Still groggy from the anesthetic, and somewhat anxious, the patient asks the surgeon how the operation went. The surgeon replies, "I'm afraid I have some bad news. The tumor we removed was cancerous." Facing her worst fears, the patient asks, "What now?" The surgeon answers, "Well, the good news is that we've removed the tumor as completely as we can . . . The rest is up to you." Spurred by the surgeon's comment, "The rest is up to you," the patient begins a re-evaluation of her life style, and the alternatives that are available to her. She makes changes in her diet and establishes consistent patterns of exercise. Reflecting on how stressful and unrewarding her life has been in the past few years before the surgery, the patient embarks on a path of personal growth, clarifying her beliefs, values and life's purpose. The patient's life takes a dramatic turn for the better, and, years later, she is happy, free of cancer and healthier than she has ever been before.

A young man has been at a dinner party, and consumed several glasses of wine. Driving home in the icy winter weather, he rounds a curve. Suddenly, in front of him he sees a person crossing the street. The young man slams on his breaks, but the car skids, hitting the pedestrian and killing him. For many weeks the young man is in inner turmoil, paralyzed by his distress. He knows that he has ruined one life, and irreparably damaged the family of the man he has killed. He feels the accident has been entirely his fault. If only he had not had as much to drink, he would have seen the person earlier and responded more quickly and appropriately. Becoming more and more deeply depressed, the young man considers taking his own life. At this time, he is visited by his uncle. Seeing the desperation of his nephew, the uncle sits next to him in silence for a few minutes. Then, placing his hands on the young man's shoulder the uncle says simply and honestly, "We walk in danger wherever we walk." The young man feels as if some light has suddenly come into his life. He changes his life path completely, studying psychology and becoming a grief counselor for the victims of drunken drivers, as well as a therapist for alcoholics and people who have been arrested for driving under the influence of alcohol. He becomes a positive force for healing and change in many people's lives.

A young woman is preparing to go to college. She has looked around at many options, and would most like to apply to a business school at one of the most prestigious universities in her area. She feels, however, that there are so many people attempting to get into that program that she doesn't stand a chance of being accepted. In order to be "realistic" and avoid disappointment, she plans only to apply to some of the more average schools. As she fills in her applications, she mentions her reasoning to her mother, explaining, "I am sure that the big university will be flooded with applications." Her mother replies, "There is always room for someone who's good." The simple truth of her mother's statement inspires the young woman to send in her application to the prestigious university. To her surprise and delight she is accepted, and goes on to become an extremely successful business consultant.

A young boy is struggling to learn to play baseball. He wants to be on a team with his friends, but is unable to throw or catch well, and is frightened by the ball. As the team practices continue, he becomes increasingly discouraged. He tells his coach that he plans to quit because he is a "bad ballplayer." The coach replies, "There are no bad ballplayers, there are only people who are not confident in their ability to learn." The coach stands facing the boy and puts the ball in the youth's glove, and has the boy take it out and hand it back to him. He then takes one step back and gently tosses the ball into the boy's glove, and has the boy toss it back. Step by step, the coach moves a little farther away, until the boy is throwing and catching the ball at a distance with ease. With a sense of confidence that he can learn, the boy returns to practice, and eventually becomes a valuable player on his team.

Each of these examples shares a common feature: a few words change the course of someone's life for the better, by shifting a limiting belief to a more enriched perspective that offers more choices. They are illustrations of how the right words at the right time can create powerful and positive effects.

Unfortunately, words can also confuse us and limit us as easily as they can empower us. The wrong words at the wrong time can be hurtful and damaging.

This book is about the power of words to be either helpful or harmful, the distinctions that determine the type of impact words will have, and the language patterns through which we can transform harmful statements into helpful ones.

The term "Sleight of Mouth" is drawn from the notion of "Sleight of Hand." The term *sleight* comes from an Old Norse word meaning "crafty," "cunning," "artful" or "dexterous." *Sleight of hand* is a type of magic done by close-up card magicians. This form of magic is characterized by the experience, "now you see it, now you don't." A person may place an ace of spades at the top of the deck, for example, but, when the magician picks up the card, it has "transformed" into a queen of hearts. The verbal patterns of Sleight of Mouth have a similar sort of "magical" quality because they can often create dramatic shifts in perception and the assumptions upon which particular perceptions are based.

Language and Neuro-Linguistic Programming

This study is founded in the patterns and distinctions of Neuro-Linguistic Programming (NLP). NLP examines the influence that language has on our mental programming and the other functions of our nervous systems. NLP is also concerned with the way in which our mental programming and nervous systems shape and are reflected in our language and language patterns.

The essence of Neuro-Linguistic Programming is that the functioning of our nervous system ("neuro") is intimately tied up with our capability for language ("linguistic"). The strategies ("programs") through which we organize and guide our behavior are made up of neurological and verbal patterns. In their first book, *The Structure of Magic* (1975), NLP co-founders Richard Bandler and John Grinder strove to define some principles behind the seeming "magic" of language to which Freud referred.

> *All the accomplishments of the human race, both positive and negative, have involved the use of language. We as human beings use our language in two ways. We use it first of all to represent our experience - we call this activity reasoning, thinking, fantasying, rehearsing. When we use language as a representational system, we are creating a model of our experience. This model of the world which we create by our representational use of language is based upon our perceptions of the world. Our perceptions are also partially determined by our model or representation . . . Secondly, we use our language to communicate our model or representation of the world to each other. When we use language to communicate, we call it talking, discussing, writing, lecturing, singing.*

According to Bandler and Grinder, language serves as a means to represent or create models of our experience as well as to communicate about it. The ancient Greeks, in fact, had different words for these two uses of language. They used the term *rhema* to indicate words used as a medium of communication and the term *logos* to indicate words associated with thinking and understanding. *Rhema* meant a saying or 'words as things'. *Logos* meant words associated with the 'manifestation of reason'. The great Greek philosopher Aristotle described the relationship between words and mental experience in the following way:

Spoken words are the symbols of mental experience and written words are the symbols of spoken words. Just as all men have not the same writing, so all men have not the same speech sounds, but the mental experiences, which these directly symbolize, are the same for all, as also are those things of which our experiences are the images.

Aristotle's claim that words "symbolize" our "mental experience" echoes the NLP notion that written and spoken words are *'surface structures'* which are transformations of other mental and linguistic *'deep structures'*. As a result, words can both reflect and shape mental experiences. This makes them a powerful tool for thought and other conscious or unconscious mental processes. By accessing the deep structure beyond the specific words used by an individual, we can identify and influence the deeper level mental operations reflected through that person's language patterns.

Considered in this way, language is not just an 'epiphenomenon' or a set of arbitrary signs by which we communicate about our mental experience; it is a key *part of* our mental experience. As Bandler and Grinder point out:

The nervous system which is responsible for producing the representational system of language is the same nervous system by which humans produce every other model of the world — visual, kinesthetic, etc. . . .The same principles of structure are operating in each of these systems.

Thus, language can parallel and even substitute for the experiences and activities in our other internal representational systems. An important implication of this is that 'talking about' something can do more than simply reflect our perceptions; it can actually create or change our perceptions. This implies a potentially deep and special role for language in the process of change and healing.

In ancient Greek philosophy, for instance, *'logos'* was thought to constitute the controlling and unifying principle in the universe. Heraclitus (540-480 B.C.) defined *'logos'* as the 'universal principle through which all things were interrelated and all natural events occurred'. According to the stoics, *'logos'* was a cosmic governing or generating principle that was immanent and active in all reality and that pervaded all reality. According to Philo, a Greek speaking Jewish philosopher (and contemporary of Jesus), *'logos'* was the intermediate between ultimate reality and the sensible world.

Map and Territory

The cornerstone of Sleight of Mouth, and the NLP approach to language, is the principle that "the map is not the territory." This principle was initially formulated by General Semantics Founder Alfred Korzybski (b. 1879 - d. 1950), and acknowledges the fundamental distinction between our maps of the world and the world itself. Korzybski's philosophy of language has been a major influence on the development of NLP. Korzybski's work in the area of *semantics*, combined with Noam Chomsky's *syntactic* theory of transformational grammar, form the core of much of the "linguistic" aspect of Neuro-Linguistic Programming.

Korzybski's major work, *Science and Sanity* (1933), asserts that human progress is largely a consequence of their more flexible nervous systems, which are capable of forming and using symbolic representations, or maps. Language, for instance, is a type of map or model of the world that allows us to summarize or generalize our experiences and pass them on to others, saving others from having to make the same mistakes or reinvent what had already been discovered. This type of linguistic generalizing ability of humans, Korzybski contended, accounted for our formidable progress over animals, but the misunderstanding, and misuse, of such symbolic mechanisms was also responsible for many of our problems. He suggested humans needed to be properly trained in the use of language to prevent the unnecessary conflicts and confusion that arose from confusing the 'map' with the 'territory'.

Korzybski's *law of individuality,* for instance, states that "no two persons, or situations, or stages of processes are the same in all details." Korzybski noted that we have far fewer words and concepts than unique experiences, and this tends to lead to the identification or "confusion" of two or more situations (what is known as "generalization" or "ambiguity" in NLP). The word "cat," for example, is commonly applied to millions of different individual animals, to the 'same' animal at different times in its life, to our mental images, to illustrations and photographs, metaphorically to a human being ("a hep-cat"), and even to the combined letters c-a-t. Thus, when someone uses the term "cat," it is not always clear whether he or she is referring to a four legged animal, a three letter word, or a two legged hominid.

Korzybski believed it was important to teach people how to recognize and transcend their language habits in order to communicate more effectively, and to better appreciate the unique characteristics of their daily experiences. He sought to develop tools that would prompt people to evaluate their experiences less by the implications of their everyday language and more by the unique facts of the particular situation. Korzybski's goal was to encourage people to delay their immediate reactions while they searched for the unique characteristics of a situation and alternative interpretations.

Korzybski's ideas and methods are one of the foundations of NLP. In fact, in 1941, Korzybski mentioned "neurolinguistics" as an important area of study relating to General Semantics.

NLP contends that we all have our own world view and that view is based upon the internal maps that we have formed through our language and sensory representational systems, as a result of our individual life experiences. It is these "neurolinguistic" maps that will determine how we interpret and react to the world around us and how we give meaning to our behaviors and experiences, more so than reality itself. As Shakespeare's Hamlet pointed out, "There is nothing either good or bad, but thinking makes it so."

In their first book, *The Structure of Magic Vol. I* (1975), NLP co-founders Richard Bandler and John Grinder pointed out that the difference between people who respond effectively as opposed to those who respond poorly in the world around them is largely a function of their internal model of the world:

Language and Experience

[P]eople who respond creatively and cope effectively...are people who have a rich representation or model of their situation, in which they perceive a wide range of options in choosing their action. The other people experience themselves as having few options, none of which are attractive to them . . . What we have found is not that the world is too limited or that there are no choices, but that these people block themselves from seeing those options and possibilities that are open to them since they are not available in their models of the world.

Korzybski's distinction between map and territory implies that our mental models of reality, rather than reality itself, determines how we will act. Therefore, it is important to continually expand our maps of the world. In the words of the great scientist Albert Einstein, "Our thinking creates problems that the same type of thinking will not solve."

A core belief of NLP is that if you can enrich or widen your map, you will perceive more choices available to you given the same reality. As a result, you will perform more effectively and wisely, no matter what you are doing. A primary mission of NLP is to create tools (such as the Sleight of Mouth patterns) which help people to widen, enrich and add to their internal maps of reality. According to NLP, the richer your map of the world, the more possibilities you will have of dealing with whatever challenges arise in reality.

From the NLP perspective, there is no single 'right' or 'correct' map of the world. Everyone has his or her own unique map or model of the world, and no one map is any more "true" or "real" than any other. Rather, the people who are most effective are the ones who have a map of the world that allows them to perceive the greatest number of available choices and perspectives. They have a richer and wider way of perceiving, organizing and responding to the world.

Experience

Our maps of the world can be contrasted with our experience of the world. "Experience" refers to the process of sensing, feeling and perceiving the world around us and our inner reactions to that world. Our "experience" of a sunset, an argument, or a vacation relates to our personal perception of and participation in such events. According to NLP, our experiences are made up of information from the external environment that we take in through our sense organs, as well as the associated memories, fantasies, sensations and emotions that emerge from inside of us.

The term "experience" is also used to refer to the accumulated knowledge of our lives. Information that is taken in through our senses becomes constantly encoded, or folded into our previous knowledge. Thus, our experience is the raw material out of which we each create our maps or models of the world.

Sensory experience refers to information received through one's sense organs (eyes, ears, skin, nose and tongue), and to the knowledge of the external world that is derived from that information. The sense organs are the faculties by which humans and other animals perceive the world around them. Each sensory channel acts as a type of filter that responds to a range of stimuli (light waves, sound waves, physical contact, etc.), and which varies for different species.

As our primary interface with the world around us, our senses are our "windows on the world." All of the information that we have about our physical existence comes to us through these sensory windows. It is for this reason that sensory experience is highly valued in NLP. NLP considers sensory experience the primary source of all of our knowledge about our external environment, and the fundamental building material out of which we construct our models of the world. Effective learning, communication and modeling are all rooted in sensory experience.

Sensory experience may be contrasted with other forms of experience, such as fantasy and hallucination, which are generated from within a person's brain rather than received through the senses. In addition to experience taken in from the senses, humans also have an internal web of knowledge and information constructed from internally generated experiences, such as "thoughts," "beliefs," "values," and "sense of self." Our internal web of knowledge creates another set of 'internal' filters which focus and direct our senses (and also operate to delete, distort and generalize data received from the senses).

Our sensory experience is the primary way we get new information about reality and add to our maps of the world. Often our preexisting internal knowledge filters out new and potentially valuable sensory experience. One of the missions of NLP is to help people enrich the amount of sensory experience they are able to receive by widening what Aldous Huxley referred to as the "reducing valve" of consciousness. NLP co-founders John Grinder and Richard Bandler constantly urged their students to "use sensory experience" rather than to project or hallucinate.

Most NLP techniques, in fact, are based on observational skills which attempt to maximize our direct sensory experience of a situation. According to the model of NLP, effective change comes from the ability to "come to our senses." To do this, we must learn to drop our internal filters and have direct sensory experience of the world around us. In fact, one of the most important basic skills of NLP is that ability to achieve the state of "uptime." Uptime is a state in which all one's sensory awareness is focused on the external environment in the 'here and now'. Uptime, and the increased amount of sensory experience which comes from uptime, helps us to more fully perceive and enjoy life and the many possibilities for learning that surround us.

Thus, our "experience" of something may be contrasted with the "maps," "theories," or "descriptions" made *about* that experience. In NLP, a distinction is made between *primary* and *secondary* experience. 'Primary' experience relates to the information we actually receive and perceive through our senses. 'Secondary' experience relates to the verbal and symbolic maps that we create to represent and organize our primary experiences. Primary experience is a function of our direct perceptions of the territory around us. Secondary experience is derived from our mental maps, descriptions and interpretations about those perceptions – and are subject to significant deletion, distortion and generalization. When we experience something directly, we have no self-consciousness or dissociative thoughts about what we are sensing and feeling.

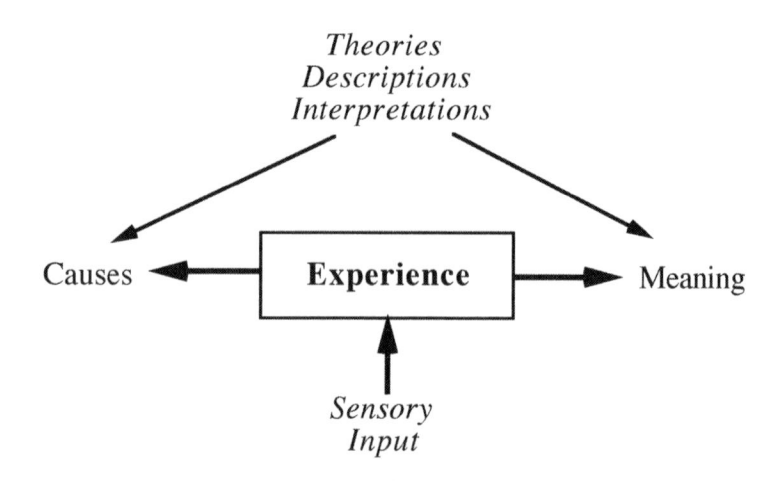

```
           Theories
         Descriptions
        Interpretations
              |
      ┌───────────────┐
Causes ←──│  Experience  │──→ Meaning
      └───────────────┘
              ↑
          Sensory
           Input
```

Our Experience is the Raw Material Out of Which we Create our Models of the World.

It is our primary experience that brings vibrancy, creativity and the sense of our own uniqueness to our lives. Our primary experience is necessarily much richer and more complete than any maps or descriptions we are able to make of it. People who are successful and enjoy life have the ability to experience more of the world directly, rather than dilute it through the filters of what they "should" experience or expect to experience.

From the NLP perspective, our subjective experience is our "reality," and takes precedence over any theories or interpretations we have relating to that experience. If a person has an 'out of the ordinary' experience, such as a "spiritual" or "past life" experience, NLP does not question its subjective validity. Theories and interpretations relating to the causes or the social implications of the experiences may be questioned and argued, but the experience itself is part of the essential data of our lives.

NLP processes and exercises place a heavy emphasis on experience. NLP based activities (especially discovery activities) tend to "lead with experience." Once we can directly experience something without the contamination of judgment or evaluation, our reflections on that experience are much richer and more meaningful.

Like other NLP distinctions and models, Sleight of Mouth helps us to become more aware of the filters and maps that can block and distort our experience of the world and its potential. By becoming more aware of them, we can also become free of them. The purpose of the Sleight of Mouth patterns is to help people enrich their perspectives, expand their maps of the world and reconnect with their experience.

Generally, Sleight of Mouth patterns can be characterized as "verbal reframes" which influence beliefs, and the mental maps from which beliefs have been formed. Sleight of Mouth patterns operate by getting people to frame or reframe their perceptions of some situation or experience. Sleight of Mouth Patterns lead people to 'punctuate' their experiences in new ways and take different perspectives.

How Language Frames Experience

Words not only represent our experience, but, frequently they 'frame' our experience. Words frame our experience by bringing certain aspects of it into the foreground and leaving others in the background. Consider the connective words "but," "and," and "even though," for example. When we connect ideas or experiences together with these different words, they lead us to focus our attention on different aspects of those experiences. If a person says, "It is sunny today *but* it will rain tomorrow," it leads us to focus more on the concern that it will be raining tomorrow, and to mostly neglect the fact that it is sunny today. If someone connects the same two expressions with the word "and"—i.e., "It is sunny today *and* it will be raining tomorrow"— the two events are equally emphasized. If someone says, "It is sunny today *even though* it will rain tomorrow," the effect is to focus our attention more on the first statement—that it is sunny today—leaving the other in the background.

It is sunny today
but
it will rain tomorrow

It is sunny today
and
it will rain tomorrow

It is sunny today
even though
it will rain tomorrow

Certain Words 'Frame' Our Experiences, Bringing Different Aspects of the into the Foreground

This type of verbal framing and "re-framing" will occur regardless of the contents being expressed. For example, the statements: "I am happy today *but* I know it will not last;" "I am happy today *and* I know it will not last;" "I am happy today *even though* I know it will not last;" create shifts in emphasis similar to the statements about the weather. The same is true with the statements: "I want to reach my outcome *but* I have a problem;" "I want to reach my outcome *and* I have a problem;" "I want to reach my outcome *even though* I have a problem."

When some structure applies across different contents in this way, we call it a *pattern*. Some people, for instance, have a habitual pattern in which they are constantly dismissing the positive side of their experience with the word "but."

This type of verbal framing can greatly influence the way we interpret and respond to particular statements and situations. Consider the following statement, *"You can do whatever you want to, if you are willing to work hard enough."** This is a very affirming and empowering belief. It connects two significant portions of experience in a type of cause-and-effect relationship: "doing whatever you want to" and "working hard enough." "Doing what you want to" is something that is very motivating. "Working hard" is not so desirable. Because the two have been linked together, however, with the statement that "you can do whatever you want to" in the foreground, it creates a strong sense of motivation, connecting a dream or wish with the resources necessary to make it happen.

Notice what happens if you reverse the order of the statement and say, "If you are willing to work hard enough, you can do whatever you want to." Even though this statement uses the exact same words, its impact is diminished somewhat, because the willingness to "work hard" has been placed in the foreground sequentially. It seems more like an attempt to convince somebody to work hard than an affirmation that "you can do whatever you want to." In this second framing, "doing what you want" appears to be more of a reward for "working hard." In the first statement, the willingness to "work hard" was framed as an internal resource for "doing what you want to." This difference, while subtle, can make a significant impact on how the message is received and understood.

---

* Many thanks to Teresa Epstein for this example.

The 'Even Though' Reframe

Identifying verbal patterns can allow us to create linguistic tools which can help to shape and influence the meaning we perceive as a result of our experience. An example is the 'even though' reframe. This pattern is applied by simply substituting the words "even though" for the word "but" in any sentence in which the word "but" is being used to diminish or discount some positive experience.

Try it out using the following steps:

1. Identify a statement in which a positive experience is 'discounted' by the word "but."

   e.g., "I found a solution to my problem, but it could come back again later."

2. Substitute the words "even though" for the word "but," and notice how it shifts the focus of your attention.

   e.g., "I found a solution to my problem, even though it could come back again later."

This structure allows people to maintain a positive focus and still satisfy the need to keep a balanced perspective. I have found this technique to be quite powerful for people who have a tendency to the "Yes, but . . ." type of pattern.

Chapter 2

Frames and Reframing

Frames

A psychological "frame" refers to a general focus or direction that provides an overall guidance for thoughts and actions during an interaction. In this sense, frames relate to the cognitive *context* surrounding a particular event or experience. As the term implies, a "frame" establishes the borders and constraints surrounding an interaction. Frames greatly influence the way that specific experiences and events are interpreted and responded to because of how they serve to 'punctuate' those experiences and direct attention. A painful memory, for example, may loom as an all-consuming event when perceived within the short term frame of the five minutes surrounding the event. That same painful experience may seem almost trivial when perceived against the background of one's lifetime. Frames also help to make interactions more efficient because they determine which information and issues fall within or outside of the purpose of an interaction.

A "time frame" is a common example of framing. Setting a time frame of ten minutes for a meeting or exercise, for example, greatly influences what can be accomplished in that meeting. It determines where people will focus their attention, what topics and issues are appropriate for them to include in the interaction, and the type and degree of effort they will exert. A time frame of one hour or three hours for the same meeting or exercise would create quite different dynamics. Shorter time frames tend to focus people on tasks, while longer time frames open up the possibility for people to also focus on developing relationships. If a time limit of 15 minutes has been set for a meeting, it is more likely that the meeting will be interpreted as being task-oriented rather than as an open-ended, exploratory brainstorming session.

Some common "frames" in NLP include the "outcome" frame, the "as if" frame and the "feedback versus failure" frame. The basic emphasis of the *outcome frame*, for instance, is to establish and maintain focus on the goal or desired state. Establishing an Outcome Frame involves evaluating any activity or information with respect to its relevance to the achievement of a particular goal or desired state.

```
┌─────────────────────────┐
│                         │
│    Topics which are        Topics which are
│    "inside" the frame      "outside" the frame
│                         │
└─────────────────────────┘
         **Frame**
  *e.g., An "outcome" Frame*
```

Frames Direct Attention and Influence How Events are Interpreted

An "outcome frame" may be usefully contrasted with a "problem frame." A problem frame places the emphasis on "what is wrong" or what is "not wanted," as opposed to what is desired or "wanted." A problem frame leads to a focus on undesired symptoms and the search for their causes. In contrast, an outcome frame leads to a focus on desired outcomes and effects, and the resources required to attain them. Thus, an Outcome Frame involves staying solution focused and oriented toward positive possibilities in the future.

Outcome Frame
What do you want?
How can you get it?
What resources are available?

Problem Frame
What is wrong?
Why is it a problem?
What caused it?
Whose fault is it?

Comparison of 'Outcome Frame' With 'Problem Frame'

The application of the Outcome Frame involves such tactics as reformulating problem statements to goal statements, and reframing negatively worded descriptions to those which are stated in positive terms. From the NLP perspective, for instance, all problems can be reperceived as challenges, or "opportunities" to change, grow or learn. Seen in this way, all "problems" presuppose desired outcomes. If someone says, "My problem is that I am afraid of failure," it can be assumed that there is an implied goal to "be confident that I am going to succeed." Similarly, if there is a problem such as "profits are down," it can be assumed that the outcome is to "increase profits."

People often unintentionally state their outcomes negatively, such as: "I want to avoid embarrassment," "I want to quit smoking," "I want to get rid of this interference," etc. Doing so places the focus of attention back onto the problem, and, paradoxically, often forms embedded suggestions in relation to the problem state. Thinking, "I want to not be so afraid," actually carries the suggestion "be afraid" as part of the thought itself. Maintaining an Outcome Frame would involve asking, "What *do* you want?" or "If you were not so afraid, what would you be feeling instead?"

While it is important to examine symptoms and their causes as part of effective problem solving, it is also important to do so in the context of reaching a desired state. If not, the exploration of the symptoms and causes will not lead to any solution. When the outcome, or desired state, remains the focus of information gathering, then solutions may often be found even if the problem state is not fully understood.

Other NLP "frames" operate in a similar manner. The focus of the "as if" frame is on acting 'as if' one has already achieved the desired goal or outcome. A feedback versus failure frame places attention on how seeming problems, symptoms or mistakes can be interpreted as feedback, which helps to make corrections leading to a desired state, rather than as failures.

Perhaps the most fundamental goal of applying the verbal patterns of Sleight of Mouth is to help people to shift their perspective 1) from a problem frame to an outcome frame, 2) from a failure frame to a feedback frame, and 3) from an impossibility frame to an 'as if' frame. The examples of the police officer, psychiatrist, doctor, coach, etc., provided at the beginning of this book, are all illustrations of shifting the frame from which some circumstance or event was being perceived. The psychiatrist, doctor, supportive uncle, mother, and coach, all helped to shift the perception of a situation that was being experienced as a "problem" or "failure" so that it was placed inside of an "outcome" or "feedback" frame. Attention was shifted from the 'problem' to the 'outcome', opening up new possibilities. (Even the police officer identifying herself as a "television repairman," is a metaphoric way of shifting to an outcome and feedback frame – placing emphasis on "repairing" what is wanted rather than "getting rid of" what is not wanted.)

Shifting Outcomes

It has been pointed out that "purpose directs activity." Thus, a particular outcome itself sets a type of frame that determines what is perceived as relevant, successful and "inside the frame;" and what is considered not relevant, unhelpful and "outside the frame." In a brainstorming session, for instance, the outcome is to "come up with new and unique ideas." Making unusual analogies, telling outrageous jokes, asking silly questions, and being a bit "bizarre," would all be relevant and helpful activities with respect to that outcome. Bringing up existing solutions and policies as "the right answer," and evaluating whether or not something is "realistic" would be inappropriate and unhelpful.

On the other hand, if, instead of brainstorming, the session involved the final stage of negotiations with a key client, the outcome of the session might be to "establish and reach consensus about the priorities for the completion and delivery of a specific product or intervention." With respect to this outcome, it is less likely that suddenly using unusual analogies, telling outrageous jokes, asking silly questions, and being a bit "bizarre," would be perceived as relevant and helpful (unless, of course, the negotiation had reached some kind of impasse which required a bit of brainstorming to get past).

Similarly, different behaviors will be perceived as relevant and useful for "getting to know each other," than for "meeting an impending deadline." Thus, shifting the outcome that is the focus of attention with respect to a particular situation or interaction will alter our judgments and perceptions about what is relevant and meaningful with respect to that situation.

The Sleight of Mouth pattern of *Another Outcome* involves making a statement that shifts people's attention to a different goal than the one that is being addressed or implied by a particular judgment or generalization. The purpose of the pattern is to challenge (or reinforce) the relevancy of that judgment or generalization.

For example, let's say that a participant in a seminar or workshop has done an exercise and feels frustrated with it because he or she "did not get the expected results." Frequently, a person feels this way because he or she had an outcome such as "doing it perfectly." With respect to this outcome, a generalization or judgment such as "not getting the expected result means you have done something wrong or are not yet competent enough," might be appropriate. Shifting the outcome of the seminar exercise from the goal of "doing it perfectly," to the outcome of "exploring," "learning," or "discovering something new," however, can greatly shift the way we approach and interpret the experiences that occur during that exercise. What is a failure with respect to "doing it perfectly," may be a success with respect to "discovering something new."

Thus, applying the pattern of shifting to *another outcome* would involve saying to the participant, "The outcome of the exercise is to learn something new as opposed to demonstrate that you already know how to do something perfectly. As you think back over the interaction, what new learnings are you aware of?"

A similar principle operates with respect to all of our life experiences. If we evaluate our response to a challenging situation with respect to the outcome of "being comfortable and secure," it may seem like we failed miserably. If we perceive the same situation with respect to the outcome of "growing stronger," we may discover that we have been quite successful.

Consider the following statement made to a client by the famous psychiatrist and hypnotherapist Milton H. Erickson, M.D. (the psychiatrist referred to in the example of the man who thought he was Jesus Christ):

It is important to have a sense of security; a sense of readiness; a full knowledge that come what may, you can meet it and handle it — and enjoy doing it. It's also a nice learning to come up against the situation that you can't handle — and then later think it over, and realize that, too, was a learning that's useful in many, many different ways. It allows you to assess your strength. It also allows you to discover the areas in which you need to use some more of your own security, which rests within yourself . . . Reacting to the good and the bad, and dealing with it adequately — that's the real joy in life.

Erickson's statement is an example of applying the Sleight of Mouth pattern of *Another Outcome*. The comment transforms what might be considered "failure" with respect to one outcome (handling the situation), into feedback with respect to another outcome ("reacting to the good and the bad, and dealing with it adequately').

```
┌─────────────────────────────────────────┐
│                                         │
│        ┌───────────────────────┐        │
│        │  Handling the situation │      │
│        └───────────────────────┘        │
│                                         │
│     Reacting to the good and the bad,   │
│       and dealing with it adequately    │
│                                         │
└─────────────────────────────────────────┘
```

Changing the Outcome Shifts the Frame of What is Relevant and Successful

Frames and Reframing

Try this pattern out for yourself:

1. Think of a situation in which you feel stuck, frustrated or a failure.

Situation: _____

> *e.g., I feel that a person is taking advantage of me and I am not able to confront that person directly about my feelings.*

2. What is the negative generalization or judgment that you have made (about yourself or others) with respect to that situation, and what outcome or outcomes are implied by that judgment?

Judgment: _____

> *e.g., Not speaking up for myself means that I am a coward.*

Outcome(s): _____

> *e.g., To make myself speak up for myself, and be strong and brave.*

3. Explore the impact it would have on your perception of the situation if you thought about it with respect to some other possible outcomes as well – e.g., safety, learning, exploration, self-discovery, respect for myself and others, acting with integrity, healing, growing, etc.

> For instance, if the outcome were switched to "treating myself and others with respect," or "treating others the way I would like to be treated," judging

oneself as a "coward" for not speaking up for oneself, may not seem as relevant or appropriate a generalization to be making.

4. What is another outcome that you could add to or substitute for your current outcome that would make your negative generalization or judgment less relevant, and make it easier to view the current consequences of this situation as feedback rather than failure?

Alternative Outcome(s): _____

e.g., Learn to act toward myself and others with congruence, wisdom and compassion.

From the NLP perspective, switching to another outcome serves to "reframe" our perception of the experience. "Reframing" is considered to be a core process for change in NLP, and is the primary mechanism of Sleight of Mouth.

Reframing

Reframing involves helping people to reinterpret problems and find solutions by changing the frame in which the problems are being perceived. *Reframing* literally means to put a new or different frame around some image or experience. Psychologically, to "reframe" something means to transform its meaning by putting it into a different framework or context than it has previously been perceived.

The frame around a picture is a good metaphor for understanding the concept and process of reframing. Depending on what is framed in a picture, we will have different information about the content of the picture, and thus a different perception of what the picture represents. A photographer or painter who is recording a particular landscape, for example, might only "frame" a tree, or choose to include an entire meadow with many trees, animals and perhaps a stream or pond. This determines what an observer of the picture will see of the original scene at a later time. Furthermore, a person who has purchased a particular picture might subsequently decide to change the frame so that it fits more esthetically in a particular room of the house.

Similarly, because they determine what we "see" and perceive with respect to a certain experience or event, psychological frames influence the way we experience and interpret a situation. As an illustration, consider for a moment the following picture.

Small Frame

Now consider what happens if the frame is expanded. Notice how your experience and understanding of the situation being represented is widened to include a new perspective.

Larger Frame

The first picture does not have much "meaning" per se. It is simply of a "fish" of some type. When the frame is widened to produce the second picture, we suddenly see a different situation. The first fish is not simply a "fish," it is a "little fish about to be eaten by a big fish." The little fish seems unaware of the situation; a situation that we can see easily due to our perspective and our "larger frame." We can either feel alarmed and concerned for the little fish, or accept that the big fish must eat in order to survive.

Notice what happens when we "reframe" the situation again by widening our perspective even more.

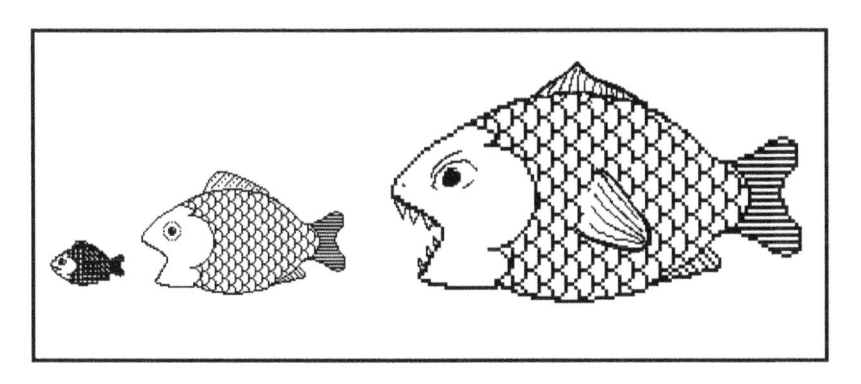

Even Larger Frame

Now we have another perspective and a new meaning altogether. By *changing the frame size*, we see that it is not only the little fish who is in danger. The big fish is also about to be eaten by an even bigger fish. In his quest to survive, the big fish has become so focused on eating the little fish that it is oblivious to the fact that its own survival is threatened by the much bigger fish.

The situation depicted here, and the new level of awareness that comes from reframing our perspective of the situation, is a good metaphor for both the process and purpose of psychological reframing. People frequently end up in the situation of the little fish, or of the fish in the middle. They are either unaware of some impending challenge in their larger surroundings like the little fish, or so focused on achieving some outcome, like the fish in the middle, that they do not notice an approaching crisis. The paradox for the fish in the middle is that it has focused its attention so much on one particular behavior related to survival that it has put its survival at risk in another way. Reframing allows us to see the "bigger picture" so that more appropriate choices and actions can be implemented.

In NLP, reframing involves putting a new mental frame around the content of an experience or situation, expanding our perception of the situation so that it may be more wisely and resourcefully handled.

Changing Frame Size

The Sleight of Mouth pattern of *Change Frame Size* applies this principle directly to our perceptions of some situation or experience. The pattern involves re-evaluating (or reinforcing) the implication of a particular action, generalization or judgment in the context of a longer (or shorter) time frame, a larger number of people (or from an individual point of view) or a bigger or smaller perspective. An event that seems unbearably painful when we consider it with respect to our own desires and expectations, for instance, may suddenly seem almost trivial when we compare it to the suffering of others.

Spectators at a sports event may end up in a frenzy if their team wins or loses a particular game, or a person makes an exceptionally good or exceptionally poor play. Years later, when considered with respect to the larger landscape of their lives, those same events may seem totally insignificant.

An action that seems acceptable if one person does it, can become destructive and harmful if a whole group does it.

Childbirth can be an intense and frightening experience for a person who is experiencing it for the first time. Being reminded that it is a process that has evolved over millions of years by millions of women, can help the person to have greater trust and less fear in what is happening within her body.

Notice that the process of changing frame size is distinct from that of shifting to another outcome. A person can maintain the same outcome, such as "healing" or "safety," but change the frame size in which he or she is evaluating progress towards that outcome. The specific symptoms of an illness, for example, may be viewed as not being "healthy" in the framework of their immediate consequences, but as a necessary process of "cleansing," or of immunizing a person with respect to their long term consequences. The field of homeopathy, for instance, is based on the premise that small amounts of a toxic substance produce immunity to its toxicity over the long term.

Similarly, what might seem like the "safe" thing to do in the short term could put a person at great risk in the longer term.

Changing frame size has to do with the breadth or width of the perspective we are taking, as distinct from the particular outcome we are considering with respect to that frame. A good literal illustration of changing frame size can be seen in the movie *Cabaret*. One scene in the film begins with a close up of the face of an angelic looking young boy who is singing in a beautiful voice. The image appears sweet and wholesome. As the camera begins to pan back, however, we see that the boy is wearing a military uniform. Next, we see that he is wearing an arm band containing a swastika. As the frame size gets larger and larger, we eventually see that the boy is singing at a huge Nazi rally. The meaning and feeling conveyed by the image is completely changed by the information coming from the changes in the frame size of the image.

Similar shifts can be made through the use of language. Phrases such as, "looking at the situation from the big picture," "considering the long term implications," or "for generations to come," can directly influence the frame size we are applying to perceive a situation, event or outcome. Frame size can also be changed by adding or including words that presuppose a larger frame. Saying something like "four score and ten years ago," or "for a hundred years to come," will naturally trigger people to think in terms of a particular time frame.

Consider the changes in frame size utilized in the following set of riddles, from a traditional Scottish lullaby:

> I gave my love a cherry that had no stone.
> I gave my love a chicken that had no bone.
> I gave my love a baby that's not crying.

How can you have a cherry that has no stone?
How can you have a chicken that has no bone?
How can you have a baby that's not crying?

When a cherry is a blossom, it has no stone.
A chicken that's an egg, has no bone.
A baby when its sleeping is not crying.

The solution to the first two riddles requires that we widen our frame of perception to the larger life cycle of a cherry or a chicken. The solution to the third riddle requires that we go the other direction, and narrow our perception to particular time periods in the baby's daily cycle. The terms "blossom," "egg" and "sleeping" bring us naturally to this shift in perception.

The size of the frame we are considering determines a great deal about the meaning and significance we are able to perceive, and can be an extremely important issue with respect to effective problem solving.

Try this pattern out for yourself using the following steps:

1. Think of a situation that you judge as difficult, disappointing or painful in some way.

Situation: _____

2. What is the current frame from which you are viewing that situation? (i.e., immediate results, long term consequences, individual, group, community, past, future, specific event, whole system, as an adult, as a child, etc.)

Current Frame: _____

3. Change the frame size by widening it and narrowing it to include more time, a larger number of people, a larger system, etc. Then, narrow it to focus on just a specific

individual, a limited time frame, a single event, etc. Notice how this shifts the perceptions you have and evaluations you make with respect to that situation. Something that seems to be a failure in the short term often becomes seen as a necessary step to success in the longer term. (Realizing that your own struggles are something that everyone goes through at some time, for instance, can help make them feel less overwhelming.)

4. What is a longer (or shorter) time frame, a larger number or smaller number of people, or a bigger or smaller perspective that would change the judgment or generalization you are making about the situation to be something more positive?

New Frame: _____

The Sleight of Mouth patterns of Changing Frame Size and shifting to Another Outcome are examples of what are known as *context* and *content* reframing in NLP.

Context Reframing

Context reframing has to do with the fact that a particular experience, behavior or event will have different implications and consequences depending on the context in which it occurs. Rain, for example, will be perceived as an extremely positive event to a group of people who have been suffering from a severe drought, but as a negative event for a group of people who are in the midst of a flood, or who have planned an outdoor wedding. The rain itself is neither "good" nor "bad." The judgment related to it has to do with the consequence it produces within a particular context.

According to Leslie Cameron-Bandler (1978, p. 131) *contextual reframing* in NLP "accepts all behaviors as useful in some context." The purpose of contextual reframing is to change a person's negative internal response to a particular behavior by realizing the usefulness of the behavior in some contexts. This allows us to see the behavior as simply "a behavior" (like the rain) and shift our attention to addressing the issues related to the larger context (i.e., instead of cursing the rain when we are flooded, we learn to focus on creating more effective drainage systems).

As an example, let's say a mother is distraught because her teenage son is constantly getting into fights at school. A context reframe would involve saying something like, "Isn't it nice to know that your son could protect his little sister if anyone bothered her on the way home from school?" This can help her to shift her perception of her son's behavior and view it in a broader perspective. Rather than being outraged and ashamed, the mother may be able to appreciate her son's behavior as useful in a particular context, and thus respond in a more constructive way.

Negative responses often serve to maintain and even escalate problematic behaviors, rather than extinguish them. Blame frequently produces a type of "polarity response" which actually serves to stimulate rather than inhibit the unwanted behavior. When the mother in the previous example is able to see the positive benefits of her son's behavior in a single context, it can help her to get a better "meta position" to that behavior, and thus begin to communicate more usefully with her son about his behavior and the context in which it is occurring.

Having his own behavior validated as useful in a particular context, rather than being attacked and criticized, also allows the son to view his own behavior from a different perspective, rather than constantly being on the defensive. As a next step, the mother and son could work to establish the positive intent and benefits related to the son's behavior at school and explore more appropriate substitutes.

Changing the frame size from which one is perceiving some event is clearly one way to perceive it within a different context.

Content Reframing

Instead of shifting contexts, *content reframing* involves altering our perspective or level of perception with respect to a particular behavior or situation. Consider an empty field of grass, for instance. To a farmer, the field is an opportunity to plant new crops; to an architect, the field is a space on which to build a dream home; to a young couple, the field is a wonderful location for a picnic; to the pilot of a small airplane that is running out of gas, it is a place to safely land; and so on. The same content (the "field") is perceived differently according to the perspective and "intent" of the viewer. This is clearly the mechanism underlying the Sleight of Mouth pattern of shifting to *another outcome*.

Using the analogy of a physical picture, for instance, one way to view a painting or photograph differently is to "reframe" it by considering the intent of the artist or photographer in creating the picture. What response did the artist or photographer intend to elicit in the observer? What emotion was the artist or photographer intending to convey? Considering something within the framework of its intention alters our perception of it.

Similarly, "content reframing" in NLP involves exploring the intention behind a person's external behavior. This is most commonly accomplished in NLP by finding the "positive intention," "positive purpose," or "meta outcome" related to a particular symptom or problematic behavior. One of the basic principles of NLP is that it is useful to separate one's "behavior" from one's "self." That is, it is important to separate the positive intent, function, belief, etc., that generates a behavior, from the behavior itself. According to this principle it is more respectful, ecological and productive to respond to the 'deep structure' than to the surface expression of a problematic behavior. Perceiving a symptom or problematic behavior in the larger framework of the positive purpose it is intended to satisfy, shifts the internal responses to that behavior, opening the door to addressing it in a more resourceful and creative manner.

As an example, an NLP practitioner was counseling the family of a teenage boy who complained that his father always objected to any future plans that the young man proposed. The practitioner said to the youth, "Isn't it nice to have a father who is trying to protect you from being hurt or disappointed in any way? I'll bet you don't know very many fathers who care that much about their children." This comment took the young man by surprise, as he had never considered that there might be some positive purpose behind his father's criticism. He had only thought of it as an attack against him. The practitioner went on to explain the difference between being a 'dreamer', 'realist', and 'critic', and the importance that each role played in effective planning. He pointed out that the function of an effective critic is to find out what might be missing from a particular idea or plan in order to avoid problems, and that the teen's father was clearly in the position of the "critic" to his son's dreams. He also explained the problems that can occur between a dreamer and a critic in the absence of a realist.

The NLP practitioner's comments were enough to shift the teenager's internal response to his father's objections from one of anger, to one that included sincere appreciation. This new framing of the father's behavior also allowed the youth to consider his father as a potential resource for helping him learn how to plan his future, rather than as a liability or roadblock. The validation of the father's intent also allowed the father to shift his perception of his own role (and thus his method of participation) in his son's life. The father realized he could take on the role of a realist, or coach, as well as that of a critic.

Thus, content reframing involves determining a possible positive intention that could underlie a problematic behavior. There are two aspects to the intent. The first is the positive internal motivation behind the behavior (e.g., the desire for safety, love, caring, respect, etc.). The second is the positive benefit that behavior could serve with respect to the larger system or context in which it is occurring (e.g., protection, shifting attention, getting acknowledgment, etc.).

One of the primary applications of content reframing in NLP is *Six-Step Reframing*. In this process, a problematic behavior is separated from the *positive intention* of the internal program or "part" that is responsible for the behavior. New choices of behavior are established by having the part responsible for the old behavior take responsibility for implementing alternative behaviors that satisfy the same positive intention but don't have the problematic by-products.

Reframing Critics and Criticism

As the example of the father and his teenage son illustrates, reframing can be an effective method for dealing with critics and criticism. "Critics" are often considered the most difficult people to handle in an interaction because of their seemingly negative focus and their tendency to find problems with the ideas and suggestions of others. Critics are frequently perceived as "spoilers," because they operate from a "problem frame" or "failure frame." (Dreamers, on the other hand, function from the "'as if' frame," and realists act from the "outcome frame" and "feedback frame.")

A major problem with criticisms, on a linguistic level, is that they are typically asserted in the form of generalized judgments, such as: "This proposal is too costly," "That idea will never work," "That's not a realistic plan," "This project requires too much effort," etc. One problem with such verbal generalizations, is that, given the way they are stated, one can only agree or disagree with them. If a person says, "That idea will never work," or, "It is too expensive," the only way one can respond directly is to say, either "I guess you are right," or "No, you are wrong, the idea will work," or, "No, it is not too expensive." Thus, criticism usually leads to polarization, mismatching and ultimately conflict, if one does not agree with the criticism.

The most challenging problems occur when a critic doesn't merely criticize a dream or a plan, but begins to criticize the "dreamer" or "realist" on a personal level. This would be the difference between saying, "That *idea* is stupid," and, "*You* are stupid for having that idea." When a critic attacks a person at the identity level then the critic is not only a "spoiler," but also a "killer."

It is important to keep in mind, however, that criticism, like all other behavior, is positively intended. The purpose of the 'critic' is to evaluate the output of the 'dreamer' and 'realist'. An effective critic makes an analysis of the proposed plan or path in order to find out what could go wrong and what should be avoided. Critics find missing links by logically considering 'what would happen if' problems occur. Good critics often take the perspective of people not directly involved in the plan or activity being presented, but who may be effected by it, or influence the implementation of the plan or activity (either positively or negatively).

Getting Positive Statements of Positive Intentions

One of the problems with many criticisms is that, in addition to being "negative" judgments, they are stated in negative terms linguistically – that is, they are stated in the form of a verbal negation. "Avoiding stress," and "becoming more relaxed and comfortable," for example, are two ways of verbally describing a similar internal state, even though they use quite different words. One statement ("avoiding stress") describes what is not wanted. The other statement ("becoming more relaxed and comfortable") describes what is wanted.

Similarly, many criticisms are framed in terms of what is not wanted, rather than what is wanted. As an example, the positive intent (or criterion) behind the criticism, "this is a waste of time," is probably the desire to "use available resources wisely and efficiently." This intention is not easy to ascertain from the "surface structure" of the criticism however, because it has been stated in terms of what is to be avoided. Thus, a key linguistic skill in addressing criticisms, and transforming problem frames to outcome frames, is the ability to recognize and elicit positive statements of positive intentions.

This can be challenging at times, because critics operate so much from a problem frame. For example, if you ask a critic for the positive intention behind a criticism such as, "This proposal is too expensive," you are likely to get a response like, "The intention is to avoid excessive costs." Notice that, while this is a "positive intention," it is linguistically stated or framed negatively—i.e., it states what is to be "avoided" rather than what is to be achieved. The positive statement of this intention would be something like, "To make sure it is affordable" or "To be certain we are within our budget."

To elicit the positive formulations of intentions and criteria, one needs to ask questions such as: "If (stress/expense/failure/waste) is what you do not want, then what is it that you *do* want?" or "What would it get for you (how would you benefit) if you were able to avoid or get rid of what you do not want?"

The following are some examples of positive reformulations of negative statements.

Negative Statement	Positive Reformulation
too expensive	affordable
waste of time	use available resources wisely
fear of failure	desire to succeed
unrealistic	concrete and achievable
too much effort	easy and comfortable
stupid	wise and intelligent

Turning Criticisms Into Questions

Once the positive intention of a criticism has been discovered and stated in positive terms, the criticism can be turned into a question. When a criticism is transformed into a question, the options for responding to it are completely different than if it is stated as a generalization or judgment. Say, for instance, that instead of saying, "It is too expensive," the critic asked, "How are we going to afford it?" When asked this question, the other person is given the possibility of outlining the details of the plan, rather than having to disagree with, or fight with the critic. This is true for practically every criticism. The criticism, "That idea will never work," can be transformed into the question: "How are you going to actually implement that idea?" "That's not a realistic plan," can be restated as: "How can you make the steps of your plan more tangible and concrete?" The complaint, "It requires too much effort," can be reformulated to, "How can you make it easier and simpler to put into action?" Typically such questions serve the same purpose as the criticism, but are much more productive.

Notice that the questions above are all 'how' questions. These types of questions tend to be the most useful. Why questions, for instance, often presuppose other judgments, which can lead back into conflict or disagreement. To ask, "Why is this proposal so expensive?", or "Why can't you be more realistic?" still presuppose a problem frame. The same is true with questions like, "What makes your proposal so expensive?" or "Who is going to pay for it?" In general, 'how' questions are most effective for refocusing on an outcome frame or feedback frame.

[Note: On the level of their deeper structure, criticisms are ontological statements – assertions of what something *'is'* or *'is not'*. How questions lead to epistemological explorations - the examination of *'how you know'* what is or is not.]

Helping Critics to be Advisors

In summary, in order to help someone to be a 'constructive' critic, or an advisor, it helps to: 1) find the positive purpose behind the criticism, 2) make sure the positive intention is stated (framed) positively, and 3) turn the criticism into a question – and in particular, into a 'how' question.

This can be accomplished by using the following sequence of questions:

1. What is your criticism or objection?
    e.g., *"What you are proposing is superficial."*

2. What is the criterion or positive intention behind that criticism? What is it that you are attempting to achieve or preserve through your criticism?
   e.g., "Deep and lasting change."

3. Given that that's the intention, what is the HOW question that needs to be asked?
   e.g., "How can you be sure that the proposal will address the key issues that are necessary for deep and lasting change?"

Practice this process by trying it out on yourself. Think of some area in your life in which you are attempting to manifest new values or beliefs, and go into a "critic" position with respect to yourself. What objections or problems do you find with yourself or what you are doing?

When you have identified some problems or objections, go through the steps defined above, in order to turn your criticisms into questions. Find the positive intention and the how question related to your self-criticism (it sometimes helps to do it with a partner). Once the criticisms have become questions, you can take them to the "dreamer" or "realist" within you in order to formulate appropriate answers.

Ultimately, the objectives of the critic phase of a project are to make sure an idea or plan is ecologically sound and preserves any positive benefits or by-products of the current way(s) of achieving the goal. When a critic asks 'how' questions, then he or she shifts from being a "spoiler" or "killer" to being an "advisor."

[Note: It is also useful to guide the critic to first acknowledge which criteria have been met before commenting on what is missing or needed.]

The Sleight of Mouth Patterns of 'Intention' and 'Redefining'

Identifying and acknowledging the positive intention of the critic, and turning the criticism into a "how" question, is an example of a type of 'verbal magic trick', using Sleight of Mouth to shift attention from a problem frame or failure frame to an outcome frame and feedback frame. It results in the transformation of a critic from a spoiler to an advisor. The process is based upon two fundamental forms of reframing that are at the core of the Sleight of Mouth patterns: Intention and Redefining.

Intention involves directing a person's attention to the purpose or intention (e.g., protection, getting attention, establishing boundaries, etc.) behind some generalization or statement, in order to either reframe or reinforce the generalization.

Redefining involves substituting a new word or phrase for one of the words or phrases used in a statement or generalization that means something similar but has different implications. Substituting a positively stated phrase for a negatively stated one is an example of "redefining."

The Sleight of Mouth pattern of Intention is based on the fundamental NLP presupposition that:

At some level all behavior is (or at one time was) "positively intended". It is or was perceived as appropriate given the context in which it was established, from the point of view of the person whose behavior it is. It is easier and more productive to respond to the intention rather than the expression of a problematic behavior.

Applying the pattern of Intention would involve responding to the positive intention(s) behind a particular generalization or judgment, rather than directly to the statement itself. As an example, let's say a customer comes into a store and shows interest in a particular item, but states, "I like this, but I'm afraid it is too expensive." To apply the pattern of intention, the salesperson might say something like, "I hear that it is important to you that you get good value for your money." This serves to direct the customer's attention to the intention behind the judgment that something is "too expensive" (in this case, the intention of "getting value"). This helps to shift the customer from responding from a "problem frame" to that of an "outcome frame."

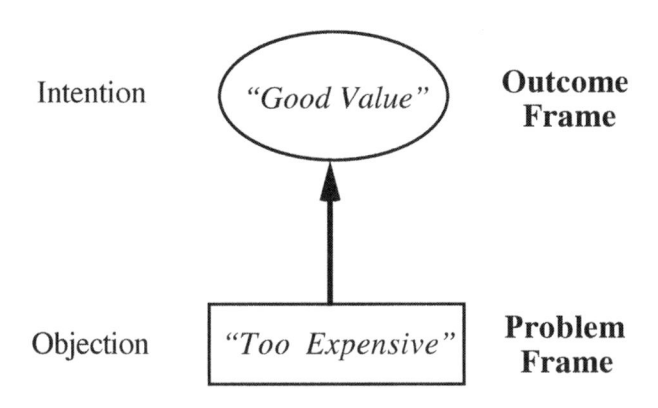

Intention — *"Good Value"* — **Outcome Frame**

Objection — *"Too Expensive"* — **Problem Frame**

Focusing on the Intention of a Limiting Judgment or Statement Helps to Shift From a Problem Frame to an Outcome Frame

Redefining would involve saying something such as, "Is it that you think the item is overpriced, or are you concerned that you cannot afford it?" Here, the statement, "I'm afraid it is too expensive," has been redefined in two different ways, in order for the salesperson to gather more specific information about the customer's objection. The first redefinition substitutes "think" for "afraid" and "overpriced" for "too expensive."

The second redefinition substitutes "concerned" for "afraid" and "cannot afford it" for "too expensive." Both reformulations mean something similar to the original objection, but have different implications, which serve to place the customer's judgment back into a "feedback frame."

"Thinking" and "being concerned" are in many ways very different from being "afraid." They imply cognitive processes more than an emotional reaction (thus, more likelihood that something will be perceived as feedback). "Overpriced" as a redefinition of "too expensive" implies that the objection is a function of the customer's expectation of what the store should be charging for the item. Redefining "too expensive" as "unable to afford it" places the source of the objection as the customer's concerns with respect to his or her own financial resources and ability to pay for the item.

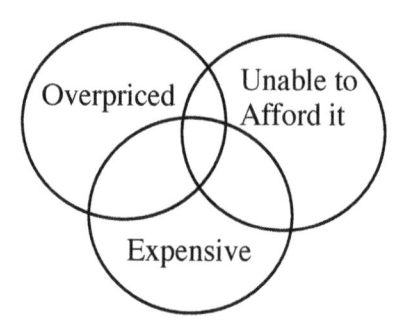

Words Can Have Overlapping Meanings, But Different Implications

The redefinition that the customer chooses provides important feedback to the salesperson. Depending on the customer's response, for example, the salesperson might decide to offer a discount for the item (if it is perceived as "overpriced") or work out a payment plan with the customer (if the concern is with "affordability").

Thus, redefining is a simple but powerful way to open up new channels of thinking and interaction. Relabeling "pain" as "discomfort," is another good illustration of the impact of the Sleight of Mouth pattern of redefining. It has a different impact, for instance, to ask a person, "How much pain are you in?" and "How much discomfort do you feel?" Often this type of verbal reframing automatically changes people's perceptions of their pain. A term like "discomfort" contains within it the embedded suggestion of "comfort." "Pain" has no such positive twist.

One-Word Reframing Exercise

One way to explore the Sleight of Mouth pattern of redefining is by making "one-word reframes" of other words. This is done by taking a word expressing a particular idea or concept and finding another word for that idea or concept that puts either a more positive or negative slant on the initial term. As the philosopher Bertrand Russell humorously pointed out, "I am firm; you are obstinate; he is a pigheaded fool." Borrowing Russell's formula, try generating some other examples, such as:

I am righteously indignant; you are annoyed; he is making a fuss about nothing.
I have reconsidered it; you have changed your mind; he has gone back on his word.
I made a genuine mistake; you twisted the facts; he is a damned liar.
I am compassionate, you are soft, he is a "pushover."

Each of these statements takes a particular concept or experience and places it in several different perspectives by "re-framing" it with different words. Consider the word "money," for example. "Wealth," "success," "tool," "responsibility," "corruption," "green energy," etc., are all words or phrases that put different "frames" around the notion of "money," bringing out different potential perspectives.

Make a list of words and practice forming some of your own one-word reframes.

e.g.,
responsible (stable, rigid)
stable (comfortable, boring)
playful (flexible, insincere)
frugal (wise, stingy)
friendly (nice, naive)

assertive (confident, nasty)
respectful (considerate, compromising)
global (expansive, unwieldy)

Once you become comfortable with one-word reframes, you can try applying them to limiting statements that you encounter in yourself or others. For example, maybe you blame yourself for being "stupid" or "irresponsible" sometimes. See if you can find redefinitions that put a more positive slant on these words. "Stupid" could be redefined as "naive," "innocent" or "distracted," for instance. "Irresponsible" could be redefined as "free spirited," "flexible," or "unaware," and so on.

You might also consider using one-word reframes to rephrase comments that you make to other people. Perhaps you can soften some of your own criticisms of others by redefining certain words that you use when talking to your spouse, children, co-workers or friends. Instead of accusing a child of "lying," for instance, one could say that he or she has "a big imagination," or is "telling fairy tales." Redefinitions can often "get the point across," and at the same time exclude unnecessary (and often unhelpful) negative implications or accusations.

This type of redefining is the essential process behind the notion of "political correctness" in language. The purpose of this type of relanguaging is to reduce the negative judgments and stigmas that often accompany the labels used to describe others that are different in some way. As opposed to being labeled "hyperactive," for instance, a child with a lot of physical energy, who has difficulty following directions, can be called "spirited." Instead of being called "deaf," a person who is hard of hearing is referred to as "hearing impaired." Rather than being called "crippled" a handicapped person can be described as "physically challenged." A person that used to be called a "janitor" might be referred to as a "maintenance technician." "Garbage collection" may be talked about as "waste management."

The intention of such relabeling is to help people view others from a broader and less judgmental perspective (although it can also be viewed as patronizing and insincere by some). When effective, such renaming also helps to shift from viewing and defining roles from a "problem frame" to an "outcome frame."

Perceiving a Situation from a Different Model of the World by Taking 'Second Position'

One simple but powerful form of reframing is to consider some situation, experience or judgment from a different Model of the World. From the NLP perspective, this is most easily and naturally done by putting yourself in another person's shoes — what is known as taking 'second position'.

Taking second position involves stepping into another person's point of view, or 'perceptual position', within a particular situation or interaction. Second position is one of the three fundamental Perceptual Positions defined by NLP. It involves shifting perspectives and viewing the situation as though you were another individual. From second position, you see, hear, feel, taste, and smell what the interaction is like from the other person's perspective; to "be in his or her skin," "walk a mile in his or her shoes," "sit on the other side of the desk," etc.

Thus, second position involves being associated in another person's point of view, beliefs and assumptions, and perceiving ideas and events from that person's model of the world. Being able to view a situation from another person's model of the world, frequently offers many new insights and understandings.

The Sleight of Mouth Pattern known as *Model of the World*, is drawn from this process. It involves being able to reframe a situation or generalization by being able to perceive and express a different mental map of the situation. A good example of the process of taking second position in order to get a different model of the world, and then putting it into words in order to widen other people's perspective is provided by criminal lawyer Tony Serra. In a 1998 interview in *Speak* magazine, Serra commented:

[W]hen you represent the criminal defendant. . . you become him, you feel like him, you walk in his shoes, and you see with his eyes and hear with his ears. You've got to know him completely to know that nature of his behavior. But you have 'the word.' That is, you can translate his feeling, his meaning and his intellect as components that are relevant to his behavior into legalese, into the words of the law, or into persuasive metaphors. You take the clay of a person's behavior and you embellish it, you make a piece of art. And that is the lawyer's creativity.

The Sleight of Mouth pattern of Model of the World is founded in the NLP presupposition that:

The map is not the territory. Every person has their own individual map of the world. There is no single correct map of the world. People make the best choices available to them given the possibilities and the capabilities that they perceive available to them from their model of the world. The 'wisest' and most 'compassionate' maps are those which make available the widest and richest number of choices, as opposed to being the most "real" or "accurate".

Identify a situation involving another person in which you were not able to perform as masterfully as you know you that you could have. What is the generalization or judgment that you have made about yourself or the other person? Enrich your perception of the situation and your generalization by considering them from at least three points of view or 'Models of the World'.

What do you see, hear and feel through your own eyes, ears and body?

Step into the shoes of the other person. How would you perceive the situation if you were that person?

Imagine you were an uninvolved observer looking at this situation. What would you notice about the interaction from this perspective? How would an (anthropologist, artist, minister, journalist) perceive this situation?

It can be a very powerful experience to pick someone who has been an important teacher or mentor to you and view the situation or generalization from that person's perspective as well.

An Example of the Right Words at the Right Time

As a practical example, of how I have applied some of the principles we have been exploring in this book for myself, I was in a bar once with Richard Bandler, to have a meeting. It was the type of place that is typically called a "biker bar"; meaning that it was full of some pretty rough and unsavory characters. This was not the type of place that I generally liked to hang out, but Richard liked it and wanted to meet there.

We started talking, and pretty soon these two large men came in. They were drunk and angry, and wanted to pick on somebody. I guess they could tell that I didn't really belong in a place like that, because pretty soon they started shouting obscenities at me and Bandler, calling us "queers," and telling us to get out of the bar.

My first strategy was to attempt to politely ignore them, which, of course, did not work. It wasn't long before one of the guys was bumping my arm and spilling my drink. So, I decided to try to be friendly. I looked over at them and smiled. One of them said, "What are you looking at?" When I averted my gaze, the other one said, "Look at me while I'm talking to you."

Things were getting pretty bad, and, to my surprise, I was getting angry. Fortunately I realized that following the normal pattern of response would only serve to escalate the situation. So, I had a brilliant idea; why not use NLP? I decided to try to discover and address their positive intention. I took a breath, and stepped into their shoes for a split second. In an even and steady voice, I said to the man nearest to me, "You know, I don't really think that you believe we are homosexuals. As you can clearly see, I am wearing a wedding ring. I think that you have a different intention." At this point, the fellow blurted out, "Yeh, we want to fight!"

Now, I know that some of you readers are probably sarcastically thinking, "Wow, Robert, what incredible progress. This Sleight of Mouth stuff must be pretty powerful." On the other hand, there was progress, because I had begun to engage them in a conversation, rather than a one-sided tirade. Seizing the opportunity, I responded, "I understand that, but it really wouldn't be much of a fight. First of all, I don't want to fight, so you wouldn't get much out of me. Besides, you are both twice my size. What kind of fight would that be?"

At this point, the second fellow (who was the 'brains' of the two) said, "No. Its a fair fight; we're drunk." Turning to look the man squarely in the eyes, I said, "Don't you think that would be just like a father coming home and beating up his fourteen year old son, and saying that it was 'fair' because the father was drunk?" I was certain that this was probably what happened to this man over and over again when he was fourteen.

Confronted with the truth, the two men could no longer continue to be abusive to Bandler and I; and eventually went to bother someone else (who turned out to be a karate expert that took them outside and whipped them soundly).

The way Bandler tells the story, I began to elicit the two men's submodalities and their decision strategy for choosing us to pick on, and eventually did therapy with them. [According to him, he was going to suggest that, since they wanted to fight, they should just go outside and fight with each other.] But that is not exactly how I remember it. It did, however, confirm my belief in the power of language and NLP.

Chapter 3
Chunking

Forms of Chunking

Reframing processes frequently alter the meaning of an experience or judgment by "re-chunking" it. In NLP, the term "chunking" refers to reorganizing or breaking down some experience into bigger or smaller pieces. *"Chunking up"* involves moving to a larger, more general or abstract level of information – for example, grouping cars, trains, boats and airplanes as "forms of transportation." *"Chunking down"* involves moving to a more specific and concrete level of information – for example, a "car" may be chunked down into "tires," "engine," "brake system," "transmission," etc. *"Chunking laterally"* involves finding other examples at the same level of information – for instance, "driving a car" could be likened to "riding a horse," "peddling a bicycle" or "sailing a boat."

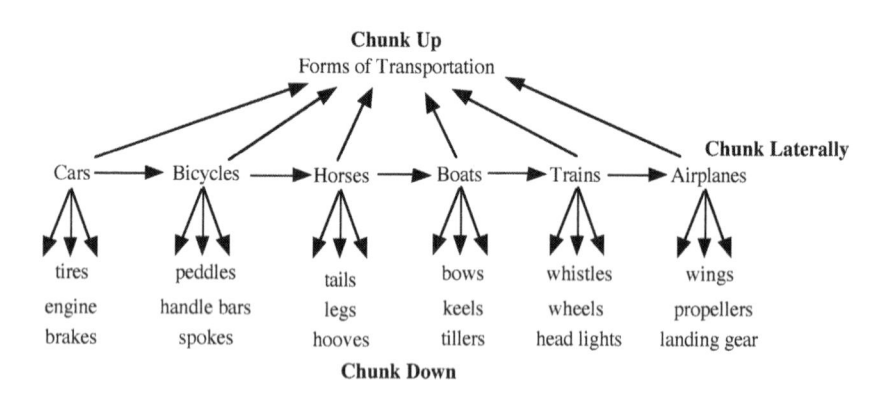

Chunk Up
Forms of Transportation

Chunk Laterally

Cars → Bicycles → Horses → Boats → Trains → Airplanes

tires	peddles	tails	bows	whistles	wings
engine	handle bars	legs	keels	wheels	propellers
brakes	spokes	hooves	tillers	head lights	landing gear

Chunk Down

"Chunking" Involves the Ability to Move Attention Between Generalities and Details

Chunking, then, has to do with how a person uses his or her attention. "Chunk-size" relates to the level of specificity or generality with which a person or group is analyzing or judging a problem or experience, and whether a judgment of generalization applies to a whole class or only certain members of the class. Situations may be perceived in terms of varying degrees of detail (micro chunks of information) and generalities (macro chunks of information). Someone could focus attention on small details, such as the spelling of individual words in a paragraph, or on larger portions of experience, such as the basic theme of the book. There is also the question of the relationships between big chunks and smaller chunks. (If a particular spelling is inaccurate, does it mean that the idea expressed by that spelling is also inaccurate?)

Given a particular situation, the way a person is chunking his or her experience may be helpful or problematic. When a person is attempting to think "realistically" it is valuable to think in smaller chunks. When brainstorming, however, attention on small chunks may lead the person to "losing sight of the forest for the trees."

Unhelpful criticisms are frequently stated in terms of fairly large 'chunks' or generalizations; such as: "That will never work," "You never follow through," or "You're always coming up with ideas that are too risky." Words like "always," "never," "ever," and "only," are known as *universals* or *universal quantifiers* in NLP. This type of language results from "chunking up" to a point that may no longer be accurate or useful. Transforming such a criticism into a 'how' question (as we explored earlier) frequently serves to help "chunk down" overgeneralizations.

Chunking down is a basic NLP process that involves reducing a particular situation or experience into its component pieces. A problem that seems overwhelming, for instance, may be chunked down into a series of smaller more manageable problems. There is an old riddle which asks, "How do you eat a whole watermelon?" The answer is an example of chunking down: "One bite at a time." This metaphor can be applied to any type of situation or experience. A very imposing goal, such as "starting a new business," may be chunked into sub-goals, such as "developing a product," "identifying potential clients," "selecting team members," "creating a business plan," "seeking investments," etc.

To develop competence with Sleight of Mouth, it is important to have flexibility in being able to move one's attention freely between little chunks and big chunks. As the Native Americans would say, "seeing with the eyes of a mouse or an eagle."

Finding the *intention* behind a particular behavior or belief, for instance, is considered the result of the ability to 'chunk up' in NLP. That is, you need to be able to find the broader classification of which the judgment or behavior is an expression (i.e., "protection," "acknowledgment," "respect," etc.). *Redefining* involves the additional abilities to 'chunk down' and 'chunk laterally', in order to identify concepts and experiences that are similar or related to those referred to in the initial statement, but which have different associations and implications.

Chunking Down

The processes of chunking up and chunking down may also be applied directly to a statement, judgment, or belief, in order to shift perceptions of them and 'reframe' them. The Sleight of Mouth pattern of *chunking down*, for instance, involves breaking the elements of a statement or judgment into smaller pieces, creating a different or enriched perception of the generalization expressed by the statement or judgment. For example, let's say someone has been diagnosed as "learning disabled" (an obvious 'problem frame' label). One could take the word "learning" and 'chunk it down' into words which reflect various components of the process to which the term "learning" refers; such as: "inputting," "representing," "storing," and "retrieving" information. One can then ask, "Does learning disabled mean someone is also 'inputting' disabled? That is, is the problem that the person is unable to input information?" Likewise, does being learning disabled mean a person is "representing disabled," "storing disabled," or "retrieving disabled"?

Such questions and considerations can stimulate us to rethink our assumptions about what such labels mean, and help to put the situation back into a 'feedback frame'. It helps to shift our attention back to people and processes, rather than categories.

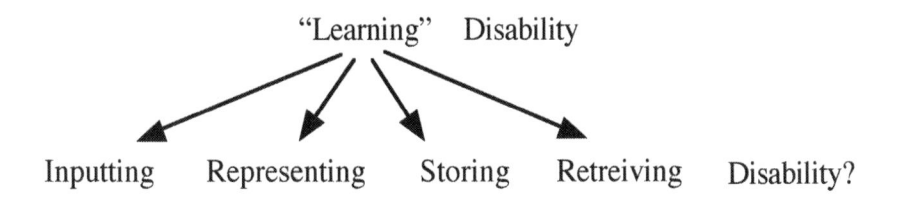

"Learning" Disability

Inputting   Representing   Storing   Retreiving   Disability?

Chunking Down a Generalization can Change Our Perceptions and Assumptions About It

Verbs and process words can be 'chunked' into the sequence of sub-processes which make them up (as in the example of "learning" above). A term like "failure," for example, could be chunked into the series of steps making up the "failure" experience, such as: setting (or not setting) a goal; establishing (or neglecting) a plan; taking (or avoiding) action; attending to (or ignoring) feedback; responding in a flexible (or rigid) way; etc.

Nouns and objects can be chunked into the smaller components which make them up. If someone says, "This car is too expensive," for instance, one could 'chunk down' by responding, "Well, actually the tires, windshield, exhaust pipe, gasoline and oil are as inexpensive as any other car. It is only the brakes and engine that cost a bit more in order to ensure performance and safety." In a statement such as, "I am unattractive," even the word "I" can be 'chunked down' by questioning, "Are your nostrils, forearm, little toes, voice tone, hair color, elbows, dreams, etc., all equally unattractive?"

Again, this process often places a judgment or evaluation in a completely different framework.

Practice this process for yourself. Find some negative label, judgment or generalization, noting the key words. 'Chunk down' one of the key words linguistically by finding *smaller* elements or chunks, which are implied by the statement or judgment. See if you can find reformulations that have richer or more positive implications than the ones stated in the label, judgment or generalization; or which stimulate a completely different perspective with respect to the label, judgment or generalization.

———————— Key Word

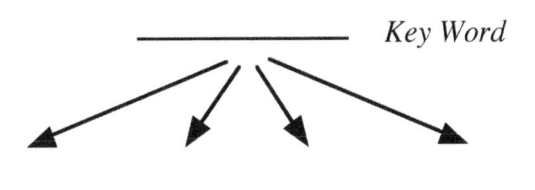

Smaller 'Chunks'

You might take a label like "attention deficit" and explore different types of attention (visual, auditory, kinesthetic, for instance; or attention to goals, oneself, context, past, internal state, etc.).

Chunking Up

The Sleight of Mouth pattern of *chunking up* involves generalizing an element of a statement or judgment to a larger classification, creating a new or enriched perception of the generalization being expressed. "Learning," for example, is a member of a larger class of processes which may be referred to as various forms of "adaptation"—which also includes processes such as "conditioning," "instinct," "evolution," etc. If a person has been termed "learning disabled," does that mean that the person is also to some degree "adaptation disabled?" And, why doesn't the person also have a "conditioning disability," "instinct disability," or "evolution disability?" Some of these terms sound almost comical, and yet they are a possible logical extension of such labels.

Again, reconsidering the judgment with respect to this type of "re-framing" leads us to consider our meaning and assumptions from a new perspective, and move it out of a 'problem frame'.

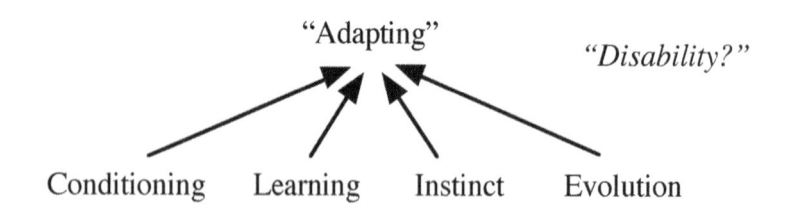

"Adapting"   "Disability?"

Conditioning   Learning   Instinct   Evolution

Chunking Up can Lead us to Reconsider the Implications of a Generalization or Judgment

Practice this process for yourself. Take the same negative label, judgment or generalization you used in the previous example. 'Chunk up' one of the key words linguistically by identifying some larger classification, into which that word could fit, that has richer or more positive implications than the ones stated in the label, judgment or generalization; or which stimulate a completely different perspective with respect to the label, judgment or generalization.

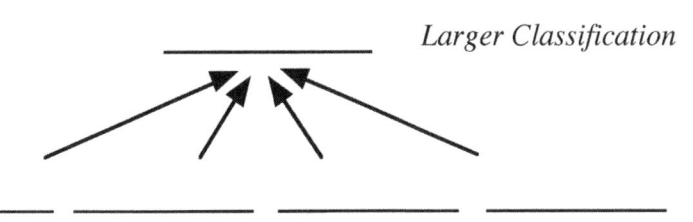

Larger Classification

Key Word   Other Processes or Object in the Same Class

"Failure," for instance, could be 'chunked up' to the class of "behavioral consequences," or "forms of feedback." Being "unattractive" could be chunked up to "varying from the norm." "Expense" could be chunked up to "cash flow considerations." And so on.

Chunking Laterally (Finding Analogies)

Chunking laterally typically takes the form of finding metaphors or analogies. The Sleight of Mouth pattern of *analogy* involves finding a relationship analogous to that defined by the generalization or judgment which gives us a new perspective on the implications of that generalization or judgment. We might say, for example, that a "learning disability" *is like* a "malfunctioning computer program." This would lead us naturally to ask questions such as, "Where is the malfunction?" "What is its cause and how can it be corrected?" "Does the problem come from a particular line of code? Is it in the whole program? The computer media? Perhaps the source of the problem is with the programmer."

Analogies such as this, stimulate us to enrich our perspective of a particular generalization or judgment, and to discover and evaluate our assumptions. They also help us to shift from a problem frame to an outcome frame or feedback frame.

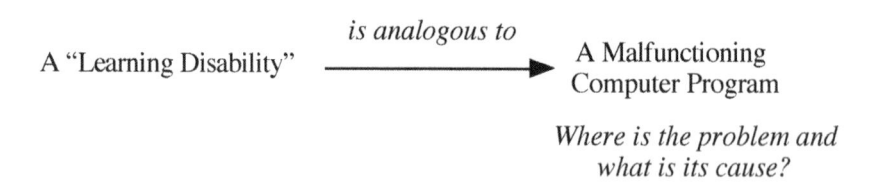

A "Learning Disability" — *is analogous to* → A Malfunctioning Computer Program

Where is the problem and what is its cause?

'Chunking Laterally' Involves Finding Analogies Which can Stimulate New Ideas and Perspectives

According to anthropologist and communication theorist Gregory Bateson, 'chunking laterally' to find analogies is a function of *abductive thinking*. Abductive thinking can be contrasted with "inductive" and "deductive" processes.

Inductive reasoning involves classifying particular objects or phenomena according to common features that they share - noticing that all birds have feathers for example. Inductive reasoning is essentially the process of 'chunking up'.

Deductive reasoning involves making predictions about a particular object or phenomenon based on its classification; i.e., *if - then* type logic. Deduction involves 'chunking down'.

Abductive reasoning involves looking for the similarities between objects and phenomena - i.e., 'chunking laterally'.

Gregory Bateson illustrated the difference between deductive logic and abductive thinking by contrasting the following statements:

Deductive	**Abductive**
Men die. Socrates is a man. Socrates will die.	Men die. Grass dies. Men are Grass.

Comparison of Abductive and Deductive Thinking Processes

According to Bateson, deductive and inductive thinking focuses more on objects and categories rather than structure and relationship. Bateson argued that thinking exclusively through inductive and deductive reasoning can cause a rigidity in one's thinking. Abductive or metaphorical thinking leads to more creativity and may actually lead us to discover deeper truths about reality.

Practice this process for yourself. Again, take the negative label, judgment or generalization you used in the previous examples. 'Chunk laterally' by finding some other process or phenomenon, which is analogous to that defined by the label, judgment or evaluation (i.e., is a metaphor for it), but which has new or richer implications than the ones stated in the label, judgment or generalization; or which stimulates a completely different perspective with respect to the label, judgment or generalization.

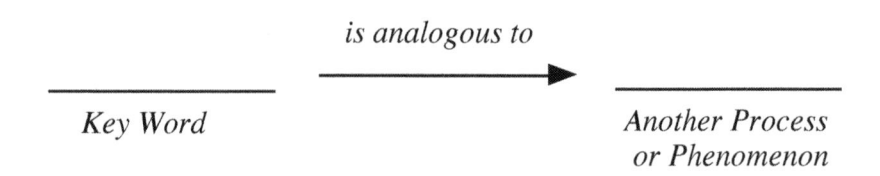

is analogous to

Key Word　　　　　　　　　　　　Another Process
　　　　　　　　　　　　　　　　　or Phenomenon

An analogy for "failure," for instance, could be Columbus' inability to establish a trade route to the Orient, and ending up in North America instead. A baby swan (or "ugly duckling") is a classic example of an enriching analogy for an "unattractive" person. An analogy could be made between "expense" and the "energy" required for physical exercise and growth. And so on.

Exercise: Finding Isomorphisms

The ability to 'chunk laterally' and create analogies is a fundamental skill for constructing therapeutic metaphors. Therapeutic metaphors involve establishing isomorphisms or parallels between the characters and events in the story and the listener's situation in order to help them find new perspectives and activate resources.

The following exercise can help you to develop and apply your lateral thinking abilities:

In groups of three; A, B and C.

1. A tells B and C about a current problem or situation for which A would like some guidance. e.g., A would like to get in a new relationship, but is hesitant because of problems he or she has experienced from previous partnerships.

2. B and C listen for the significant elements in A's situation or problem. e.g., "The focus on the past is preventing A from moving forward in his or her life."

3. B and C concur regarding the important contextual elements, characters, relationships and processes in A's situation. B paraphrases these to A to check for accuracy.

4. B and C get together and construct a metaphor to deliver to A. B and C may use the following sources for inspiration:

    Fantasy
    Universal themes
    General Life experiences

Personal Life Experiences
Nature: Animals, Seasons, Plants, Geology, Geography etc.
Folk Tales
Science Fiction
Sports

e.g., "My grandfather taught me how to drive. He told me that I could drive quite safely looking only in the rear view mirror, providing the road ahead is exactly the same as the road behind."

5. Rotate until each player has been in the A role.

Punctuation and Repunctuation

The various forms of chunking (up, down and laterally) provide a powerful set of linguistic tools to help us enrich, reframe, and "re-punctuate" our maps of the world. Different "punctuations" of our perception of the world allow us to create different meanings of the same experience. For example, in the use of written language, we punctuate a series of words in different ways; as a question, statement or demand. The commas, exclamation points and question marks allow us to know which meaning is implied. A similar action occurs in the organization of our experience.

Punctuation is defined in the dictionary as "the act or practice of inserting standardized marks or signs to clarify the meaning and separate structural units." In NLP, the term "punctuation" is used to refer to how an individual chunks an experience into meaningful units of perception. This type of cognitive punctuation functions analogously to the way linguistic punctuation operates in written and spoken language.

Consider for a moment the following words:

that that is is that that is not is not is not that it it is

At first glance, these words seem like gibberish. They have no meaning. But notice how your experience of them changes if they are punctuated in the following manner:

That that is, is. That that is not, is not. Is not that it? It is!

Suddenly, there is at least some meaning to them. The punctuation, which is on a different level than the words themselves, organizes and 'frames' them in a way that shifts our perception of them.

The words could be punctuated in other ways as well. Compare the previous punctuation with the following examples:

That! That is. Is that? That is not, is not, is not! That it? It is.

That? That is!
Is that that?
Is not!
Is!
Not!
Is!
Not that!
It, it is.

The content of our experience is like the first string of words. It is relatively neutral and even void of any real meaning. Cognitive processes, such as chunking, time perception, and representational channels, determine where we place our mental and emotional question marks, periods and exclamation points. Our mental punctuation influences which perceptions are clustered together, where our focus of attention is placed, what types of relationships are perceptible, etc. For example, considering an event in terms of its 'long term future' implications will give it a different significance than evaluating it with respect to the 'short term past'. Viewing a particular detail with respect to the "big picture" is different than seeing it in relationship to other details.

People don't usually argue, become depressed, or kill each other over the content of their experience and maps of the world in and of itself. Rather, they fight over where to place the exclamation points and question marks that give the content different meanings.

For instance, take a piece of information like, "Profits were down last quarter." A dreamer, realist and critic would perceive or 'punctuate' the exact same data in different ways, based on different beliefs, values and expectations.

Critic: Profits were down last quarter. This is terrible! We're ruined (exclamation point)!

Realist: Profits were down last quarter. We have had difficult times in the past (comma), what can we do to make ourselves 'leaner' (question mark)?

Dreamer: Profits were down last quarter. It's just a bump in the road (semi colon); we're past the most difficult phase now. Things are bound to look up.

Sleight of Mouth is largely about how language leads us to punctuate and repunctuate our maps of the world, and how these punctuations give meaning to our experience.

Chapter 4
Values and Criteria

The Structure of Meaning

Meaning has to do with the intention or significance of a message or experience. The term, from the Middle English *menen* (Old English *maenan*), is akin to Old High German *meinen*, which meant "to have in mind." Thus, meaning relates to the inner representations or experiences that are associated with external cues and events.

NLP processes and models, such as those characterized by Sleight of Mouth, were developed to explore and discover "how" we symbolize, signify or represent experiential data, and how we interpret or give that data inner significance in our maps of the world—in other words, how we make "meaning." From the NLP perspective, meaning is a function of the relationship between "map and territory." Different maps of the world will produce different inner meanings for the same experiential territory. The same incident or experience in the external world will take on different meanings or significance to different individuals, or different cultures, depending on their internal maps. Having a lot of money, for instance, may be looked upon as "success" for some people, but a "risk" or a "burden" by others. As another example, belching, in an Arabic culture, typically signifies, "thanks for the satisfying meal." In other cultures, however, it may mean that the person is suffering from indigestion, is unmannered, or rude.

All animals have the ability to create codes and maps of the world and to give meaning to their experience of these maps. Meaning is the natural consequence of interpreting our experience. What meaning we make and how we make it is connected with the richness and flexibility of our internal representations of the world. A limited map of an experience will most likely produce a limited meaning. NLP emphasizes the importance of exploring different perspectives and levels of experience in order to create the possibility of discovering different potential meanings with respect to a situation or experience.

Because meaning is a function of our *internal representations* of our experience, altering those internal representations can alter the meaning an experience has for us. Sensory representations constitute the 'deep structure' of our language. Feeling "success" is a different experience than visualizing it or talking about it. Shifting the color, tone, intensity, amount of movement, etc., (the "submodality" qualities) of internal representations can also alter the meaning and impact of a particular experience.

Meaning is also greatly influenced by *context*. The same communication or behavior will take on different meanings in different contexts. We will respond differently if we see someone apparently shot or stabbed on the stage of a theater, than if we see the same behavior in the alley behind the theater. Thus, perception of context and contextual cues is an important aspect of the ability to make meaning of a message or event.

The mental *frames* we place around our perception of a situation, message, or event serves as a type of internally generated context for our experience. Perceiving a situation from a "problem frame," will focus our attention on certain aspects of that situation, and attach different meanings to events, than if we perceive the same situation from an "outcome frame" or a "feedback versus failure frame." Assumptions about the *intent* behind a behavior or communication also create a type of frame that influences the way in which they are interpreted. This is what makes the NLP processes of Framing and Reframing such powerful tools with which to transform the meaning of a situation or experience.

Another influence on meaning is the *medium* or *channel* through which a message or experience is received or perceived. A spoken word will trigger different types of meaning than a visual symbol, a touch or a smell. Media theorist Marshall McLuhan claimed that the medium through which a particular message was transmitted had more impact on how that message was received and interpreted than the message itself.

Thus, the way a person makes meaning of a communication is largely determined by the para-messages and *meta messages* that accompany that communication. Non verbal "meta messages" are like guides and markers on transmitted messages which tell us how to interpret a message in order to give it the appropriate meaning. The same words, said with different intonation and voice stress patterns, will take on different meaning (i.e., there is a difference between "No?", "No.", and "*No!*").

One of the fundamental principles of NLP is that *the meaning of a communication, to the receiver, is the response it elicits in that receiver, regardless of the intention of the communicator.* There is a classic example of a medieval castle that was under siege by foreign troops. As the siege went on, the people within the castle began to run out of food. Determined not to give up, they decided to show their defiance by putting every last bit of their food in a basket and catapulting it over the wall at troops outside. When the foreign soldiers, who were also getting low on supplies, saw the food, they interpreted it to mean that the people in the castle had so much food that they were throwing it at the soldiers to taunt them. To the surprise of the people in the castle, the troops, who had become disheartened by their interpretation of the message, abruptly abandoned the siege and left.

Fundamentally, meaning is a product of our *values* and *beliefs*. It relates to the question, "Why?" The messages, events and experiences that we find most "meaningful" are those which are most connected to our core values (safety, survival, growth, etc.). Beliefs relating to cause-and-effect and the connection between perceived events and our values largely determine the meaning we give to those perceived events. Altering beliefs and values can immediately change the meaning of our life experiences. Sleight of Mouth Patterns operate to shift the meaning of events and experiences by updating or altering the values and beliefs associated with them.

Values and Motivation

According to Webster's Dictionary, *values* are "principles, qualities or entities that are intrinsically valuable or desirable." The term "value" originally meant "the worth of something," chiefly in the economic sense of exchange value. The use of the term was broadened to include a more philosophic interpretation during the 19th century; under the influence of thinkers and philosophers such as Friedrich Nietzsche. These philosophers coined the term *axiology* (from the Greek *axios*, meaning "worthy") to describe the study of values.

Because they are associated with worth, meaning and desire, values are a primary source of motivation in people's lives. When people's values are met or matched, they feel a sense of satisfaction, harmony, or rapport. When their values are not met, people often feel dissatisfied, incongruent, or violated.

As an exploration of your own values, consider for a moment how you would respond to the following questions, "In general, what motivates you?" "What is most important to you?" "What moves you to action, or 'gets you out of bed in the morning?'"

Some possible answers might be:

Success
Praise
Recognition
Responsibility
Pleasure
Love and Acceptance
Achievement
Creativity

Values such as these greatly influence and direct the outcomes that we establish and the choices that we make.

The goals that we set for ourselves are, in fact, the tangible expression of our values. A person who has a goal to "create an effective team," for instance, most likely values "working together with others." A person whose goal is to "increase profits" probably values "financial success." Similarly, a person who has a value of "stability" will set goals that are related to achieving stability in his or her personal or professional life. Such a person will seek different outcomes than a person who values "flexibility," for example. A person who values stability may be content with a 9 to 5 job that has consistent pay and involves well established tasks. A person who values flexibility, on the other hand, may try to find work involving a range of tasks and a variable time schedule.

A person's values will also shape how that individual "punctuates" or gives meaning to his or her perception of a particular situation. This determines which kinds of mental strategies a person selects to approach that situation and, ultimately, that person's actions in that situation. A person who values "safety," for example, will constantly evaluate a situation or activity from whether or not it harbors any potential "danger." A person who values "fun" will assess the same situation or activity seeking opportunities for humor or play.

Values, then, are the basis for motivation and persuasion, and serve as a powerful perceptual filter. When we can connect our future plans and goals to our core values and criteria, those goals become even more compelling. All Sleight of Mouth patterns revolve around using language in order to relate and link various aspects of our experience and maps of the world to core values.

Criteria and Judgment

In NLP, values are often equated with what are known as "criteria", but the two are not entirely synonymous. Values relate to what we desire and want. *Criteria* refer to the standards and evidences we apply in order to make decisions and judgments. The term comes from the Greek word *krites*, meaning "judge." Our criteria define and shape the types of desired states that we will seek, and determine the evidences we will use to evaluate our success and progress with respect to these desired states. For example, applying the criterion of "stability" to a product, organization or family, will lead to certain judgments and conclusions. Applying the criterion of "ability to adapt" may lead to different judgments and conclusions about the same product, organization or family.

Criteria are often associated with "values," but they are not synonymous. Criteria may be applied to any number of different levels of experience. We can have environmental criteria, behavioral criteria and intellectual criteria as well as emotionally based criteria. From this perspective, values are similar to what are called *core criteria* in NLP.

Values and core criteria are classic examples of "subjective" experience; in contrast with "facts" and observable actions, which represent "objectivity." Two individuals can claim to have the same values and yet act quite differently in similar situations. This is because, even though people may share similar values (like "success," "harmony," and "respect"), they may have very different forms of evidence for judging whether these criteria have been met or violated. This can be the source of either conflict or creative diversity.

One of the challenges in defining, teaching, debating, or even talking about values and criteria is that the language used to express them is often very general and 'non-sensory based'. Values and core criteria are expressed by words such as: "success," "safety," "love," "integrity," etc. These types of words, known as *nominalizations* in NLP, are notoriously "slippery." As labels, they tend to be much farther removed from any specific sensory experience than words like "chair," "run," "sit," "house," etc. This makes them much more susceptible to the processes of generalization, deletion and distortion. It is not uncommon for two individuals to claim to share the same values and yet act quite differently in similar situations, because their subjective definitions of the values vary so widely.

People, of course, also frequently operate from different values. One person, or group, may seek "stability" and "security" while another desires "growth" and "self development." Recognizing that people have different values and criteria is essential for resolving conflicts and managing diversity. Culture contact, mergers between organizations and transitions in a person's life often bring up issues related to differences in values and criteria.

The principles and patterns of Sleight of Mouth can be used to help resolve problems and issues relating to values and criteria in a number of ways:

1. "Chaining" criteria and values by *redefining* them
2. Chunking Down to define *"criterial equivalences"*
3. Chunking Up to identify and utilize *"hierarchies" of values and criteria*

Chaining Criteria and Values by Redefining Them

Situations often arise in which there seem to be differences in the core values or criteria of individuals or groups. A company, for example, may have a core value of "globalization." Some individuals within the company, however, may be driven by the criterion of "security." These types of seemingly fundamental differences can create conflict and dissension if not properly addressed in some way.

One way to deal with perceived conflicts in values is to use the Sleight of Mouth pattern of *redefining* in order to create a "chain" linking the different criteria. As an example, "globalization" can be easily reframed to "working together with diverse people." "Security" can be reframed to "the safety of being part of a group." In many ways, "working together with diverse people" and "being part of a group" are quite similar. Thus, the simple verbal reframes have closed the gap between the two seemingly incompatible criteria.

As another example, let's say a company has a highly valued criterion of "quality;" but a particular person or team within that company values "creativity." These two values might initially seem at odds with one another. "Quality," however, could be reframed as "continual improvement." "Creativity" could be reframed as "producing better alternatives." Again, the simple reframes help people to see the connection between the two seemingly disparate criteria.

Try this out yourself using the spaces provided below. Write two seemingly opposed criteria in the spaces titled Criterion #1 and Criterion #2. Then, reframe each criterion using a word or phrase that overlaps with the criterion but offers a different perspective. See if you can find reframes that "chain" the two initial criteria together in a way that make them more compatible.

One example might be:

<u>Professionalism</u> —> <u>*Personal Integrity*</u>   <u>*Self Expression*</u> <— <u>Freedom</u>
Criterion #1   —>   Reframe #1   Reframe #2 <— Criterion #2

Try finding reframes that help to chain the two criteria listed below:

<u>Customer Service</u> —> _____   _____ <— <u>Increased Profit</u>
Criterion #1   —> Reframe #1   Reframe #2 <— Criterion #2

Write your own examples for Criterion #1 and Criterion #2 in the spaces below, and find simple verbal reframes that will help to create a chain linking the two.

_____ _____   _____ _____

Criterion #1 —> Reframe #1   Reframe #2 <— Criterion #2

_____ _____   _____ _____

Criterion #1 —> Reframe # 1   Reframe #2 <— Criterion #2

Chaining criteria is a form *chunking laterally* in order to link seemingly opposing values. Another way to avoid or resolve potential limitations and conflicts that can arise from the language used to express values is to *chunk down* values statements into more specific expressions, or *criterial equivalences*.

Chunking Down to Define "Criterial Equivalences"

"Criterial equivalence" is the term used in NLP to describe the specific and observable evidences that people use to define whether or not a particular criterion has been met. "Criteria" are related to goals and values. "Criterial equivalences" are related to the experiences and rules people use to evaluate their success in achieving particular criteria. Criteria and values are usually very general, abstract and ambiguous. They can take many shapes and forms. Criterial equivalences are the specific sensory or behavioral demonstrations or observations that are used to know if a criterion of value has been satisfied. Criterial equivalences are the result of evidence procedures. An *evidence procedure* links the *why* (the criteria and values) to the *how* (the observations and strategies used to attempt to satisfy the criteria).

The type of sensory evidence, or criterial equivalences, that a person uses to evaluate an idea, product or situation will determine to a large extent whether it is judged as being interesting, desirable or successful, etc. People often differ in the sensory channels, level of detail and perspectives that they use to evaluate their success in meeting their criteria. Effective persuasion, for example, involves the ability to identify and then meet a person's core criteria by matching their criterial equivalence. Establishing criteria and criterial equivalences is also an important part of team building, creating and managing organizational culture, and strategic planning.

Defining criterial equivalences involves asking, "How do you know if some behavior or consequence fits a particular criterion or value?" On a personal level, we hold or represent the "deeper structure" of our values to ourselves non-linguistically in the form of inner pictures, sounds, words and feelings. To explore some of your own criterial equivalences, try the following:

1. Think of some value or criterion that is important for you to satisfy (quality, creativity, uniqueness, health, etc.)
2. How do you know, specifically, that you have met this value or criterion? Is it something you see? Hear? Feel? Do you know it based solely on your own evaluation, or do you need verification from outside of yourself (i.e., from another person or an objective measurement)?

The sensory perceptions that form our criterial equivalences greatly influence how we think and feel about something. Consider the ways in which your sensory perceptions influence your degree of motivation. Think of an advertisement on television that made you want to own the product being advertised, for example. What was it about the ad that inspired you to go out and buy the product? Was it the color, brightness, music, words, tone of voice, movement, etc. These particular features are known as "submodalities" in NLP, and often play a significant role in people's motivation strategies.

Explore this for yourself by trying out the following exercise:

1. Imagine that you have already achieved a goal or outcome that matches the criterion you identified above, and are really enjoying it. Get in touch with what you are seeing, hearing, doing and feeling while enjoying these benefits.
2. Adjust the sensory qualities of your internal experience in such a way that it feels more motivating or compelling. Does the experience become more compelling and attractive if you add more color? Brightness? Sound? Words? Movement? What happens if you bring the image closer or move it farther away? What happens if you make the sounds or words louder or softer? What do you experience if you make the movement quicker or slower? Identify which qualities make the experience feel the best.

Reality Strategies

Criterial equivalences are closely related to a person's *reality strategy.* Reality strategies involve the sequence of mental tests and internal criteria an individual applies in order to evaluate whether or not a particular experience or event is "real" or "really happened." It is essentially the strategy by which we distinguish "fantasy" from "reality."

It is a common childhood experience to think that something really happened that was actually a dream or a fantasy. Even many adults are unsure whether or not a powerful experience they had as a child was real or imagined. Another common experience is when you have been absolutely certain you told someone something and they claim you didn't, and later you realized you rehearsed it in your mind but never actually talked about it with the person.

From the NLP perspective, we will never know exactly what reality is, because our brain doesn't *really* know the difference between imagined experience or remembered experience. The fact is, the same brain cells are used to represent both. There is no specific part of the brain that has been designated for "fantasy" and "reality." Because of that, we have to have a strategy that tells us that information received through the senses passes certain tests that imagined information does not.

Try a little experiment. Think of something that you could have done yesterday but know you didn't do. For example, perhaps you could have gone shopping yesterday, but you didn't. Then think of something you know you did do—like go to work or talk with a friend. Contrast the two in your mind—how do you determine that you didn't do one and did do the other? The difference can be subtle, but the qualities of your internal pictures, sounds and kinesthetic feelings will probably differ in some way. As you contrast your imagined experience with your real one, check your internal representations—are they located in the same place in your field of vision? Is one clearer than the other? Is one a movie and one a still picture? Are there differences in the qualities of your internal voices? What about the quality of feelings you have associated with those two experiences?

The quality of information that we have in our senses is somehow coded more precisely for the real experience than the imagined one, and that's what makes the difference. You have a "reality strategy" that lets you know the difference.

Many people have tried to change or "re-program" themselves by visualizing themselves being successful. For all the people who naturally use this as a strategy, it will work fine. For all the people that use a voice that says, "You can do it," this visual programming won't work. If I want to make something real for you, or convince you about something, I have got to make it fit your criteria for your reality strategy. I have to make it consistent with the required qualities of your internal pictures, sounds and feelings (i.e., submodalities.) So, if I assist you in changing your behavior in some way, I want to make sure that it is going to fit in with you as a person. By identifying your reality strategy, you can determine precisely *how you* need to represent a change in behavior in order to be convinced that it is something that is possible for you to accomplish.

In many ways, NLP is the study of how we create our maps of reality, what holds that reality or map in a stable form, how it is destabilized, and what makes a map effective or not. NLP assumes that there are different realities expressed in our different maps of the world.

The system or strategies of reality that we create, and how that system interacts to form our maps of reality, has been a focus in NLP since its inception. Reality strategies are the glue which hold our maps together – how we "know" something to be so. Consider the following example of eliciting a person's reality strategy with respect to her name:

Q: What is your name?

L My name is Lucy.

Q: How do you know your name is Lucy?

L: Well, that is what I have been called all my life.

Q: How do you know, as you sit here right now, that you have been called that "all your life?" Do you hear something?

L: Yes. I just hear a voice saying, "My name is Lucy."

Q: If you didn't have a voice saying your name is Lucy, how would you know your name is Lucy?

L: I see a banner in my mind's eye, the word "Lucy" is written on it.

Q: If you couldn't see this banner, or it was out of focus and you couldn't read the word, how would you know that your name is Lucy?

L: I would just know.

Q: If you saw many banners with different names on them, how would you know the one that says "Lucy" is your name?

L: Its a feeling.

This example illustrates some common features of a "reality strategy." The person "knows" Lucy is her real name because she has it "cross-referenced" in multiple representational systems. Ultimately, "Lucy" had a feeling that was associated with that name. If Lucy could make arrangements so that she would not experience or notice that feeling, it would be interesting to find out if Lucy would still know her name. If such an exercise is taken far enough, a person can even come to doubt something as fundamental as his or her own name.

When a person truly begins to get to the root of his or her reality strategy, it can become a bit disorienting, and even frightening; but it also opens up the doorway to new learnings and discoveries. As an example, there was an psychoanalyst, studying NLP, who was very interested in his reality strategy. He discovered that he had constant internal dialog. The psychoanalyst realized that he was verbally labeling all of his experience to himself. For example, he would walk into a room and internally say, "a picture," "a couch," "a fireplace," etc. When asked if he could silence the voice, he was reluctant to give it up because he was afraid he would lose contact with reality as he knew it. When asked if there was anything he could do which would allow him to comfortably let go of his internal voices, he said, "I need something to hold on to." He was instructed to hold a spoon and maintain contact with reality kinesthetically. By doing so, he was able to expand his reality strategy and literally open himself up to a new "non-verbal" way of experiencing reality.

To explore your own reality strategy, try out the following exercise.

Reality Strategy Exercise

Part 1:

(a) Pick some trivial thing that you did yesterday, and something you could have done but did not do. Make sure that the thing that you could have done but did not do is something that is completely within your range of behavior. If you could have put peanut butter on your ice cream, but you don't like peanut butter on your ice cream, you wouldn't really have done that anyway. Pick examples of things that you have done before (such as brushing your teeth and having a cup of tea). The only difference should be that you "actually" did do one of them yesterday – i.e., you brushed your teeth, but did not have a cup of tea (even though you could have had tea).

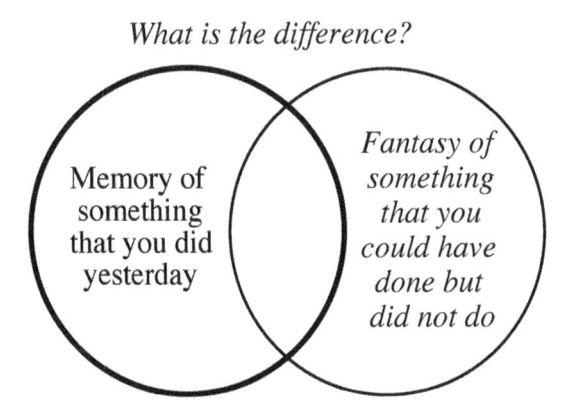

What is the difference?

Memory of something that you did yesterday

Fantasy of something that you could have done but did not do

Explore Your 'Reality Strategy' by Contrasting a Memory of Something that Did Happen Yesterday with Something that Could Have Happened But Did Not.

(b) Determine how you know the difference between what you did and what you could have done, but did not do. What you come up with first will typically be the most obvious reality check. You might have a picture of one and not of the other. After you make the picture, you may notice other things about it. Check the submodality differences for instance. Maybe one is a movie and the other is a still picture. Maybe one has more color or is brighter than the other. To explore successively deeper layers of your reality strategy, take each distinction that you discover and apply it to the memory that 'did not' actually happen. That is, make the sensory qualities of your representation of the event that did not happen more and more like the one that did happen. How do you still know that one happened and one did not? Keep making the one that 'did not' happen more and more like the one that 'did' happen until you actually cannot tell the difference.

The following is a list of some of the ways in which people know something "really" happened:

1) *Timing* – What comes to mind first? Often we determine an experience is "real" because it is the first association we make when asked to think of something.

2) *Involvement of Multiple Representational Systems* – i.e., there are sights, sounds, feelings, tastes and smells associated with the experience. Usually, the more senses that are involved in a memory, the more "real" it seems.

3) *Submodalities* – The sensory quality of an internal experience is one of the most common reality strategies. If a mental image is associated, intense, clear, life size, etc., it seems more "real."

4) *Continuity* – The fit of a particular memory (its "logical flow") with the memory of other events immediately

preceding and following the one upon which we are focusing. If something doesn't "fit in" with our other memories, it is likely to seem less "real."

5) *Probability* – Probability is an evaluation of the likelihood that something could occur based on information that we have about past behaviors. Sometimes we perceive something as not being "real" because it is 'improbable' or unlikely to have occurred, given the rest of the information that we have. (This begins to overlap with our belief or convincer strategies.)

6) *Context* – The degree of detail relating to the surroundings or background of some memory is another cue about how "real" it is. Often, manufactured experiences delete details about the surrounding context because they are not considered important.

7) *Congruency* – The degree to which some experience fits into our beliefs relating to our personal habits and values also effects our perception of its "reality." We are less likely to perceive the memory of some possible action we could have taken as "real" if it is not congruent with our beliefs about ourselves.

8) *'Meta' Memory* – A person will often have a memory of having created or manipulated the imaginary experience. This 'meta' memory can be a key part of a person's reality strategy. Such 'meta' memory processes can be enhanced by having people learn how to 'mark' internal experiences that have been fabricated or manipulated; by putting an imaginary picture frame around them, for instance.

9) *Accessing Cues* – A key part of many reality strategies, that is often outside of people's consciousness, is the physiology associated with memory. Memories are typically accompanied by an eye movement up and to the left (for right handed people), while fantasies are accom-

panied by an eye movement up and to the right. While people are not usually consciously aware of such subtle cues, they may use them unconsciously to distinguish reality from fantasy.

Part II:

(c) Pick two things that happened during your childhood and determine how you know that they were real. You're going to find that it is a bit harder to determine exactly what happened back then. In Part I, you took something that happened less than 24 *hours* ago, and shifted your perception of reality with respect to it. When you consider something that happened 24 *years* ago, it's an even more interesting decision process, because your pictures may not be as clear, and may possibly be distorted. In fact, for distant memories, sometimes people know the real things that happened because they are actually fuzzier than the experiences they have made up.

(d) Think of something that did not happen in your childhood, but if it had would have made a powerfully positive impact on your life. Create an internal representation of this event. Then make the submodalities and other qualities of this fantasy match the qualities that you use in your reality strategy. How does this change your experience of your past?

In both Part I and Part II of this exercise, try to get to a point where you really have to think about which experience was real. But be careful as you begin to change the qualities of the experience that you didn't have to be represented like the experience you did have. The object of this exercise is not to confuse your reality strategies, but to find out what reality checks exist for you. Remember, your goal is to elicit your reality strategy, not disrupt it. If the process starts getting scary (which it sometimes can), you may begin to hear a swishing sound, or maybe you'll feel yourself spinning. In such cases it is appropriate and ecological to stop for a while.

Confusion with respect to one's reality strategy can lead to deep uncertainty. In fact, the inability to distinguish imagination from "reality" is considered one of the symptoms of psychosis and other severe mental disorders. Thus, understanding, enriching and strengthening one's own reality strategy can be an important source of increasing one's mental health.

The value of knowing your reality strategy is that you can use it for future pacing new experiences, so that they already seem "real." People like Leonardo da Vinci, Nicola Tesla and Wolfgang Mozart were able to create fantasies in their heads, and, by making them fit the criteria of their reality strategies, turn those fantasies into realities. They can also be used to help people develop a stronger sense of their own point of view and become clearer about their own thoughts and experiences.

When applied to generalizations and beliefs as one of the Sleight of Mouth patterns, exploring reality strategies serves to help people chunk down to discover the (frequently unconscious) representations and assumptions upon which they have built a particular belief or generalization. This can help them to either reaffirm or question the validity of the generalization, belief or judgment. It helps people to recognize that their beliefs are indeed "beliefs," as opposed to "reality." This can automatically give people more choice, and serves as a type of "meta frame" around the belief. The person becomes free to ask, "Is this really what I want to believe?" "Is this the only generalization that can be drawn from those representations and experiences?" "Am I really so certain about the experiences from which this belief is drawn to want to hold on to this belief so strongly?"

Chunking Up to Identify and Utilize Hierarchies of Values and Criteria

It is also possible to chunk up values and criteria in order to identify deeper levels of values and criteria—i.e., their hierarchy of criteria. A person's or group's *hierarchy of criteria* is essentially the order of priorities that they apply in order to decide how to act in a particular situation. Hierarchies of values and criteria relate to the *degree* of importance or meaning which people attach to various actions and experiences.

An example of a 'hierarchy of criteria' would be a person who values 'health' more than 'financial success'. Such a person would tend to put his or her health "first." This person would probably structure his or her life more around physical activities than professional opportunities. A person whose hierarchy of criteria placed "financial success" over health would have a different life-style. He or she might sacrifice health and physical well-being in order to "get ahead" monetarily.

Clarifying people's hierarchies of values is important for successful mediation, negotiation and communication. Values hierarchies also play an important role in persuasion and motivation.

One of the main ways to elicit a person's hierarchy of criteria is through the process of finding what are known as "counter examples." Counter examples are, in essence, 'exceptions to the rule'. The following questions use the process of finding counter examples to reveal a person's hierarchy of criteria:

1. What is something that you could do, but do not do? Why?
    e.g., "I would not go into a toilet that has been marked for the opposite sex, because it is against the rules."
    Criterion = 'Follow the Rules'.

Values and Criteria

2. What could make you do it *anyway*? (Counter example)
   e.g., "I would go into a toilet marked for the opposite sex if there were no other choices, and I really had to go badly." Higher Criterion = 'Expediency in a Crisis'.

As the example illustrates, the identification of counter examples can help to uncover 'higher level' criteria which override others. To get a sense of your own hierarchy criteria by exploring counter examples, answer the following questions:

1. What would motivate you to try something new?
2. What would cause you to *stop* doing something, even if it satisfied your answer to question 1? (Counter example A)
3. What would make you *start* doing something *again*, even if you stopped for the reasons you identified in question 2? (Counter example B)
4. What would cause you to *stop* doing it *again*? (Counter example C)

As you reflect on your answers notice which criteria have emerged, and in what order of priority. Perhaps you would do something that you felt would be "creative," exciting" or "fun." These would be your first level of "criteria." You might stop doing something that was creative, exciting and fun, if you felt you felt that you were being "irresponsible" to your family (Counter example A). In this case, the criterion of "responsibility" would override "creativity" or "fun." You might, however, do something that you thought was "irresponsible" anyway if you felt it was "necessary for your growth as a person" (Counter example B). "Growth" would thus be higher on your 'hierarchy of criteria' than "responsibility" or "fun." Going more deeply, you might find that you would quit doing something that was "necessary for your growth as a person" if you believed it would "jeopardize the safety of yourself or your family" (Counter example C). Thus, "safety" would be higher on your "ladder" of criteria than the others.

Incidentally, another way to identify counter examples (and thus hierarchies of criteria) is to ask:

1. What would motivate you to try something new?
   e.g., "If it were safe and easy."
2. What would motivate you to try something new, even if it did not did *not* satisfy your answer to question 1? (i.e., If it was *not* safe and easy.)
   e.g., "If I could learn a lot from doing it."

Hierarchies of criteria are one of the main sources of difference between people, groups and cultures. Similar hierarchies of criteria, on the other hand, are the basis for compatibility between groups and individuals. Hierarchies of criteria are a key aspect of motivation and marketing. Consider, for instance, the following hypothetical example of using the process of finding counter-examples to identify a customer's hierarchy of criteria for purchasing beer:

Q: What type of beer do you usually buy?

A: Well, I usually get XYZ beer.

Q: Why XYZ beer?

A: It's the kind of beer I always get. I'm just used to it I guess. (*Criterion 1 = Familiarity*)

Q: Yes, its important to be familiar with what you're buying isn't it. Have you ever bought any other kind of beer? (*Identify counter-example*)

A: Sure. At times.

Q: What made you decide to buy it even though you weren't used to it? (*Elicit higher level criterion related to counter-example*)

A: It was on sale. A big discount from its usual price. (*Criterion 2 = Save Money*)

Q: Saving money can sure help out sometimes. I'm wondering, have you ever bought a beer that you weren't used to buying that wasn't on sale? (*Identify next counterexample*)

A: Yes. I was paying back some friends for helping me move into my new house. (*Criterion 3 = Show Appreciation to Others*)

Q: Good friends can be hard to come by. Its good to show them how much you appreciate them. Is there anything that would motivate you to buy a beer that was unfamiliar and wasn't inexpensive even though you didn't need to pay someone back for a favor? (*Identify next counter example*)

A: Well sure, I've bought more expensive beers when I've been out with the guys at work. I'm no cheapskate. (*Criterion 4 = Impress Others*)

Q: Yes, I guess there are certain situations where the kind of beer you buy can make a statement about your priorities. I'm really curious to know if there's anything that might get you to buy a more expensive unfamiliar beer if there was no one you owed a favor to or that you wanted to make a statement to? (*Identify next counterexample*)

A: I suppose I might do it if I really wanted to reward myself for doing something difficult. (*Criterion 5 = Appreciate Self*)

Assuming that this person is representative of a larger population of potential beer buyers, the interviewer has now uncovered a particular hierarchy of criteria that may be appealed to in order to sell an unfamiliar and more expensive beer to people that might not normally purchase it.

This process of eliciting hierarchies of criteria by identifying counter examples can also help in the process of effective persuasion. By getting people to answer these types of questions you can help them to break out of their habitual ways of thinking and can learn about the ordering of their values.

This information can then be used to get around boundaries that are often taken for granted. As an example, this method of questioning was once taught to a group of men who were shy about meeting women because they didn't think they had anything to offer a woman. They were instructed to go out and interview women and learn to identify values in women that could help them realize that they had more choices socially. The following is an example of one such interview:

Man: What kind of man would you most like to go out with?

Woman: Someone who is rich and handsome, naturally.

M: Have you ever gone out with someone who wasn't particularly rich or handsome?

W: Yes. There was this guy I knew who was really witty. He could make me laugh about practically anything.

M: Are the only people you go out with rich and handsome or witty, or do you ever consider going out with other kinds of people?

W: Well sure. I went out with this person who was so intelligent. He seemed to know something about everything.

M: What would make you consider going out with someone who wasn't rich, handsome or witty, and who didn't particularly impress you with their intelligence?

W: There was this one guy I really liked who didn't have any of those things but he just seemed to know where he was going in life and had the determination to get there.

M: Have you ever gone out with anyone who didn't have money, good looks, wit, intelligence or determination?

W: No. Not that I can remember.

M: Can you think of anything that would motivate you?

W: Well, if they did something or were involved in something that was unique or exciting I'd be interested.

M: Anything else?

W: If they really cared about me and helped me to get in touch with myself as a person, or brought out something special about me.

M: How would you know if someone really cared about you? . . .

This dialogue demonstrates how some simple questions may be used to get from surface level beliefs to deeper beliefs and values that can broaden a person's choices and flexibility.

Recognizing that people have different criteria (and different hierarchies of criteria) is essential for resolving conflicts and managing diversity. Some individuals and cultures value the 'achievement of tasks' more than they do the 'preservation of relationships'. Others have exactly the reverse set of priorities.

Hierarchy of Criteria is a key Sleight of Mouth pattern that involves re-evaluating (or reinforcing) a generalization according to a criterion that is more important than the criteria that are currently being addressed by the generalization.

The following technique is a procedure that applies this pattern in order to identify and override conflicts related to different levels of criteria.

Hierarchy of Criteria Technique

Criteria at different levels of one's "hierarchy of criteria" often bounce back and forth between "self" and "others," and move successively closer to core values by shifting to deeper 'levels' of experience. That is, behavioral level criteria (e.g., "to do or achieve something for others") are often overridden by those related to capabilities (e.g., "to learn something for myself"). Criteria at the level of capability are overridden by those at the level of beliefs and values (e.g., "to be responsible to others," or "follow the rules"). Beliefs and values, however, will be overridden by criteria at the level of identity (e.g., "to be a certain type of person," or "to maintain personal integrity").

Different levels of criteria are also often associated with particular representational systems or submodality qualities associated with their "criterial equivalences." Knowing about these different aspects of criteria can help you to 'pace and lead' or 'leverage' various levels of criteria in order to overcome conflicts and achieve desired outcomes more effectively. In the following procedure, spatial sorting and the counter example process are used to identify different levels of criteria, and their representational characteristics, in order to help transform inner resistance to establishing a new pattern of behavior.

Before beginning, lay out four different locations, side-by-side, as shown in the following diagram.

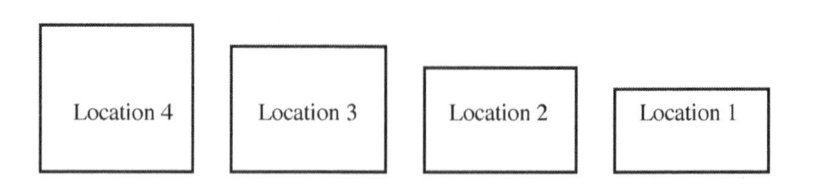

| Location 4 | Location 3 | Location 2 | Location 1 |

Spatial Layout for the Hierarchy of Criteria Technique

1. In Location #1 identify a **behavior** that you want to do, but stop yourself from doing.
   e.g., Exercising consistently.

2. Step into location #2 and identify the **criteria** that motivate you to want the new behavior.
   *e.g., I want to exercise in order to "**be healthy**" and "**look good**."*

   Identify the sensory representation or 'criterial equivalence' used to determine the criteria.
   e.g., an image of myself in the future being healthy and looking good

3. Move to Location #3 and elicit the criteria that stop you from actually doing the desired behavior.
   (**NOTE**: These will be **higher level criteria** because, by definition, they override the criteria for motivation.)
   *e.g., I do not exercise consistently because there is "**no time**" and "**it hurts**."*

   Identify the sensory representation or 'criterial equivalence' used to determine the criteria.
   e.g., a feeling of stress and tension associated with having no time and being sore

4. Step to location #5 and elicit a higher level criterion that **overrides the limiting criteria** of step 3. For example, you could ask, "*What is something that is important enough that I can always make time for it and would do it even if it hurts? What value does that satisfy that makes it more important?*"
   *e.g., "**Responsibility to my family.**"*

Identify the sensory representation or 'criterial equivalence' used to determine this criterion.
e.g., I visualize my family looking safe and happy, feel good about it, and tell myself how important that is.

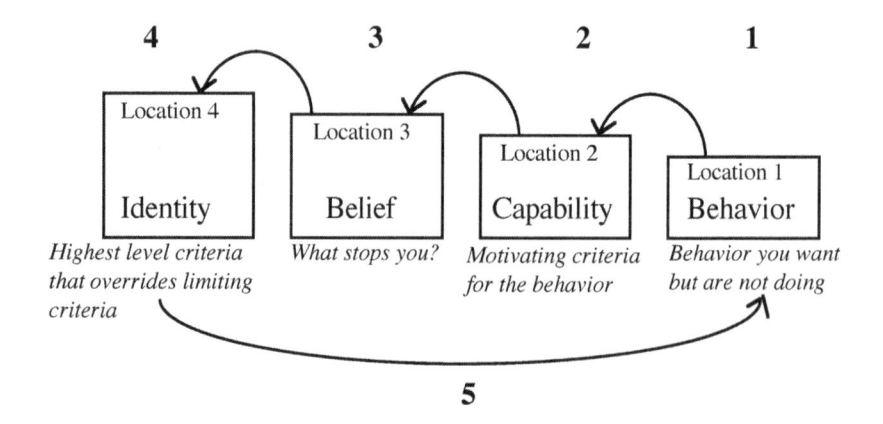

```
    4              3              2              1
┌───────────┐
│ Location 4│   ┌───────────┐
│           │   │ Location 3│   ┌───────────┐
│           │   │           │   │ Location 2│   ┌───────────┐
│           │   │           │   │           │   │ Location 1│
│ Identity  │   │  Belief   │   │ Capability│   │ Behavior  │
└───────────┘   └───────────┘   └───────────┘   └───────────┘
Highest level criteria   What stops you?   Motivating criteria   Behavior you want
that overrides limiting                    for the behavior      but are not doing
criteria

                              5
```

Sequence of Steps for the Hierarchy of Criteria Technique

5. You are now set up to use the following sequence of techniques:

   a. **Leveraging** – Keeping in mind your highest level criterion, go back to location #1, bypassing locations #2 and #3. Apply the highest level criterion to the desired behavior in order to override the limiting objections. For example, you can say, "*Since my behavior is a model for my family, wouldn't I be showing more responsibility by finding the time to keep healthy and look my best?*"

   b. **Utilizing the 'criterial equivalence' of the highest criterion** – Step to location #2 and adjust the qualities of the internal representation of the criteria associated with the desired behavior so that they

match the 'criterial equivalence' you use to determine your highest level criterion.

> e.g., *Visualize yourself being healthy and looking good, see your family looking safe and happy, feel good about it, and tell yourself how important that is.*

c. **Pacing the limiting criteria** – Step from location #2 into location #3 and explore options that will allow you to achieve the desired behavior, that will match the criteria on all three levels and doesn't violate the limiting criteria. For example, *"Is there some kind of consistent exercise program that doesn't take much time, wouldn't be painful and in which I could involve my family?"*

Chapter 5

Beliefs and Expectations

Beliefs and Belief Systems

In addition to values and criteria, one of the most fundamental ways that we frame our experience and give it meaning is through our beliefs. Beliefs are another one of the key components of our 'deep structure'. They shape and create the 'surface structures' of our thoughts, words and actions in many ways. Beliefs determine how events are given meaning, and are at the core of motivation and culture. Our beliefs and values provide the reinforcement (*motivation* and *permission*) that supports or inhibits particular capabilities and behaviors. Beliefs and values relate to the question, **"Why?"**

Beliefs are essentially judgments and evaluations about ourselves, others and the world around us. In NLP, beliefs are considered to be closely held generalizations about 1) causation, 2) meaning and 3) boundaries in: (a) the world around us, (b) our behavior, (c) our capabilities and (d) our identities. The statements, "The shifting of continental plates causes earthquakes," and "God's wrath causes earthquakes," for instance, would reflect different beliefs about cause in the world around us. Statements such as: "Pollen causes allergies," "It is unethical to conceal information," "It is not possible for a human to run a mile in less than four minutes," "I will never be successful because I am a slow learner," and "Behind every behavior is a positive intention," all represent beliefs of one form or another.

Beliefs function at a different level than behavior and perception and influence our experience and interpretation of reality by connecting our experiences to our criteria or value systems. To gain practical meaning, for example, values must be connected to experiences through beliefs. Beliefs connect values to the environment, behaviors, thoughts and representations, or to other beliefs and values. Beliefs define the relationship between values and their causes, 'criterial

Beliefs and Expectations

equivalences', and consequences (this will be covered in more depth in Chapter 6). A typical belief statement links a particular value to some other part of our experience. The belief statement, "Success requires hard work," for instance, links the value "success" to a class of activity ("hard work"). The statement, "Success is mainly a matter of luck," connects the same value to a different class of activity ("luck"). Depending upon which belief a person had, he or she would most likely adopt a different approach to attempting to reach success. Furthermore, the way in which a situation, activity, or idea fits (or does not fit) with the beliefs and value systems of an individual or group will determine how it will be received and incorporated.

Neurologically, beliefs are associated with the limbic system and hypothalamus in the midbrain. The limbic system has been linked to both emotion and long term memory. While the limbic system is a more "primitive" structure than the cortex of the brain in many ways, it serves to integrate information from the cortex and to regulate the *autonomic nervous system* (which controls basic body functions such as heart rate, body temperature, pupil dilation, etc.). Because they are produced by deeper structures of the brain, beliefs produce changes in the fundamental physiological functions in the body and are responsible for many of our unconscious responses. In fact, one of the ways that we know that we really believe something is because it triggers physiological reactions; it makes our "heart pound," our "blood boil," or our "skin tingle" (all effects that we cannot typically produce consciously). This is how a polygraph device is able to detect whether or not a person is "lying." People show a different physical reaction when they believe what they are saying than when they are "just saying" it as a behavior (like an actor might recite a line), or when they are being untruthful or incongruent.

It is the intimate connection between beliefs and deeper physiological functions that also creates the possibility for them to have such a powerful influence in the area of health and healing (as in the case of the placebo effect). Beliefs tend to have a self-organizing or "self-fulfilling" effect on our behavior at many levels, focusing attention in one area and filtering it out of others. A person who deeply believes he or she has an incurable illness will begin to organize his or her life and actions around that belief, making many subtle and often unconscious decisions which reflect that belief. A person who deeply believes that his or her illness will be cured will make quite different decisions. And because expectations generated by our beliefs effect our deeper neurology, they can also produce dramatic physiological effects. This is illustrated by the example of the woman who adopted a baby, and because she believed that "mothers" were supposed to provide milk for their babies, actually began to lactate and produced enough milk to breast feed her adopted child!

The Power of Beliefs

Beliefs are a powerful influence on our lives. They are also notoriously difficult to change through typical rules of logic or rational thinking. There is an old story, related by Abraham Maslow, about a patient who was being treated by a psychiatrist. The patient wouldn't eat or take care of himself, claiming that he was a corpse. The psychiatrist spent many hours arguing with the patient trying to convince him he wasn't a corpse. Finally the psychiatrist asked the patient if corpses bled. The patient replied, "Of course corpses don't bleed, all of their body functions have stopped." The psychiatrist then convinced the patient to try an experiment. The psychiatrist would carefully prick the patient with a pin and they would see if he started to bleed. The patient agreed. After all, he was a corpse. The psychiatrist gently pricked the patient's skin with a needle and, sure enough, he began to bleed. With a look of shock and amazement the patient gasped, *"I'll be darned...corpses **DO** bleed!"*

It is common wisdom that if someone really believes he can do something he will do it, and if he believes something is impossible no amount of effort will convince him that it can be accomplished. What is unfortunate is that many sick people, such as those with cancer or heart disease, will often present their doctors and friends with the same belief mentioned in the story above. Beliefs like *"It's too late now;" "There's nothing I can do anyway;" "I'm a victim...My number came up;"* can often limit the full resources of the patient. Our beliefs about ourselves and what is possible in the world around us greatly impact our day-to-day effectiveness. All of us have beliefs that serve as resources as well as beliefs that limit us.

The power of beliefs was demonstrated in an enlightening study in which a group of children who were tested to have average intelligence was divided at random into two equal groups. One of the groups was assigned to a teacher who was told that the children were "gifted." The other group was given to a teacher who was told that the children were "slow learners." A year later the two groups were retested for intelligence. Not surprisingly, the majority of the group that was arbitrarily identified as "gifted" scored higher than they had previously, while the majority of the group that was labeled "slow" scored lower! The teacher's beliefs about the students effected their ability to learn.

In another study, 100 cancer "survivors" (patients who had reversed their symptoms for over 10 years) were interviewed about what they had done to achieve success. The interviews showed that no one treatment method stood out as being more effective than any other. Some had taken the standard medical treatment of chemotherapy and/or radiation, some had used a nutritional approach, others had followed a spiritual path, while others concentrated on a psychological approach and some did nothing at all. The only thing that was characteristic of the entire group was that they all believed that the approach they took would work.

Another good example of the power of beliefs to both limit us and empower us is that of the 'four minute mile'. Before May 6, 1954, it was believed that four minutes was an unbreakable barrier to the speed with which a human being could run a mile. In the nine years prior to the historic day in which Roger Bannister broke the four minute ceiling, no runners had even come close. Within six weeks after Bannister's feat, the Australian runner John Lundy lowered the record by another second. Within the next nine years nearly two hundred people had broken the once seemingly impenetrable barrier.

Certainly, these examples seem to demonstrate that our beliefs can shape, effect or even determine our degree of intelligence, health, relationships, creativity, even our degree of happiness and personal success. Yet, if indeed our beliefs are such a powerful force in our lives, how do we get control of them so they don't control us? Many of our beliefs were installed in us when we were children by parents, teachers, social upbringing and the media, before we were aware of their impact or able to have a choice about them. Is it possible to restructure, unlearn or change old beliefs that may be limiting us and imprint new ones that can expand our potential beyond what we currently imagine? If so, how do we do it?

Neuro-Linguistic Programming and the Sleight of Mouth patterns offer some powerful new tools with which we can reframe and transform potentially limiting beliefs.

Limiting Beliefs

The three most common areas of limiting beliefs center around issues of *hopelessness, helplessness* and *worthlessness*. These three areas of belief can exert a great deal of influence with respect to a person's mental and physical health.

1. **Hopelessness:** Belief that the desired goal is not achievable regardless of your capabilities.

2. **Helplessness:** Belief that the desired goal is possible but that you are not capable of achieving it.

3. **Worthlessness:** Belief that you do not deserve the desired goal because of something you are or have (not) done.

Hopelessness occurs when someone does not believe a particular desired goal is even possible. It is characterized by a sense that, *"No matter what I do it won't make a difference. What I want is not possible to get. It's out of my control. I'm a victim."*

Helplessness occurs when, even though he or she believes that the outcome exists and is possible to achieve, a person does not believe that he or she is capable of attaining it. It produces a sense that, *"It's possible for others to achieve this goal but not for me. I'm not good enough or capable enough to accomplish it."*

Worthlessness occurs when, even though a person may believe that the desired goal is possible and that he or she even has the capability to accomplish it, that individual believes that he or she **doesn't deserve** to get what he/she wants. It is often characterized by a sense that, *"I am a fake. I don't belong. I don't deserve to be happy or healthy. There is something basically and fundamentally wrong with me as a* *person and I deserve the pain and suffering that I am experiencing."*

To be successful, people need to shift these types of limiting beliefs to beliefs involving **hope for the future**, a **sense of capability and responsibility**, and **a sense of self-worth and belonging**.

Obviously, the most pervasive beliefs are those regarding our identity. Some examples of limiting beliefs about identity are: *"I am helpless/worthless/a victim." "I don't deserve to succeed." "If I get what I want I will lose something." "I don't have permission to succeed."*

Limiting beliefs sometimes operate like a "thought virus" with a destructive capability similar to that of a computer virus or biological virus. A 'thought virus' is a limiting belief that can become a 'self-fulfilling prophesy' and interfere with one's efforts and ability to heal or improve. (The structure and influence of thought viruses are covered in more depth in Chapter 8.) Thought viruses contain unspoken assumptions and presuppositions which make them difficult to identify and challenge. Frequently, the most influential beliefs are often out of our awareness.

Limiting beliefs and thought viruses often arise as seemingly insurmountable "impasses" to the process of change. At such an impasse, a person will feel, "I've tried everything to change this and nothing works." Dealing effectively with impasses involves finding the limiting belief that is at their core, and holding them in place.

Transforming Limiting Beliefs

Ultimately, we transform limiting beliefs and become 'immunized' to 'thought viruses' by expanding and enriching our models of the world, and becoming clearer about our identities and missions. Limiting beliefs, for instance, are often developed in order to fulfill a positive purpose, such as, protection, establishing boundaries, feeling a sense of personal power, etc. By acknowledging these deeper intentions and updating our mental maps to include other, more effective ways to fulfill those intentions, beliefs can often be changed with a minimum amount of effort and pain.

Many limiting beliefs arise as a result of unanswered 'how' questions. That is, if a person does not know *how* to change his or her behavior, it is easy for the person to build the belief, "That behavior *can't* be changed." If a person does not know how to accomplish a particular task, the person may develop the belief, "I am *incapable* of successfully completing that task." Thus, it is often also important to provide the answers for a number of "how to" questions in order to help a person transform limiting beliefs. For example, in order to address a belief such as, "It is dangerous to show my emotions," we must answer the question, "*How* do I show my emotions and still stay safe?"

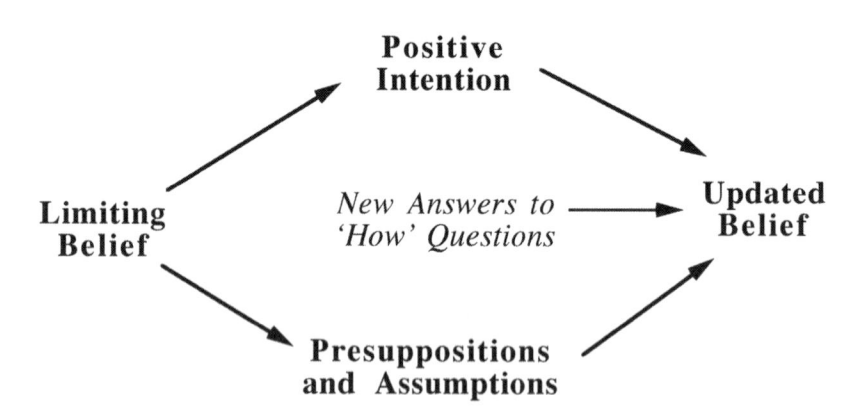

```
                    Positive
                   Intention
                ↗            ↘
Limiting     New Answers to    Updated
 Belief      'How' Questions →  Belief
                ↘            ↗
                Presuppositions
                and Assumptions
```

Limiting Beliefs May be Transformed or Updated by Identifying the Positive Intentions and Presuppositions which Underlie the Belief and Providing Alternatives and New Answers to 'How' Questions.

Beliefs, both empowering and limiting, are often built in relation to feedback and reinforcement from significant others. Our sense of identity and mission, for instance, is usually defined in relation to significant others, or "mentors," who serve as reference points for the larger systems of which we perceive ourselves as members. Because identity and mission form the larger framework which surrounds our beliefs and values, establishing or shifting significant relationships can exert a strong influence on beliefs. Thus, clarifying or altering key relationships, and messages received in the context of those relationships, often spontaneously facilitates changes in beliefs. Establishing new relationships is often an important part of promoting lasting belief change, especially relationships which provide positive support at the level of identity. (This is one of the principles at the base of the NLP belief change technique of Reimprinting.)

In summary, limiting beliefs can be updated and transformed by:

- Identifying and acknowledging the underlying positive intention.

- Identifying any unspoken or unconscious presuppositions or assumptions at the base of the belief.

- Widening the perception of the cause-effect chains or 'complex equivalences' related to the belief.

- Providing 'how to' information with respect to alternatives for fulfilling the positive intention or purpose of the limiting belief.

- Clarifying or updating key relationships which shape one's sense of mission and purpose, and receiving positive support at an identity level.

Expectation

Beliefs, both empowering and limiting, are related to our expectations. *Expectation* means "to look forward to" some event or outcome. According to Webster's dictionary, it "implies a high degree of certainty to the point of making preparations or anticipating certain things, actions or feelings." Expectations influence our behavior in different ways, depending on where they are directed. Sigmund Freud (1893) pointed out:

> *There are certain ideas which have an affect of expectancy attached to them. They are of two kinds: ideas of my doing this or that — what we call* intentions — *and ideas of this or that happening to me —* expectations *proper. The affect attached to them is dependent on two factors, first on the degree of importance which the outcome has for me, and secondly on the degree of uncertainty inherent in the expectation of the outcome.*

People's beliefs and expectations about outcomes and their own personal capabilities play an important role in their ability to achieve desired states. Freud's distinction between "intentions" and "expectations" refer to what are known in modern cognitive psychology (Bandura, 1982) as 'self-efficacy' expectation and 'outcome' expectation. *Outcome expectancy* is a result of a person's estimate that a given behavior will lead to certain outcomes. *'Self-efficacy' expectation* relates to the conviction that one can personally successfully execute the behavior required to produce the desired outcome.

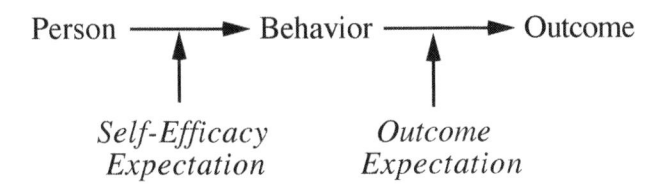

```
Person  ──────▶  Behavior  ──────▶  Outcome
           ▲                ▲
           │                │
      Self-Efficacy      Outcome
       Expectation     Expectation
```

The Relationship of 'Self-Efficacy' Expectation to 'Outcome' Expectation

These types of beliefs and expectations often determine how much effort people will invest, and how long they will sustain their efforts, in dealing with stressful or challenging situations. In self-managed activities, for instance, people who are skeptical about the possibility of the outcome occurring, or about their abilities to perform, tend to undermine their own efforts when they approach their limits. Typically, a lack of outcome expectancy leads to a feeling of 'hopelessness' which causes the person to give up out of apathy. The absence of 'self-efficacy' expectancy, on the other hand, leads to a sense of inadequacy which makes the person feel 'helplessness'.

Strong positive expectations, on the other hand, can push people to put out extra effort, and release dormant abilities. A good example of the influence of strong expectations is the so-called "placebo effect." In the case of the placebo, a person is given a "fake" drug or pill that has no medically active ingredients. If the patient believes the pill is "real," however, and expects to get better, he or she will often begin to manifest real physical improvements. In fact, some placebo studies report quite dramatic results. In these instances, the person's expectation actually triggers behavioral capabilities that are latent but largely untapped.

In relationship to learning and change, outcome expectancy relates to the degree to which a person expects that the skills or behaviors he or she is learning or engaging in will actually produce the desired benefits within the environmental system that constitutes his or her reality. Self-efficacy expectation relates to the degree of confidence one has in his or her own personal effectiveness or ability to learn the skills, or enact the behaviors necessary to reach an outcome.

Attaining desired outcomes through effective performance in challenging situations can help to strengthen a person's confidence in his or her existing capabilities. This is because people usually do not perform to their fullest potential, even though they possess the skills. It is under conditions that test their limits that people find out what they are able to do.

Expectations relating to the projected outcomes of one's behavior are the primary source of motivation. From this view, how people feel, and what they do, depends on the value that they attach to, and the causes they attribute to, anticipated consequences. Strong "positive" outcome expectations, for instance, can push people to put out extra effort in hope of reaching some desired state. Expected consequences that are perceived as "negative," on the other hand, will lead to either avoidance or apathy.

From an NLP perspective, expectations are a classic example of the relationship between map and territory, and the influence of internal maps on behavior. According to NLP, an "expectation" is a mental map relating to future actions and consequences. The map may be of one's own behavior, the results of one's behavior, or events which may befall us. When such maps are very strong, they can have more influence on us than our ongoing reality.

All people create expectations, and hope that the world will meet them. The slippage between the world at large and the expectations we form with respect to that world is the basis of many of our disappointments in life. As NLP cofounder Richard Bandler points out, "Disappointment re-

BELIEFS AND EXPECTATIONS

quires adequate planning." The strong anticipation of the prospect of success or failure is also the basis for what are known as "self fulfilling prophesies."

Thus, expectations serve as another type of powerful 'frame' around our experiences; in many ways influencing or determining the beliefs and judgments we draw from those experiences. Knowledge of the impact of expectations has been used throughout the centuries to influence people's perceptions and their evaluations of particular events and situations. Consider, for instance, the following comments made by Adolf Hitler in his book *Mein Kampf*:

The great masses' receptive ability is only very limited, their understanding is small, but their forgetfulness is great. As a consequence of these facts, all effective propaganda has to limit itself only to a very few points and to use them like slogans until even the very last man is able to imagine what is intended by such a word. As soon as one sacrifices this basic principle and tries to become versatile, the effect will fritter away, as the masses are neither able to digest the material offered nor to retain it. Thus the result is weakened and finally eliminated.

The greater the line of its representation has to be, the more correctly from the psychological point of view will its tactics have to be outlined.

For example, [during World War I] it was completely wrong to ridicule the adversary as was done in Austrian and German propaganda in comic papers. It was basically wrong for the reason that when a man met the adversary in reality he was bound to receive an entirely different impression; something that took its most terrible revenge, for now the German soldier, under the direct impression of the resistance of the enemy, felt himself deceived by those who so far were responsible for his enlightenment, and instead of strengthening his fighting spirit or even his firmness, quite the contrary occurred. The man despaired.

Compared with this, the war propaganda of the British and the Americans was psychologically right. By introducing the German as a barbarian and a Hun to its own people, it thus prepared the individual soldier for the terrors of war and helped guard him against disappointment. The most terrible weapon which was now being used against him then appeared to him only as the proof of the enlightenment already bestowed upon him, thus strengthening his belief that his government's assertions were right, and on the other hand it increased his fury and hatred against the atrocious enemy. For the cruel effect of the weapon of his enemy, which he learned to know by his own experience, appeared to him gradually as the proof of the already proclaimed "Hunnish" brutality of the barbaric enemy, without, however, making him think for even a moment that his own weapons could have, perhaps, or even probably, a still more terrible effect.

Thus the English soldier could not even for a moment have the impression that his country had taught him the wrong facts, something which was unfortunately the case to such an extent with the German soldier that he finally rejected everything that came from this side as "swindle" and "bunk" (Krampf).

No doubt, a great deal of Hitler's influence as a leader came from his awareness, understanding and application of the principles underlying Sleight of Mouth – and, unfortunately, he stands as an archetypic example of the misuse of these principles. His statements above illustrate the impact that expectations have as 'frames' which influence the conclusions that people derive from their experience. The

German soldiers felt disappointed, deceived, and disheartened when they discovered that their adversaries were not silly buffoons as they had been led to expect. On the other hand, the experience of the British and American soldiers confirmed their expectation that their adversaries would be brutal Huns—strengthening their belief in their cause and "increasing their fury and hatred" against their enemy.

Thus, our expectations exert a strong impact on our motivation and the conclusions we derive from our experience.

Expectations about reinforcement, for example, exert greater influence upon behavior than the reinforcement itself. Experiments, done with students who have received rewards for doing particular behavioral tasks, show that the effort exerted by students decreases significantly when they are led to expect that the same actions will not be rewarded on future occasions – whether or not they are in fact rewarded later on. Thus, beliefs and expectations about future reinforcement have more influence on behavior than the objective fact that the behavior has received reinforcement in the past.

The strength of an expectation is a function of the robustness of the representation of the anticipated consequence. In the view of NLP, the more a person is able to see, hear and feel some future consequence in his or her imagination, the stronger will be the expectation. Thus, expectations may be intensified by enriching the internal images, sounds, words and feelings associated with a possible future action or consequence. Likewise, expectations may be weakened by diminishing the quality or intensity of the internal representations associated with the potential future consequences.

As the example of the students above indicates, the strength of an expectation is also influenced by underlying beliefs about cause-and-effect. If students believe, "The experiment is over," they will no longer expect to be receiving reinforcement for the same tasks they were being reinforced for earlier. In this sense, expectations are often reflections of underlying beliefs. If we believe, "Hard work pays off," then we will expect to be rewarded for our labors. If we believe, "So and so is a good student," then we will expect him or her to do well in class.

Underlying beliefs can also create resistances or "counter-expectations" which come in the form of interfering inner representations. As Freud described it:

> *The subjective uncertainty, the counter-expectation, is itself represented by a collection of ideas to which I shall give the name of "distressing antithetic ideas"...In the case of an intention, these antithetic ideas will run: "I shall not succeed in carrying out my intentions because this or that is too difficult for me and I am unfit to do it; I know, too, that certain other people have failed in a similar situation." The other case, that of an expectation, needs no comment: the antithetic idea consists of enumerating all the things that could possibly happen to me other than the one I desire.*

Thus, expectations may be either 'positive' or 'negative'. That is, they may either support desired outcomes or oppose them. Expectations which run counter to one another can create confusion or inner conflict. NLP offers a number of tools and strategies to help develop positive expectations and deal with negative expectations. The basic NLP approach to establishing or altering expectations involves either:

a) working directly with the internal sensory representations associated with the expectation.

b) working with the underlying beliefs which are the source of the expectation.

Expectations and the Sleight of Mouth Pattern of Consequences

The Sleight of Mouth pattern of *Consequence* uses expectations to either reinforce or challenge generalizations and beliefs. The pattern involves directing attention to a potential effect (positive or negative) resulting from a belief or the generalization defined by the belief. Anticipated positive consequences will strengthen and reinforce beliefs and judgments – even if the judgment itself is negative or limiting (an application of the principle that 'the ends justify the means'). How many times have we heard someone say, "I'm only saying this (or doing this) for your own good."

Negative consequences, of course, will challenge generalizations and call them into question.

The Sleight of Mouth pattern of Consequences is related to the NLP presupposition that:

No response, experience or behavior is meaningful outside of the context in which it was established or the response it elicits next. Any behavior, experience or response may serve as a resource or limitation depending on how it fits in with the rest of the system.

Thus, anticipated consequences operate as a type of frame with respect to other experiences. Identifying a positive consequence is another way to reestablish an outcome frame with respect to limiting or negative judgments or generalizations.

A good illustration of how this pattern might be applied relates to the example of the psychiatrist and the patient who claimed that he was a "corpse," which was cited earlier in this chapter. The psychiatrist was attempting to use logic to convince the patient that he wasn't a corpse by pricking the patient with a needle in order to demonstrate to him that he still bled. The psychiatrist's efforts were thwarted, however, when the patient gasped in amazement, "I'll be darned...corpses DO bleed!"

If the psychiatrist had been familiar with the Sleight of Mouth pattern of consequence, and the principles that we have been exploring thus far in this book, instead of being stymied by his patient, he would have been able to make use of the patient's comments. For example, the psychiatrist could have said, "Well if corpses can bleed, I wonder what else they can do? Perhaps corpses can sing, dance, laugh, digest food, and even learn. Let's try out some of those things as well. You know, you might discover that it is possible to have a pretty good life as a corpse (some people seem to), and still maintain the positive benefits that you get from being a corpse." Rather than trying to attack and challenge the belief, it can be reframed from a problem to an advantage. (As Einstein pointed out, you cannot solve a problem with the same thinking that has created the problem.)

I applied this particular pattern successfully myself with a woman who had been diagnosed as "obsessive compulsive." She believed that bugs got on her. She called them "real imaginary fleas"; "imaginary" because nobody else accepted that they were real. But they were "real" because when they got on her, she felt it. She couldn't ignore it. They gave her the terrible feeling that she was being "invaded."

The woman spent an immense amount of time trying to protect herself from the "fleas." She had seventy two different pairs of gloves: for driving her car, cooking, putting on her clothes, etc. She always bought clothes that were longer than her arms so that she would have no exposed skin. She was constantly scrubbing her skin to wash off the fleas. She scrubbed her skin so hard it was red and raw all the time.

The fact that the fleas were "imaginary" gave them some interesting options. For example, everybody had these fleas, but some had more of them than others; especially her parents. She loved her parents dearly, of course; but, as they had the most

Beliefs and Expectations

fleas, she couldn't spend much time with them. Because the fleas were imaginary, they could even come through the telephone. So when her parents called, fleas would flow from the receiver, and she would be forced to hang up on them.

This woman was in her early thirties and had been struggling with this compulsion for more than fifteen years. Of course, people had tried many times to convince her that this belief system was crazy; always to no avail. I took the time to get rapport with her, and to find out about her 'criterial equivalences' and reality strategies. Then, at a certain point, I said, "You know, all your life you have been trying to get rid of the fleas. You have always tried to wash them off and make them go away. Maybe that's an ineffective way to deal with them. Has anybody ever treated your 'real imaginary' allergy to the 'real imaginary' fleas?"

I explained that her situation matched all the symptoms of an allergy. Some people, for instance, have an allergy to pollen in the air; they can't see pollen but it gets in their noses and they feel bad. Instead of having to hide from the pollen, wash it off, or make it go away, however, these people can use medicines that treat their immune system to reduce the allergy symptoms.

Then I pulled out a bottle of 'placebos' and said, "These are 'real imaginary' pills. They are 'imaginary' because they don't have any real drugs in them, but they are 'real' because they will cure your allergy and change your feeling." Using what I knew about her criterial equivalences and reality strategy, I described how the placebos would work, and how they would make her feel differently. I carefully explained the power of the 'placebo effect' and cited a number of studies in which placebos had been effectively used to treat allergic reactions. Because this explanation fit so well as a consequence of her own belief system, she couldn't find any holes in my logic, and agreed to try the pills.

Interestingly, when she came back the next week, she was really frightened. She was frightened because those "real imaginary pills" had worked. She sat down and said, "How will I know what kind of clothes to buy? How will I know how to interact with my parents? How will I know who to let touch me? How will I know what to do or where to go in the world around me?" She was saying that this belief had substituted for a number of decision-making strategies that she had never developed. As I pointed out earlier, limiting beliefs are frequently the result of unanswered 'how' questions. In order to ecologically change her belief, she needed to appropriately address all of these unanswered 'how' questions.

Once the woman began to believe that it was possible for her to be free from the "fleas," she had to face her beliefs about her own capabilities. A new 'outcome expectation' caused her to reevaluate her own 'self-efficacy expectation'. With coaching, the woman was able to learn a number of effective decision-making strategies, and became free once and for all of her obsession.

To explore the pattern of consequence for yourself, identify a limiting belief or generalization that prevents you or someone else from performing as effectively as you know you that you can. Enrich your perception of this situation or experience by considering: "What is a positive effect of the belief or the generalization defined by the belief?" [One way to do this is to consider the problem or difficulty from more than one time frame. For instance, view the situation with respect to an hour, a day, week, a month, a year, and many years from now.]

> e.g., Limiting belief: *I feel like a coward when I become fearful in challenging situations.*

> Positive consequence: Fear *prevents people from rushing into something*, which helps them to *act more ecologically*. Therefore fear isn't such a bad thing because it causes people to be more deliberate and act more ecologically. In the long run, your fear will make you a wiser and more determined person.

Mapping Key Beliefs and Expectations

In general, people change their behavior by acquiring new reference experiences and cognitive maps in order to form a 'plan'. The same behavior, however, does not always produce the same outcome. Certain factors, such as the 'path' to the outcome, the degree of relational support one receives, the amount of variability of the system, and the tools one has available, will determine the probability that a certain behavior will obtain a desired outcome within that system.

Managing change and reaching outcomes involves having the cognitive maps, reference experiences, relational support and tools necessary to establish the most appropriate kinds of assumptions and expectations to have with respect to a particular goal, task or situation.

Our expectations, for instance, greatly influence the degree of confidence we will have about achieving a particular goal. The basic belief issues that arise in regard to reaching our outcomes come from expectations related to a number of fundamental components of change:

1. The desirability of the outcome.

2. Confidence that the specified actions will produce the outcome.

3. The evaluation of the appropriateness and difficulty of the behavior (regardless of whether it is believed that it will produce the desired result).

4. The belief that one is capable of producing the required behaviors necessary to complete the plan leading to the outcome.

5. The sense of responsibility, self worth and permission one has in relation to the required behaviors and outcome.

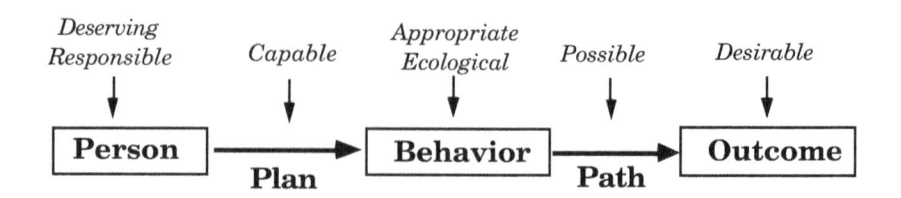

```
Deserving                  Appropriate
Responsible    Capable     Ecological     Possible    Desirable
     │            │             │             │           │
     ▼            ▼             ▼             ▼           ▼
 ┌────────┐             ┌──────────┐              ┌─────────┐
 │ Person │ ──────────► │ Behavior │ ───────────► │ Outcome │
 └────────┘    Plan     └──────────┘     Path     └─────────┘
```

Belief Issues Related to Change

For example, consider someone who is attempting to become well, learn something new or be successful in a business project. Belief issues may arise with respect to any one of the elements of change identified above.

A first issue relates to the desirability of the outcome. How much does the person *really* want to be healthy, learn, or succeed? All things being equal, everyone no doubt wants all of these things. But it is rarely the case that all things are equal, and the fact is that health, learning or success may not always be at the top of a person's hierarchy of criteria. Someone might argue, "Health is not really a priority for me right now." "I have so many things demanding my attention, learning something new is not that important". "Other people need me. It would be selfish to be concerned with my own success."

Even if a person desires health, learning or success very highly, he or she may question whether it is possible to achieve them. A person might say, "It is not possible to get well no matter what I do." "Old dogs can't learn new tricks." " I shouldn't build false hope about succeeding. There is nothing I can do that will make any difference."

A person may deeply desire an outcome and believe it is possible to achieve, but be in doubt as to whether a particular behavioral path is the most appropriate way to achieve the outcome. They might contend, "I believe it is possible to achieve my outcome, but not by using this (plan/technique/

program/etc.)" Others might think that a particular pathway is effective, but object to the efforts or sacrifices required by a particular path, or worry about the consequences it will have on other areas of their lives. A person may believe, for instance, that exercising or eating a better diet will help him or her become healthier, but not want to go through the hassle of changing his or her lifestyle. Others might believe that a particular course will help them to learn something important, but not feel that they have the time to do it. Similarly, a person may believe that a new job may lead to success, but be concerned about the impact it would have on his or her family.

It is also possible that people can desire the outcome, think it is possible, and believe that the proposed behavioral path is appropriate to achieve the result, yet doubt their abilities to perform the required actions. They might think, "I am not (skilled/consistent/intelligent/focused/etc.) enough to successfully do what I have to do in order to complete the path necessary to reach my desired outcome."

Even when people want an outcome, trust that it is possible, believe in the actions that have been defined in order to reach that outcome, and have confidence in their own abilities to perform the necessary skills and actions, they may question whether it is their responsibility to perform the required actions or reach the outcome. A person may complain, "It is not my responsibility to make myself healthy, learn or become successful. That is the job of the experts. I want to be able to rely on someone else." People may also doubt whether they deserve to be healthy, to learn or to succeed. This is an issue of self esteem. Sometimes people feel unworthy of health, intelligence or success. If a person does not believe that he or she deserves to reach a goal or is responsible to do what needs to be done in order to achieve it, then it doesn't matter if he or she is capable, knows the appropriate path or desires it.

Assessing Motivation for Change

It is important to be able to assess and address this whole system of beliefs in order to help people achieve their goals, or do so ourselves. Plans and actions cannot be effectively carried out if there is too much conflict or doubt. On the other hand, as the placebo effect demonstrates, empowering beliefs and assumptions can release capabilities and 'unconscious competencies' that are inherent in a particular person or group, but which have not yet been mobilized.

One way to determine the motivation of a person or group is to make an assessment of the five key beliefs we have identified as relevant to the process of change. The beliefs can be assessed by making a specific statement of the belief as illustrated in the following examples:

1. The desirability of the outcome.
   Statement: "The goal is desirable and worth it."

2. Confidence that the outcome is attainable.
   Statement: "It is possible to achieve the goal."

3. The evaluation of the appropriateness or difficulty of the behaviors needed to reach the outcome (regardless of whether it is believed they will produce the desired result).
   Statement: "What has to be done in order to achieve the goal is appropriate and ecological."

4. The belief that one is capable of producing the required behaviors.
   Statement: "I/we have the capabilities necessary to achieve the goal."

5. The sense of self worth or permission one has in relation to the required behaviors and outcome.
   Statement: "I/we have the responsibility and deserve to achieve the goal."

After the beliefs have been stated, individuals may rate their degree of confidence in relation to each of the statements on a scale of 1 to 5, with 1 being the lowest and 5 being the highest degree of belief. This can provide an immediate and interesting profile of potential problem areas of motivation or confidence. Any statements which are given a low rating indicate possible areas of resistance or interference which will need to be addressed in some way.

The Belief Assessment Sheet on the next page provides a simple but effective instrument for quickly assessing the relevant areas of belief in relation to a goal or plan.

Belief Assessment Sheet

Write down a one-sentence description of the goal or outcome to be achieved:

Goal/Outcome: _____

In the spaces provided below, rate your degree of belief in the outcome in relation to each of the statements on a scale of 1 to 5, with 1 being the lowest and 5 being the highest degree of belief.

a. "The goal is desirable and worth it."

| 1 | 2 | 3 | 4 | 5 |

b. "It is possible to achieve the goal."

| 1 | 2 | 3 | 4 | 5 |

c. "What has to be done in order to achieve the goal is appropriate and ecological."

| 1 | 2 | 3 | 4 | 5 |

d. "I (You / We) have the capabilities necessary to achieve the goal."

| 1 | 2 | 3 | 4 | 5 |

e. "I (You / We) have the responsibility and deserve to achieve the goal."

| 1 | 2 | 3 | 4 | 5 |

Building Confidence and Strengthening Belief

Once you have assessed your degree of confidence and congruence with respect to these key areas of belief, you can strengthen your belief in areas of doubt by considering the following questions:

1) What else would you need to know, add to your goal, or believe in order to be more congruent or confident?

2) Who would be your mentor for that belief?

3) What message or advice would that mentor have for you?

Using the 'As If' Frame to Strengthen Beliefs and Expectations

The *'as if' frame* is a process by which an individual or group acts 'as if' the desired goal or outcome has already been achieved, or by which an individual or a group pretends to be some other person or entity. The 'as if' frame is a powerful way to help people identify and enrich their perception of the world, and or their future desired states. It is also a useful way to help people overcome resistances and limitations within their current map of the world.

The 'as if' frame is often used to challenge limiting beliefs by creating counter examples or alternatives. For example, if a person says, "I can't do X" or "It is impossible to do X," the 'as if' frame would be applied by asking, "What would happen if you could do X?" or "Act as if you could do X. What would it be like?" or "If you were (already) able to do X, what would you be doing?" For instance, if a company executive were unable to describe what his or her desired state for a particular project is going to be, a mentor might say, *"Imagine it is five years from now. What is going on that is different?"*

Acting 'as if' allows people to drop their current perception of the constraints of reality and use their imagination more fully. It utilizes our innate ability to imagine and pretend. It also allows us to drop the boundaries of our personal history, belief systems, and 'ego'. In fact, it helps to recognize and utilize the notion of "I" as a function, instead of a rigid nominalization.

Many NLP processes and techniques apply the 'as if' frame. In the process of creating goals, outcomes, and dreams, for instance, we first act "as if" they are possibilities. We create pictures of them visually in our mind's eyes, and give those pictures the qualities we desire. We then begin to bring them to life by acting "as if" we were experiencing the feelings and practicing the specific behaviors that fit those dreams and goals.

The 'as if' frame is very important in creating a space in which we can begin to stimulate the neurology that can support attaining our goals. Milton Erickson said many times, "You can pretend anything and master it."

The 'as if' frame is one of the key tools for mentors and advisors. The following exercise applies the 'as if' frame as a means to help someone bypass limiting beliefs.

'As If' Exercise

1. The explorer is to think of some goal or situation about which he or she has some doubt. The explorer is to express the limiting belief verbally to the mentor — i.e., "It is not possible for me to . . .", "I am not capable of . . .", "I don't deserve . . .", etc.

2. The mentor respectfully encourages the explorer by saying things like:

   "What would happen if (it was possible/you were capable/you did deserve it)?"

   "Act 'as if' (it was possible/you were capable/you did deserve it). What would it be like?"

   "Imagine that you had already dealt with all of the issues relating to your belief that (it is not possible/you are not capable/you do not deserve it), what would you be thinking, doing or believing differently?"

3. If other objections or interferences arise from the explorer, the mentor is to continue asking:

   "Act 'as if' you have already dealt with that interference or objection. How would you be responding differently?"

Chapter 6

The Basic Structure of Beliefs

The Linguistic Structure of Beliefs

The main purpose of our beliefs and belief systems is to link core values to other parts of our experience and maps of the world. As was pointed out earlier, the belief statement, "Success requires hard work," links the value "success" to a particular class of activity ("hard work"). The statement, "Success is mainly a matter of luck," connects the same value to a different cause ("luck"). As these statements illustrate, beliefs are fundamentally statements of relationships between various elements of our experience.

Linguistically, beliefs are typically expressed in the form of verbal patterns known as "complex equivalences" and "cause-effects." *Complex equivalences* are linguistic statements which imply "equivalences" between different aspects of our experience ("A = B," or "A means B"). This type of language pattern is typically used to make definitions of values and establish evidences for whether or not values have been met or violated. To say, "A resting heart rate of 60 beats per minute is healthy," "Having a lot of money *means* you are successful," or "Love *means* never having to say you're sorry," are examples of complex equivalences reflecting beliefs.

Cause-effect statements (characterized by words such as: "cause," "make," "force," "leads to," "results in," etc.) link values causally to other aspects of our experience. Such linguistic structures are used to define the causes and consequences of particular values. Benjamin Franklin's classic adage, "Early to bed and early to rise *makes* a man healthy, wealthy and wise," is an assertion of causal factors leading to the achievement of certain values. The saying that "power corrupts" or "love heals" are statements relating to the consequences of expressing particular values.

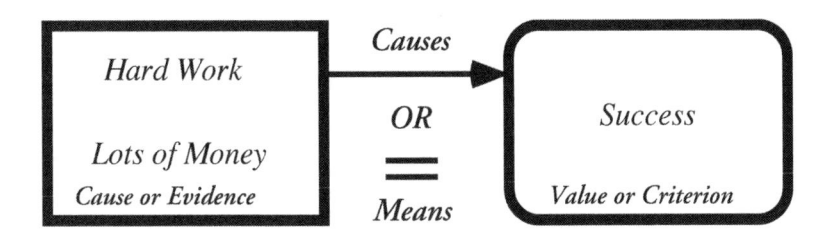

Beliefs are Typically Expressed in the Form of Either a Complex Equivalence or Cause-Effect

Complex equivalences and cause-effect generalizations are fundamental structures from which we build our maps of the world.

Complex Equivalence

Complex Equivalence involves talking about two or more experiences as if they are the same, or 'equivalent'. Complex equivalences are distantly related to criterial equivalences, but are quite distinct from them. Criterial equivalences are established in the form of sensory based evidences for a particular value or criteria. They involve 'chunking down' to specific indicators of some value or core criterion. A complex equivalence is more of a 'definition' than an 'evidence procedure'. It tends to be more of a lateral chunking process. A complex equivalence for a particular value or criterion, for instance, may be in the form of some other generalization or nominalization.

In the statement, "He is in poor health, he must really hate himself," for example, the speaker is implying that "poor health" is in some way equivalent to "self hatred." These two experiences are somehow the "same thing" in the speaker's map of the world (although they may have no connection at all in reality). Some other examples of 'complex equivalences' would be statements such as, "Thinking or acting outside of the social norms *means* that you are mentally unstable;" "Safety *means* having the power to fight unfriendly forces;" "If you don't say much, then it must *mean* you don't have much to say."

Each statement establishes a kind of 'equivalence' between two terms. Perhaps more accurately defined as "simplistic equivalence," the danger of such statements is that a complex relationship on a deep structure level is oversimplified at the level of surface structure. As Einstein said, "Everything should be made as simple as possible, but not any simpler."

Our 'interpretations' of events and experiences come from the establishment and application of clusters of complex equivalences. On the positive side, the connections established by some interpretations may help to either simplify or explicate complex relationships. On the problematic side, however, complex equivalences may distort or oversimplify systemic relationships. Patients (and the families of patients), for example, often interpret their symptoms in a very negative way, or in a way that continues to maintain the symptom.

From the perspective of Sleight of Mouth, the issue is not so much whether one has found the "correct" complex equivalence, but rather whether one is able to find interpretations which offer a new perspective, a wider map or a way of thinking which is different than the type of thinking which is creating the problem to begin with.

Cause-Effect

The perception of cause and effect is the foundation of our models of the world. Effective analysis, investigation and modeling of all types involve identifying the *causes* which underlie observable phenomena. Causes are the underlying elements responsible for creating and maintaining a particular phenomenon or situation. Successful problem solving, for example, is based upon finding and treating the cause(s) of a particular symptom or set of symptoms. What you identify as the cause of a particular desired state or problem state determines where you will focus your efforts.

For instance, if you believe that an allergy is caused by an external "allergen," then you will try to avoid that allergen. If you believe an allergy is caused by the release of "histamine," then you will take an "antihistamine." If you believe an allergy is caused by "stress," then you will attempt to reduce stress, and so on.

Our beliefs about cause and effect are reflected in the language pattern of "cause-effect," in which a causal connection is either explicitly or implicitly implied between two experiences or phenomena within a verbal description. As with complex equivalences, such relationships may or may not be accurate or valid at the level of deep structure. For instance, in the statement, "Criticizing him will make him respect the rules," it is not clear just how, specifically, the action of criticism will in fact *make* the individual being referred to develop respect for the rules. Such an action may just as easily cause the opposite effect. This type of statement leaves many potentially important missing links unspecified.

Of course, this does not mean that all cause-effect statements are invalid. Some are valid but incomplete. Others have validity, but only under certain conditions. In fact, cause-effect statements are a form of unspecified verbs. The primary danger of cause-effect statements is the implication that the relationship being defined is overly simple and/or mechanical. Because complex systems are made up of many mutually causal links (such as the human nervous system, for example), many phenomena are the result of multiple causes rather than a single cause.

Additionally, the elements involved in a cause-effect chain may each have their own "collateral energy." That is, each has its own energy source and does not respond in a predetermined way. This makes the systems much more complex because energy does not flow through the system in a fixed mechanical way. Gregory Bateson pointed out that if you kick a ball, you can determine where it will end up with a fair degree of accuracy by calculating the angle of the kick, the amount of force put into the kick, the friction of ground, etc. If you kick a dog, on the other hand, with the same angle, with same force, on the same terrain, etc., it will be much more difficult to predict where it will end up, because it has its own "collateral energy."

Causes are often less obvious, broader and more systemic in nature than the particular phenomenon or symptom that is being explored or studied. A drop in profit or productivity, for instance, may be the result of something related to competition, organization, leadership, change in the market, change in technology, communications channels, or something else.

The same is just as true for many of our beliefs relating to physical reality. We cannot actually see, hear or feel atomic particles interacting with one another, nor can we directly perceive *"gravitational"* or *"electro-magnetic"* forces. We can only perceive and measure their results. We postulate the imaginary construct *"gravity"* to explain the effects. Concepts such as *"gravity,"* *"electro-magnetic force,"* *"atoms,"* *"cause-and-effect,"* *"energy,"* even *"time"* and *"space"* were in many ways just arbitrary constructs that came from our imagination (not the outside world) in order to categorize and bring order to our sensory experiences.

The Basic Structure of Beliefs

Albert Einstein wrote:

"Hume saw clearly that certain concepts, as for example that of causality, cannot be deduced from the material of experience by logical methods . . . All concepts, even those which are closest to experience, are from the point of view of logic freely chosen conventions."

What Einstein is saying is that our senses do not actually perceive things like "causes", they can only perceive that first one event happened and then another event happened right after the first one. For example, we may perceive a sequence of events such as, first, '*a man chops on a tree with an axe*' and then '*the tree falls down*', or '*a woman says something to a child*' and then '*the child starts crying*', or '*there is an eclipse of the sun and then an earthquake the next day*'. According to Einstein, we can say that "the man caused the tree to fall down," "the woman caused the child to cry" or "the eclipse caused the earthquake," but that only the **sequence** of the events is what is perceived – "**cause**" is a freely chosen internal construct that we apply to the relationship we perceived. For instance, one could just as easily say, "gravity caused the tree to fall," "the child's unfulfilled expectations caused him to cry" or "forces from inside the earth caused the earthquake" depending on which frame of reference we choose to take.

Einstein's point is that the basic rules we use to operate in the world, and the rules that the world itself operates from, are not observable in the content of our experience. As he put it, "*A theory can be tested by experience, but there is no way from experience to the setting up of a theory.*"

This same dilemma applies with equal force to psychology, neurology, and probably every area of human endeavor. *The closer we get to the actual primary relationships and rules that determine and run our experience, the further we are from anything that is directly perceivable.* We cannot physically sense the fundamental principles and rules that generate our behavior and experiences, only their effects. When the brain, for instance, tries to perceive itself, there will be certain unavoidable blind spots.

Types of Causes

According to the Greek philosopher Aristotle (*Posterior Analytics*) there were four basic types of causes to be considered in all investigation and analysis: (1) "antecedent," "necessitating" or "precipitating" causes, (2) "constraining" or "efficient" causes, (3) "final" causes, and (4) "formal" causes.

1. Precipitating Causes
Past events, actions or decisions that influence the present state of the system through a linear chain of action-reaction.

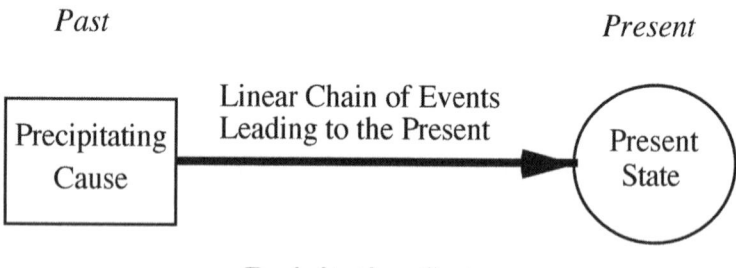

Past *Present*

[Precipitating Cause] → Linear Chain of Events Leading to the Present → (Present State)

Preipitating Cause

2. Constraining Causes
Present relationships, presuppositions and boundary conditions which maintain the current state of the system (regardless of how it got there).

THE BASIC STRUCTURE OF BELIEFS

Present

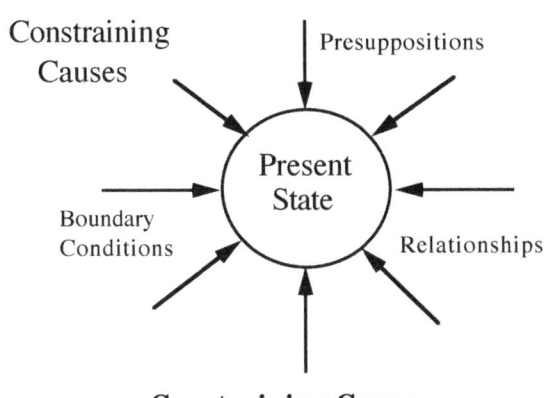

Constraining Cause

3. Final Causes
Future objectives, goals or visions which guide or influence the present state of the system giving current actions meaning, relevance or purpose.

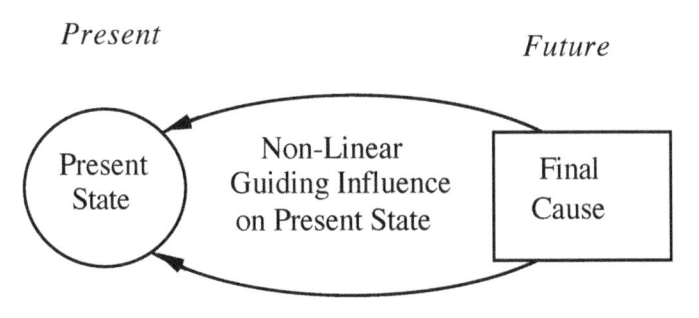

Final Cause

4. Formal Causes
Fundamental definitions and perceptions of something - i.e., basic assumptions and mental maps.

Looking for *precipitating causes* leads us to see the problem or outcome as a result of particular events and experiences from the past. Seeking *constraining causes* leads us to perceive the problem or outcome as something brought out by ongoing conditions within which the current situation is occurring. Considering *final causes* leads us to perceive a problem or outcome as a result of the motives and intentions of the individuals involved. Attempting to find the *formal causes* of a problem or outcome leads us to view it as a function of the definitions and assumptions we are applying to the situation.

Clearly, any one of these causes taken to be the whole explanation by itself is likely to lead to an incomplete picture. In today's science, we look mostly for *mechanical causes*, or what Aristotle referred to as 'antecedent' or precipitating causes. When we study a phenomenon scientifically, we tend to look for the linear cause-and-effect chain which brought it about. For instance, we say, "Our universe was caused by the 'big bang', which happened billions of years ago." Or we say, "AIDS is caused by a virus that enters the body and interferes with the immune system." Or "This organization is successful because it took those particular steps at those particular times." These understandings are certainly important and useful but do not necessarily tell us the whole story of these phenomena.

Identifying *constraining causes* would involve examining what holds a particular phenomenon's current structure in place, regardless of what brought it there. Why is it, for instance, that many people who have the AIDS virus do not manifest any physical symptoms? If the universe has been expanding after the 'big bang', what determines the current rate at which it is expanding? What constraints will cause the universe to stop expanding? What are the current constraints or lack of constraints that could cause an organization to fail or suddenly take off, regardless of its history?

Searching for *final causes*, would involve exploring the potential aims or ends of these phenomena with respect to the rest of nature. For instance, is AIDS simply a scourge, is it a lesson, or is it an evolutionary process? Is God "playing dice" with the universe, or is it heading toward something? What are the visions and goals that make an organization successful?

Identifying the *formal causes* of the "universe," a "successful organization" or of "AIDS" would involve examining our basic assumptions and intuitions about the phenomena. What exactly do we mean when we talk about our "universe" or about "success," an "organization" or about "AIDS?" What are we presupposing about their structure and their "nature?" (These were the type of questions that lead Albert Einstein to reformulate our whole perception of time, space and the structure of the universe.)

The Influence of Formal Causes

In many respects, our language, beliefs and models of the world function as the 'formal causes' of our reality. Formal causes relate to our fundamental definitions of some phenomenon or experience. The notion of "cause" itself, is a type of 'formal cause'.

As the term implies, "formal causes" are associated more with the 'form' of something than its content. The "formal cause" of a phenomenon is that which gives the definition of its essential character. It could be said that the "formal cause" of a human being, for instance, is the deep structure relationships encoded in that person's DNA. Formal causes are also intimately related to language and mental maps in that we create our realities by conceptualizing and labeling our experience.

We call a bronze statue of a four-legged animal with a mane, hooves and a tail a "horse," for instance, because it displays the form or 'formal' characteristics we have associated with the word and concept of 'horse'. We say, "The acorn grew into an oak tree," because we define something that has a trunk, branches and a certain shape of leaves as being an 'oak tree'. Thus, tapping into formal causes are one of the primary mechanisms of Sleight of Mouth.

Formal causes actually say more about the perceiver than the phenomenon being perceived. Identifying formal causes involves uncovering our own basic assumptions and mental maps about a subject. When an artist like Picasso puts the handlebars of a bicycle together with the bicycle seat to make the head of a 'bull', he is tapping into 'formal causes' because he is dealing with the essential elements of the form of something.

This type of cause is related to what Aristotle called "intuition." Before we can begin to investigate something like "success," "alignment" or "leadership," we have to have the idea that such phenomena might possibly exist. For instance, identifying 'effective leaders' to model implies that we have an intuition that these individuals are in fact examples of what we are looking for.

Seeking the formal causes of a problem or outcome, for instance, would involve examining our basic definitions, assumptions and intuitions about that problem or outcome. Identifying the formal causes of "leadership," a "successful organization" or "alignment" would involve examining our basic assumptions and intuitions about these phenomena. What exactly do we mean when we talk about our "leadership" or about "success," an "organization" or about "alignment?" What are we presupposing about their structure and their "nature?"

A good example of the influence of formal causes is that of the researcher who wanted to interview people who had experienced "remissions" from terminal cancer, in order to find any potential patterns in their healing process. He secured permission from the local authorities to be able to gather data from a regional medical records center. When he approached the computer operator to get the names of people currently in remission, however, she said she was unable to give him the information. He explained that he had the appropriate authorization, but she said that wasn't the problem. The issue was that the computer had no category for "remissions." He asked if she could get a list of all the people who had been given a terminal diagnosis of cancer ten to twelve years previously. She said, "Yes." He then asked if she could get a list of all of the people that had died of cancer from that time period. "Of course," came the reply. He then checked to see if they were equal. It turned out that there were several hundred people who had been given a terminal diagnosis but were not reported dead. After sorting out those who had moved out of the area or had died of other causes, the researcher ended up with the names of over two hundred people who were in "remission" but slipped through the cracks of the medical records center because there was no category for them. Because this group of people had no "formal cause," they did not exist for the center's computer.

Something similar happened to another group of researchers who were interested in researching the phenomenon of remission. They interviewed medical doctors to find the names and histories of people who had remissions from terminal illnesses. The doctors, however, kept saying that they had no such patients. At first the researchers were concerned that perhaps the incidence of remission was much lower than they thought. At one point, one of the researchers decided to ask if the doctors had any patients who had made "remarkable recoveries" instead of "being in remission." The doctors immediately responded, "Oh yes, we have a lot of those."

Formal causes are sometimes the most difficult types of causes to identify because they become part of the unconscious assumptions and premises from which we operate, like the water in which a fish is swimming.

Sleight of Mouth and the Structure of Beliefs

In summary, complex equivalences and cause-effect statements are the primary building blocks of our beliefs and belief systems. They are the basis upon which we choose our actions. Statements such as "If X = Y then do Z" involve initiating a causal action based on the perception of an equivalence. It is ultimately these types of structures which determine how we concretely apply what we know.

According to the principles of Sleight of Mouth and NLP, in order for 'deeper structures' such as values (which are more abstract and subjective) to reach the tangible environment in the form of concrete behaviors, they must be linked to more specific cognitive processes and capabilities through beliefs. At some level, each one of Aristotle's causes must be addressed.

Thus, beliefs are the answers to questions such as:

1. "How, specifically, do you define the quality or entity you value?" "What other qualities, criteria and values is it related to?" (Formal Causes)

2. "What causes or creates this quality?" (Precipitating Causes)

3. "What consequences or outcomes result from that value?" "What is it leading to?" (Final Causes)

4. "How, specifically, do you know if some behavior or experience fits a particular criterion or value?" "What specific behaviors and experiences accompany this criterion or value?" (Constraining Causes)

For example, a person may define "success" as "achievement" and "self satisfaction." The person may believe that "success" comes from "doing your best," and that it leads to

The Basic Structure of Beliefs

"security" and "acknowledgment from others." The person may know that he or she has been successful when the person "feels a certain sensation" in his or her "chest and stomach."

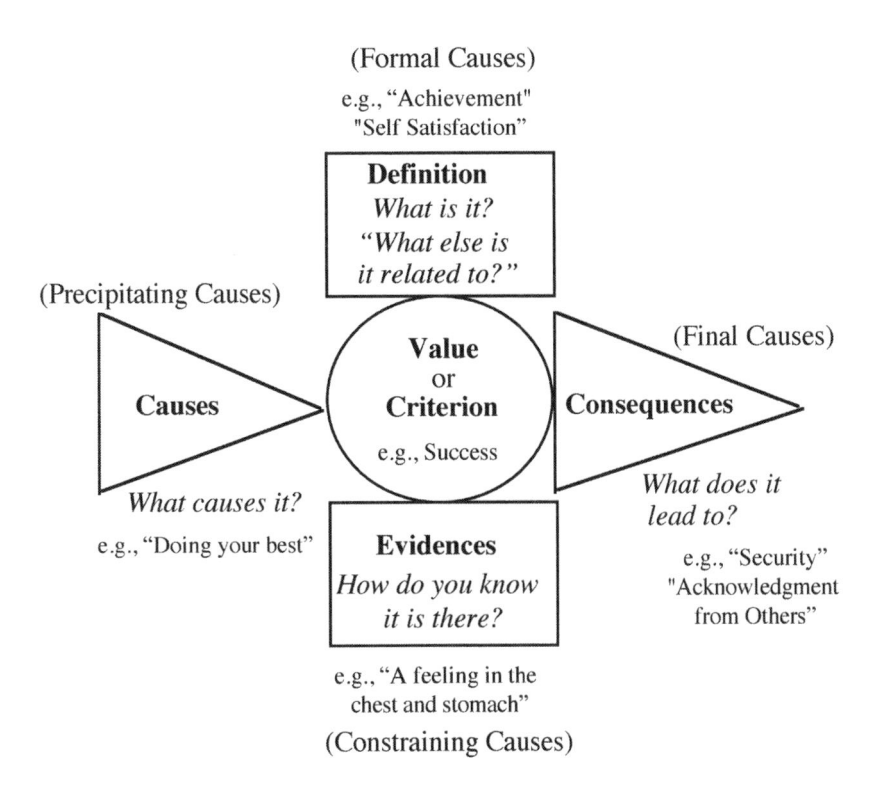

```
                        (Formal Causes)
                        e.g., "Achievement"
                        "Self Satisfaction"
                      ┌──────────────────┐
                      │   Definition     │
                      │   What is it?    │
                      │  "What else is   │
                      │  it related to?" │
(Precipitating Causes)└──────────────────┘
                            Value                    (Final Causes)
                             or
         Causes            Criterion    Consequences
                          e.g., Success
         What causes it?                  What does it
         e.g., "Doing your best"          lead to?
                          ┌──────────────┐   e.g., "Security"
                          │  Evidences   │   "Acknowledgment
                          │ How do you know│    from Others"
                          │  it is there?│
                          └──────────────┘
                        e.g., "A feeling in the
                         chest and stomach"
                        (Constraining Causes)
```

Beliefs Connect Values to Various Aspects of Our Experience

In order for a particular value to become operational, this entire system of beliefs must be specified to some degree. For a value such as "professionalism" to be enacted behaviorally, for example, one must build beliefs about what professionalism is (the "criteria" for professionalism); how you know it is being enacted (the "criterial equivalences"); what causes it; and what it leads to. These beliefs are as significant as the value itself in determining how people will act.

Two people can share the same value of "safety," for example. One person, however, may believe that safety is caused by "being stronger than one's enemies." The other person may believe that safety is caused by "understanding and responding to the positive intentions of those who threaten us." These two will seek safety in quite different ways. Their approaches may even appear to contradict one another. The first one will seek safety by building power (having "a bigger stick" than those he or she perceives as an "enemy"). The other will seek safety through communication, gathering information and looking for options.

Clearly, an individual's beliefs relating to his or her core values will determine the person's "mental map" with respect to those values; and thus, how the person attempts to manifest those values. In order to adequately teach or establish values, all of these belief issues must be appropriately addressed. For people in a system to act coherently with core values, they must all share certain beliefs, as well as values, to some degree.

Sleight of Mouth patterns can be viewed as verbal operations that shift or reframe the various elements and linkages which make up the complex equivalences and cause-effects which form beliefs and belief statements. All Sleight of Mouth patterns revolve around using language in order to relate and link various aspects of our experience and maps of the world to core values.

In the model of Sleight of Mouth, a complete 'belief statement' must minimally contain either a complex equivalence or cause-effect assertion. A verbalization such as, "People don't care about me," for instance, is not yet a full 'belief statement'. It is a generalization related to the value of "caring"; but does not yet reveal the beliefs associated with the generalization. To elicit the *beliefs* related to this generalization, one would need to ask, "*How do you know* that people don't care about you?" "What *makes* people not care about you?" "What are the *consequences* of people not caring about you?" and "What does it *mean* that people don't care about you?"

Such beliefs are often elicited through 'connective' words, such as: "because," "whenever," "if," "after," "therefore," etc. - i.e., "People don't care about me *because*. . ." "People don't care about me *if*. . ." "People don't care about me *therefore*. . ."

Again, from the NLP perspective, the issue is not so much whether one has found the "correct" cause-effect belief, but rather what types of practical results one is able to achieve if one acts "as if" a particular equivalence or causal relationship exists.

Values Audit

The purpose of our beliefs is to guide us in areas where we do not know reality. That is why beliefs have such a profound influence on our perceptions and visions of the future. To reach our outcomes and manifest our values, we must believe that it is possible for something to occur even though we are not certain that it will happen.

The Values Audit is a tool which applies linguistic connectives to help define and establish key beliefs related to establishing and manifesting core values. The values "auditing" process uses verbal prompts and key words to help you make sure you have fully explored the supporting system of beliefs necessary to bring values into action.

We build and strengthen our beliefs and values based on the cognitive maps, reference experiences, relational support and tools that we have available to us. These form the 'reasons' why we believe something in the first place. In order to bolster our own beliefs with respect to our values and goals, or to influence the beliefs of others, we must identify 'good reasons' why someone should believe in those values and goals. The more reasons that we have to believe in something, the more likely it is that we will believe in it. This involves finding and supplying the answers to several important "why" questions, such as:

a) Is something desirable? Why is it desirable?

b) Is it possible to achieve it? Why is it possible?

c) What is the path that must be followed to achieve it? Why is this the appropriate path?

d) Am I (Are we) capable of completing the path? Why am I (are we) capable?

e) Do I (we) deserve to complete the path and get what we want? Why do I (we) deserve it?

According to Aristotle, answering these types of questions would involve finding the underlying 'causes' related to the various issues. In other words, we must discover:

a) What *causes* it to be desirable.
b) What *causes* it to be possible.
c) What *causes* this to be the appropriate path.
d) What *makes* me/us capable.
e) What *makes* me/us deserving.

Linguistically, Aristotle's different types of causes are reflected in certain key words known as 'connectives'. Connectives are words or phrases that link one idea to another; such as:

because   *before*   *after*
while   *whenever*   *so that*
in the   *if*   *although*
same way that   *therefore*

Connectives

We relate ideas together, and values to experiences, through these types of 'connective' words. For instance, if we were to make a value statement such as, "learning is important," and follow it with the word "because," we would be lead to identify some 'cause' which brought us to our conclusion. As an example, we might say, "Learning is important because it helps us to grow and survive." In this case, an important link has been made to a consequence (or 'final cause') related to learning.

Different connective words can be used as a means to explore or 'audit' the various 'causes' related to a particular value or criterion. One simple method is to choose a particular value and systematically go through each of the connectives to find any other related supporting associations or assumptions.

For example, if a person wanted to strengthen his or her belief in and commitment to the value of "health," the process would start with the statement of that particular value: "Health is important and desirable." Holding this value statement constant, the individual would then go through each connective to explore all of the supporting reasons.

In this case it would be important to begin each new sentence prompted by the connective with the word "I". This helps to insure that the individual remains associated in the experience and avoids merely making 'rationalizations'. Thus, the series of new statements would be created in the following manner:

Health is important and desirable,
because I _____

Health is important and desirable,
therefore I _____

Health is important and desirable,
whenever I _____

Health is important and desirable,
so that I _____

Health is important and desirable,
*although I _____

Health is important and desirable,
if I _____

Health is important and desirable,
in the same way that I _____

An example of how someone would complete these sentences might be:

Health is important and desirable *because* I need strength and energy in order to create and survive.
Health is important and desirable *therefore* I will begin the appropriate steps to take care of myself.
Health is important and desirable *whenever* I want to be prepared for the future.
Health is important and desirable *so that* I can enjoy myself and be a good role model for others.
Health is important and desirable *if* I want to be happy and productive.
Health is important and desirable **although* I have other goals and responsibilities to be fulfilled.
Health is important and desirable *in the same way that* I need the necessary foundations and resources to reach my dreams.

After finishing the new statements, it is interesting to read each of the entries deleting the prompt words - with the exception of "although". (It is important to retain the word "although" or that particular response will appear negative.) The series of responses can form a surprisingly coherent and valuable statement of reasons to commit to the core value that you have selected:

Health is important and desirable. I need strength and energy in order to create and survive. I will begin the appropriate steps to take care of myself. I want to be prepared for the future. I can enjoy myself and be a good role model for others. I want to be happy and productive. Although I have other goals and responsibilities to be fulfilled, I need the necessary foundations and resources to reach my dreams.

As you can see, this creates a coherent set of ideas and affirmations that can help to strengthen a person's commitment to and belief in the value of health. The paragraph defines elements of a pathway for expressing the value, provides motivation, and even addresses possible objections. Because the group of statements identify a multiplicity of reasons (or causes) and puts them into words, it becomes a powerful source of positive affirmations. It provides an overall explanation justifying commitment to the value. It also provides a rich source of ideas for addressing doubts.

Try this process on one of your own values by going through the following steps, and referring to the Values Audit Worksheet.

1. Identify a core value that is important for you to establish or strengthen. Write down the value you want to strengthen in the space marked 'Value' below to complete the value statement.

2. For each of the 'prompt' words, read your value statement, add the prompt word(s), and complete the sentence with whatever 'spontaneously' comes to mind.

3. When you are finished, read your answers all together and notice what has changed and been strengthened.

Values Audit Worksheet

Value: _____ is important and desirable.
What is a core value that is important for you to establish or strengthen?

because I _____
Why is it desirable and appropriate to have this as a value?

therefore I _____
What is a behavioral consequence of having this value?

whenever I _____
What is a key situation or condition relating to this value?

so that I _____
What is the positive purpose of this value?

*although I _____
What alternatives or constraints are there with respect to this value?

if I _____
What constraints or results relate to this value?

in the same way that I _____
What is a similar value that you already have?

After you have finished filling in each statement, read each of the entries, deleting the prompt words and beginning with the word "I" (the exception is the word "although"; it is important to retain the word "although" or that particular response will appear negative.)

Belief Audit

The "auditing" process, using linguistic connectives, can be applied to strengthen other beliefs as well, by establishing "beliefs about beliefs." These can serve as additional justifications and support to have confidence in a particular belief.

As an example, let's say a person has doubts about whether he or she deserves to be healthy and attractive. Applying the Belief Audit process would involve repeating this belief and adding different connectives to the end of the statement. Filling in the blank created by adding the connectives serves to create links between that belief and other beliefs and experiences, and 'reframe' possible interferences.

Try it out using the following procedure.

'Belief Audit' Procedure

1. Identify a belief that you need in order to achieve a desired outcome, but about which you have some doubt (refer to the Belief Assessment Sheet in Chapter 5). Write down the belief you want to strengthen in the space marked 'Belief' below.

2. For each of the 'prompt' words below, repeat the sentence expressing the belief. Then add the prompt word(s) and complete the sentence with whatever 'spontaneously' comes to mind.

3. When you are finished, read your answers all together and notice what has changed and what has been strengthened.

Belief: _____

The Basic Structure of Beliefs

because I/you _____
Why is it (are you) desirable / possible / appropriate (capable / deserving / responsible) to reach the outcome?

therefore I/you_____
What is an effect or requirement of this belief?

after I/you _____
What has to happen to support this belief?

while I/you _____
What else is going on concurrently with this belief?

whenever I/you_____
What is a key condition relating to the belief?

so that I/you_____
What is the intention of this belief?

if I/you_____
What constraints or results relate to this belief?

*although I/you _____
What alternatives or constraints are there to this belief?

in the same way that I/you_____
What is a similar belief that you already have?

As you try this process with one of your own beliefs, you will realize that some of the prompts are easier to respond to than others. You may also find that it is easier or more appropriate to respond to the prompts in a different order than they are listed. Of course you can feel free to answer the prompts in the order that feels most natural and comfortable for you or your group, and it is okay to leave some of the prompts blank. You will find, however, that the prompts which seem most difficult to answer often lead to some of the most surprising and insightful results.

Auditing a Belief From a Different Perspective

Sometimes it is difficult or unfruitful to audit a belief from your own perspective. In fact, doubts often arise because we are stuck in our point of view and cannot see any other choices.

Another way to use the Belief Audit process is to do it while considering the vision and belief from the shoes of another person, or 'mentor'. This can open up new 'perceptual space' and help to remove unconscious blocks to creativity. It can also help you to find unconscious or unnecessary assumptions.

This form of the Belief Audit can be done by identifying a person, either actual or hypothetical, who does have full confidence in the particular belief you have doubts about. Then you, or a partner, can step into the shoes of that person and 'role play' his or her responses to the various prompts. To facilitate the role play, you would want to use the word "you" instead of "I" when initially responding to the prompts.

To test the influence of the other perspective on your own confidence level, you can then repeat the responses generated by the other perspective substituting the word "I" for "You". It often helps to have another person read the responses to you first, so you can get a sense of the statement from both perspectives.

For example, if the statement generated from the role-played perspective is "You deserve to be healthy and attractive because You are a precious product of nature," you would repeat the response in first person. That is, you would say, "I deserve to be healthy and attractive because I am a precious product of nature."

Using Counter Examples to Reevaluate Limiting Beliefs

The Values Audit and Belief Audit apply principles of NLP and Sleight of Mouth in order to help us become more *open to believe* in our goals, our values, our capabilities and ourselves. They are simple but powerful processes that help us to establish new and empowering beliefs.

There are times, however, where we may encounter interference from limiting beliefs. In such situations, it is also important to have tools to help us become *open to doubt* those generalizations or judgments that limit us. Processes such as finding the intention, chunking down, chunking up, finding analogies, and identifying higher level criteria offer several methods softening and reframing limiting beliefs. Another very powerful pattern, that works with the structure of beliefs, is to identify "counter examples" to the beliefs.

A *counter example* is an example, experience, or piece of information, which does not fit a particular generalization about the world. Counter examples are essentially exceptions to a rule. For example, a person may say that "all Masai are cattle thieves," stating a generalization about a group of people. To challenge this representation, we would search for any examples which do not fit that generalization – perhaps a time when a Masai returned a missing cow to someone.

Finding counter examples is a simple but powerful way to evaluate and challenge potentially limiting beliefs, and to deepen our understanding of other beliefs. Counter examples do not necessarily disprove a belief statement, but they do challenge its 'universality', and frequently put it in a broader perspective. (In Chapter 4, for instance, we used counter examples to identify hierarchies of criteria.) As was mentioned earlier, beliefs and criticisms become limiting when they are stated as 'universals'; characterized by language such as "all," "every," "always," "never," "none," "no one," etc. It is different to say, "I am not succeeding because I lack the necessary experience," than to say, "I'll never succeed because I lack the necessary experience." Similarly, there are different implications and expectations connected with the statement, "I am sick because I have cancer," than the statement, "I will always be sick because I have cancer." Beliefs stated as universals frequently have more impact on our expectations and motivation.

For a statement to be truly universal, of course, we should find no counter examples. With respect to Sleight of Mouth, establishing a counter example involves finding an example that does not fit the cause-effect or complex equivalence statements which make up a belief or belief system, and which shifts and enriches our perception of the generalization or judgment being asserted. So, if someone claims, "All employees are mistrustful of their bosses," then we would seek any examples of employees who trusted their bosses. We should also find out if there are bosses who are mistrusted by people other than their employees.

Finding a counter example, by the way, does not mean that a belief statement is 'wrong', it generally means that the system or phenomenon that is being explored or studied is more complex than it has been perceived to be, or that its most fundamental elements have not yet been discovered. This opens up the potential for other perspectives and possibilities.

As we have already established, the structure of belief statements typically takes the form of either:

A **means** B (complex equivalent): *e.g., Frowning means you are unhappy.*

or

C **causes** D (cause-effect): *e.g., Allergens cause allergies.*

To seek **counter examples** we would first ask:

Does A ever occur without B?
e.g., Do people ever frown when they are happy?

or

Are there times when C is present but does not cause D?
e.g., Can people be around an allergen and not have an allergy?

You can also reverse, or 'convert', the terms and ask:

Does B ever occur without A?
e.g., Are people ever unhappy, yet do not frown?

or

Is there any D that is not caused by C?
e.g., Can someone have an allergic reaction even though no allergy is present?

Finding counter examples often leads us to a deeper understanding of the phenomenon we are considering, and helps to enrich our 'map' of the territory. Often, there is a superficial validity to certain generalizations (like the relationship between frowning and unhappiness or allergens and allergies), but the deeper processes to which they refer are, in fact, much more complex.

Keep in mind that, because beliefs are linked with deep level neurology, a change in beliefs by finding a counter example can often produce immediate and dramatic effects. Finding counter examples, for instance, is the core of the NLP Allergy Technique (which involves finding something as similar as possible to the allergen, but which does not produce the allergic reaction).

Some Verbal Frames for Eliciting Limiting Belief Statements

In order to practice finding counter examples for limiting beliefs, you will need some examples of limiting beliefs. We can utilize verbal prompts, similar to those applied in the Values Audit and Belief Audit, in order to generate limiting belief statements.

As with all beliefs, and the verbalization of beliefs, limiting beliefs typically take the form of "cause-effect" and "complex equivalence" statements. That is, we believe that something is the *result* or *consequence* of something else, or that something is *evidence of* or *means* something else. The following prompts use these verbal forms as a way to explore and elicit clusters of limiting beliefs relating to the sense of hopelessness, helplessness and worthlessness. Filling in the statements with respect to some situation or area in your life where you feel stuck or at an "impasse" can help you to uncover important limiting beliefs which can then be addressed by the various Sleight of Mouth patterns that we have been exploring in this book.

If I get what I want then _____.
What would you lose or could go wrong if you get what you want?

Getting what I want would mean_____.
What would it mean negatively about you or others if you got what you wanted?

_____ causes things to stay the way they are now.
What prevents things from changing?

Getting what I want will make _____.
What problems could be caused by getting what you want?

The Basic Structure of Beliefs

The situation will never change because _____.
What constraints or blocks keep things the way they are?

I can't get what I want because _____.
  What stops you from getting what you want?

It is not possible for me to get what I want because _____.
  What makes it impossible for you to get what you want?

I am not capable of getting what I want because _____.
  What personal deficiency prevents you from getting your outcome?

Things will never get better because _____.
  What will always prevent you from truly succeeding?

I'll always have this problem because _____.
  What prevents you from reaching your outcome that can never be changed?

It is wrong to want to be different because _____.
  What makes it wrong or inappropriate to want to change?

I don't deserve to get what I want because _____.
What have you done, or not done, that makes you unworthy of getting what you want?

Generating Counter Examples

Choose a belief (complex equivalent or cause-effect) to work with and write it in the spaces provided below.

(A)_____ **because** (B)_____

*e.g., (A) I am not capable of learning to operate a computer **because** (B) I am not a technically oriented person.*

Finding counter examples would involve 1) searching for cases in which there was **A but not B**; i.e., cases in which people learned to operate computers who were not technically oriented.

You can also identify counter examples by 2) seeking instances in which there was **B but not A**; i.e., situations in which people who were technically oriented did not learn to operate computers.

Here are a couple of other examples:

*I will never succeed academically **because** I have a learning disability.*

1. Are there examples of people who did not succeed academically even though they did not have any learning disabilities? (i.e., people who did not take advantage of the opportunities provided for them)

2. Are there examples of people who did have learning disabilities (such as Albert Einstein) yet did succeed academically?

*I don't deserve to get what I want **because** I have not made enough effort.*

1. Can you think of examples of individuals who do not deserve to get what they want even though they have made a lot of effort? (e.g., thieves or assassins who put a lot of effort into their crimes)

2. Can you think of any individuals who make no effort at all (such as a new born baby), yet still deserve to get what they want?

You can search for counter examples either in your own personal life experiences or in the accomplishments and achievements of others. The actions and achievements of others generally convince us that something is possible or desirable. Counter examples coming from our life experiences convince us that we personally have the capabilities and deserve it.

Generally finding even one person who has been able to accomplish something that is believed impossible builds our sense of hope and 'outcome expectation', strengthening our confidence that something is possible. Finding examples from our own life experiences goes a step further, intensifying our confidence, not only that something is possible, but that we are capable of reaching it already to some degree — i.e., it strengthens our self-efficacy expectation.

Once a meaningful counter example has been found, it can be presented to the person who is struggling with the limiting belief. Remember, the purpose of finding counter examples, and of Sleight of Mouth in general, is not to attack or humiliate someone for having a limiting belief; rather, it is to help the person widen and enrich his or her map of the world, and shift from a problem frame or failure frame to an outcome frame or feedback frame.

As an example, if a child says, "I'll never to learn to ride this bike, I keep falling down all the time," a parent could respond, "You were able to keep your balance for almost 10 feet a little while ago. So you are not falling all the time. Keep practicing and you will able to keep your balance longer and longer." This counter example is arrived at from "chunking down" the child's experience and narrowing the frame size to focus on the moments of success. Because it is drawn from the child's own behavior, it is likely to help reinforce the child's belief in the development of his or her own capabilities. This supports the child to become open to believe that he or she can, indeed, learn to maintain his or her balance.

A parent could also make a statement like, "Remember how your brother fell down all the time when he was first learning to ride his bicycle? Now he rides his bike easily all the time. Falling down is just a part of learning." In this case, the counter example is established by "chunking up," widening the frame, and pointing to the achievements of others. This will serve to build the child's confidence, or "outcome expectation," that it is possible to learn to ride a bicycle, even if one falls down a lot. This can help the child to become open to doubt that falling down means one will ultimately fail to learn.

Both counter examples help to put the limiting generalization—"I'll never to learn to ride this bike, I keep falling down all the time"—back into a feedback frame instead of a failure frame.

Chapter 7

Internal States and Natural Belief Change

The Natural Process of Belief Change

The purpose of all of the Sleight of Mouth patterns we have explored up to this point is to assist us to become more open to believe in our goals, our values, our capabilities and ourselves. They can also help us to 'reframe' negative generalizations, stimulating us to become more open to doubt evaluations and judgments which limit us. Sleight of Mouth patterns are simple but effective verbal structures that aid us in the establishment of new and empowering beliefs, and in changing limiting beliefs. They are powerful tools for conversational belief change.

People often consider the process of changing beliefs to be difficult and effortful; and accompanied by struggle and conflict. Yet, the fact remains that people naturally and spontaneously establish and discard hundreds, if not thousands, of beliefs during their lifetimes. Perhaps the difficulty is that when we consciously attempt to change our beliefs, we do so in a way that does not respect the natural cycle of belief change. We try to change our beliefs by "repressing" them, disproving them, or attacking them. Beliefs can become surprisingly simple and easy to change if we respect and pace the natural process of belief change.

I have spent a great deal of time studying and modeling the process of natural belief change. I have worked with many people, individually and in seminars, over the past twenty years, and have witnessed the sometimes miraculous consequences which result when people are able to release old limiting beliefs and establish new and empowering ones. This transition can often be both rapid and gentle.

I have also seen my two children (who are 10 and 8 years old at the time of this writing) change many, many potentially limiting beliefs in their short lives; and establish more enriching ones. Perhaps most importantly, they did it without psychotherapy or medication (although a little mentoring and Sleight of Mouth is often helpful). These limiting beliefs covered a variety of topics and activities, including:

I'll never learn to ride this bicycle.
I am not good at math.
I'll never live through this pain.
It is too hard for me to learn to ski.
Learning to play the piano (or this particular song) is difficult and boring.
I am not a good baseball player.
I can't learn how to pump the swing by myself.

At a certain point in their lives, my children actually made statements such as these. The degree to which they believed their own words threatened their motivation to keep trying to succeed. When such beliefs are taken to an extreme, people give up, and can actually cease to enjoy or attempt to do such activities for the rest of their lives.

The process through which my children changed their beliefs occurred as a natural cycle in which they became more and more *open to doubt* the limiting belief, and more and more *open to believe* that they could be successful. This has led me to formulate what I call the *Belief Change Cycle* (see *Strategies of Genius Volume III*, 1995).

The Belief Change Cycle

The natural cycle of belief change can be likened to the changing of the seasons. A new belief is like a seed that becomes planted in the Spring. The seed grows into the Summer where it matures, becomes strong and takes root. During the process of its growth, the seed must at times compete for survival with other plants or weeds that may already be growing in the garden. To successfully accomplish this, the new seed may require the assistance of the gardener in order to help fertilize it or provide protection from the weeds.

Like crops in the Autumn, the belief eventually serves its purpose, and begins to become outdated and wither. The 'fruits' of the belief, however, (the positive intentions and purposes behind it) are retained or 'harvested', and separated from the parts that are no longer necessary. Finally, in the Winter, the parts of the belief which are no longer needed are let go of and fade away, allowing the cycle to begin again.

As we prepare for the different stages in our lives or careers, we repeat this cycle many times: (a) We begin by *'wanting to believe'* that we will be able to manage the new challenge successfully and resourcefully. As we enter that stage of life and learn the lessons that we need in order to manage, we (b) become *'open to believe'* that we may, in fact, have the capabilities to be successful and resourceful. As our capabilities become confirmed, we (c) become confident in our *'belief'* that we are successful and resourceful and that what we are doing is right for us now.

Sometimes our new conviction comes in conflict with existing limiting beliefs that contradict the new generalization or judgment we are attempting to establish. Frequently, these interfering beliefs are generalizations that have served to support or protect us at some time in the past, by establishing limits and priorities perceived as necessary for safety or survival at that time in our lives. As we recognize that we are passing that stage of life or work, we begin to become (d) *'open to doubt'* that the boundaries and decisions associated with that stage are really what is most important, priorital or 'true' for us anymore.

When we are able to move on to the next stage in our lives or careers, we can look back and see that what used to be important and true for us is no longer the case. We can recognize that we (e) *'used to believe'* that we were a certain way and that certain things were important. We can also retain the beliefs and capabilities that will help us in our current phase, but we realize that our values, priorities and beliefs are now different.

All one needs to do is to reflect upon the cycles of change that one has gone through since childhood, adolescence, and the stages of adulthood, to find many examples of this cycle. As we enter and pass through relationships, jobs, friendships, partnerships, etc., we develop beliefs and values which serve us, and let them go again as we transition to a new part of our life's path.

The fundamental steps of this cycle include:

1. Wanting to Believe

'Wanting to believe' has to do with our expectations and our motivations for establishing a new belief. When we 'want to believe' something, it is usually because we think that the new belief will produce positive consequences in our lives. 'Wanting to believe' something also involves the acknowledgment that we do not yet 'believe' it - the new belief has not yet passed our 'reality strategy' or the 'criterial equivalences' necessary for us to know that we have incorporated fully into our current model of the world.

2. Becoming Open to Believe

Becoming 'open to believe' is an exciting and generative experience, typically accompanied by a sense of freedom and exploration. When we are 'open to believe', we are not yet convinced that the new belief is completely valid. Rather, we are gathering and weighing evidence which could support the belief. Being open to believe involves being fully immersed in the outcome frame, the feedback frame and the 'as if' frame. We know that we do not believe it yet, but think, "Maybe it is possible." "It could be." "What would my life be like if I did take on this new belief?" "What would I have to see, hear or feel to become convinced that the new belief is valid and useful?"

3. Currently Believing

The generalizations that we 'currently believe' make up our ongoing belief system. When we believe something (whether it is positive or negative; empowering or limiting), we fully commit to that belief as our current "reality." We congruently act "as if" that belief were true for us. It is at this point that the belief begins to take on the "self-fulfilling" properties associated with believing something (as in the 'placebo effect'). When we fully believe something, there are no questions or doubts in our minds.

Frequently, when we first attempt to take on a new belief, it comes into conflict with existing beliefs. A child who wants to believe, "I am able to ride a bicycle," must often contend with previous generalizations derived from the experience of falling down on many previous attempts. Similarly, a child who wants to believe, "It is safe for me to cross the street on my own," may first have to address and let go of the belief that his or her parents have established previously that, "You cannot cross the street by yourself, without an adult to help you."

It is not uncommon for such conflicting beliefs to arise as we begin to seriously consider believing in something new or different. Thus, the attempt to fully take on a new belief can frequently trigger or bring out conflicts and resistance with respect to other beliefs that have already been established as part of our existing belief system.

4. Becoming Open to Doubt

In order to reevaluate and let go of existing beliefs that are interfering with the establishment of a new belief, we must become 'open to doubt' the existing belief. The experience of being open to doubt is the complement of being open to believe. Rather than thinking that some new belief might be true, when we are 'open to doubt' we are open to consider that some belief that we have been holding onto for a long time might not be the case. We think, "Maybe it is not valid, or no longer valid." "Perhaps it is not so important or necessary to believe it." "I have changed my belief about other things before." "What counter examples do I have that might call this old belief into question?" "If I view it from a larger perspective, what other possibilities do I become aware of?" "What is the positive purpose that this belief has served, and are there other ways to achieve that positive intention that are less limiting and more enriching?"

Becoming open to doubt typically involves reframing beliefs formulated in terms of the problem frame or failure frame so that they may be put back into an outcome frame or feedback frame. Sleight of Mouth patterns provide powerful verbal tools to help us reframe and become open to doubt existing, interfering beliefs.

5. The 'Museum of Personal History' – Remembering What We 'Used to' Believe

When we stop believing something, we do not usually develop amnesia for the belief, or forget that we used to believe it. Rather, the emotional and psychological affect that the belief produces within us changes dramatically. We remember that we "used to" believe it, but know that it no longer has any meaningful influence on our thoughts or behavior – it no longer fits our criteria for "reality."

When we truly change a belief, we no longer need to exert any effort to deny or suppress the belief. Our relationship to it is more like the experience we have of seeing historical items in a museum. When we see Medieval weapons and torture instruments in a glass case at a museum, we are curious and reflective; not frightened, angry or disgusted. We know that people once used these weapons, but that we have gone beyond that now. In fact, it is important to remember the mistakes and limiting beliefs of our ancestors, so that we do not repeat them.

A similar experience happens with respect to our own discarded beliefs. We know that we 'used to believe' them, but now no longer believe them. The belief in Santa Claus is a classic example of this experience. Most adults (in cultures that celebrate Christmas) remember that, as children, they believed that the character "Santa Claus" lived at the North Pole and would ride through the sky on a magic sled to deliver gifts to children all over the world on Christmas Eve. When a person no longer believes in Santa Claus, he or she does not need to angrily and vehemently deny the existence of the fictitious character. Rather, one can look back on it nostalgically, and remember the positive intention of the belief to create the sense of magic and excitement.

Similarly, this is the way we recall other beliefs that we have let go of. We can remember them and think, "I used to believe that I (could not ride a bicycle, could not cross the street on my own, was not capable of establishing a healthy pattern of behavior, did not deserve to succeed, etc.), but I no longer believe it. It is no longer part of my reality. I have other ways to satisfy the positive intention and purpose of the old belief."

6. *Trust*

In many ways, trust is the cornerstone of the natural process of belief change. Merriam Webster's Dictionary defines *trust* as "assured reliance on the character, ability, strength, or truth of someone or something." Thus, trust is characterized by confidence or belief in "something future or contingent." People trust, for instance, that a person will "be true to his word," or that "things will turn out for the best."

Emotionally, trust is related to hope. *Hope* is a function of our belief that something is possible. A person who has hope that he or she will recover from a serious illness, must believe that such a recovery is possible. The feeling of trust, however, is often stronger than hope. It has to do with the expectation that something will happen, rather than simply the belief that it could happen.

Trust, in fact, is often something we must rely on when we have no proof. In this sense, trust extends beyond belief (to the level of identity or even spiritual experience). In the natural cycle of belief change, "trust" is typified by a state that allows us to go beyond our beliefs; to the state from which our beliefs are formed.

The experience in 'trusting' in something that is beyond one's beliefs, or trusting in a larger system than oneself, can help to make the process of belief change smoother, more comfortable, and more ecological.

When they are used effectively, Sleight of Mouth patterns serve as verbal tools which help to support this natural cycle of belief change; leading people to become open to believe new and empowering beliefs, and open to doubt those beliefs and generalizations which limit them.

Belief Change and Internal States

As the steps involved in the process of natural belief change illustrate, our internal state is an important influence on belief change. Our internal states are in many ways the containers for our beliefs. If one is in a positive, optimistic state, it is much more difficult to hold onto negative and limiting beliefs. On the other hand, it is difficult to remain congruent about positive and empowering beliefs when our internal state is one of frustration, disappointment or fear.

A person's *internal state* relates to the psychological and emotional experience that a person is having at a particular point in time. Internal states determine much about our choice of behavior and response. Internal states function as both a type of filtering mechanism with respect to our perceptions and a gateway to particular memories, capabilities and beliefs. Thus, a person's state exerts an enormous influence on his or her current 'world view'.

There is an old, and very relevant, New Guinea Proverb which states, *"Knowledge is only a rumor until it is in the muscle."* A belief (positive or negative) is just a "rumor" until it is "in the muscle." That is, until we have incorporated a particular belief or value somatically, feeling and emotionally experiencing its implications, it is merely a disassociated set of concepts, words or ideas. Beliefs and values are given "power" by their connection to our physiology and internal states.

Similarly, our ongoing physical, psychological and emotional state will exert a great deal of influence on the types of beliefs we are inclined to enact. Consider, for example, the influence of the following lists of states on your experience:

"Positive" Internal States	"Negative" Internal States
Calm	Upset
Relaxed	Tense
Flexible	Rigid
Flowing	Stuck
Centered	Anxious
Confident	Frustrated
Optimistic	Doubtful
Focused	Distracted
Receptive	Closed
Trusting	Fearful

As you can easily tell from your own life experiences, it is probably much easier to associate to—and be 'open to believe'—empowering and positive beliefs when we are in positive internal states than when we are in negative internal states.

A basic premise of NLP is that the human brain functions similarly to a computer - by executing "programs" or mental strategies that are composed of ordered sequences of instructions or internal representations. Certain programs or strategies function better for accomplishing certain tasks than others, and it is the strategy that an individual uses that will to a great extent determine whether his performance is one of mediocrity or excellence. The efficacy and ease with which a particular mental program is carried out is to a large degree determined by the physiological state of the individual. Clearly, if a computer has a bad chip or power surges in its electrical supply its programs will not be able to execute effectively.

The same is true for the human brain. The level of arousal, receptivity, stress, etc., of the individual will determine how effectively he can carry out his own mental programs. Deep physiological processes, such as heart rate, breathing rate, body posture, blood pressure, muscle tension, reaction time and galvanic skin response, etc., accompany changes in a person's internal state, and greatly influence a person's ability to think and act. Thus, an individual's internal state has important influences on his or her ability to perform in any situation.

Our internal states have to do with the "neurological" part of Neuro-Linguistic Programming. The state of our physiology and neurology acts as a type of filter upon how our attention is focused; and thus upon what we hear (and do not hear), and how we interpret what we do hear.

Recognizing, reacting to, and influencing people's internal states is an important skill for effectively using Sleight of Mouth.

Recognizing and Influencing Internal States

We are constantly changing and accessing different states as we move through the different experiences and contexts of our lives. For most of us, these state changes have remained largely outside of our ability to choose. We respond to stimuli (anchors) that are both internal and external to ourselves as though we were on "automatic pilot."

It is possible, however, to learn how to choose one's state. Being able to influence and direct one's state increases an individual's flexibility and creates a higher probability of maintaining positive beliefs and expectations, and achieving desired outcomes. The ability to recognize useful states and intentionally access such states in particular situations gives us more choices about how we will experience and react to those situations. In NLP, the terms 'state selection' and 'state management' refer to the ability to choose and achieve the most appropriate state for a given situation or challenge.

One goal of NLP is to help people to create a "library" of useful or resourceful states.

By becoming more aware of the patterns and cues that influence internal states, we can increase the number of choices we have in responding to a particular situation. Once we are aware of the factors that define and influence the characteristics of our internal states we can sort them and "anchor" them to help make them available for use. Some of the methods used in NLP to sort and anchor internal states include: spatial location, submodalities (colors, tones, brightness, etc.), and non-verbal cues.

In order to better recognize and understand your own internal states, and to assist in developing your capacity for state 'selection' and 'management', it is necessary to learn how to take an internal inventory of your neurological processes. There are three methods of doing this in NLP: physiology inventory, submodality inventory, and emotions inventory.

A *physiological inventory* involves becoming aware of one's body posture, gestures, eye position, breathing and movement patterns.

A *submodality inventory* involves noticing the sensory submodalities which are most prominent within our internal sensory experience, i.e. the brightness, color, size and position of mental images; the tone, timbre, volume and location of voices and sounds; and the temperature, texture, area, etc., of kinesthetic sensations.

An *emotions inventory* involves taking an account of the constellation of components that make up our emotional states.

These three types of inventories are related to our criterial equivalences and reality strategies. Developing an ability to take inventory in all three ways leads to a greater flexibility along with the pleasant side benefit of increasing your mastery over the psychological states you inhabit. This allows you to make the appropriate adjustments if the state you are in is interfering with your ability to reach your desired outcomes.

As an example, as you sit reading this paragraph right now, place tension in your shoulders, sit off balance; allow your shoulders to press up towards your ears. A typical stress state. How is your breathing? Is this a comfortable state? Do you find the physiology useful for learning? Where is your attention? What beliefs about learning do you maintain in this state?

Now change your position, move around a little bit, maybe stand up and sit down again. Find a balanced, comfortable position. Move your attention through your body and release any excess tension, and breathe deeply and comfortably. Where is your attention in this state? What beliefs about learning are connected with this state? Which state is more conducive to learning?

As the simple exercise above illustrates, non-verbal cues are often one of the most relevant and influential aspects of monitoring and managing internal states. It is important to acknowledge the influence of behavior, even very subtle aspects of physiology, on people's internal states. Different states or attitudes are expressed through different patterns of language and behaviors.

Exercise: Accessing and Anchoring a State

The cognitive and physical distinctions and cues identified by NLP may be used to systematically access and mobilize different parts of our nervous system. The following exercises illustrate some ways to use the basic NLP tools in order to help you better select and manage your own internal state.

Anchoring is one of the simplest and most powerful tools for selecting and accessing internal states. Anchoring involves establishing cues or triggers for a specific desired state. As an example, the following steps can be used to establish two important and useful types of 'anchors':

1. Select a specific physical location on the ground in front of you to be a 'spatial' anchor for the state you would like to create access to, now or in the future (being 'open to believe', for example).

2. Remember a specific time when you experienced the state you want to achieve. Recover the state fully. See through your own eyes, hear through your own ears, and feel the sensations, breathing patterns etc.

3. Make an inventory of the physical cues, submodalities (qualities of imagery, sound and feeling), and emotional sensations associated with the state.

4. Select a specific color, symbol or some other visual cue, some sound and/or word, or some other specific internal cue to remind you of (i.e., be an 'internal' anchor) the state.

5. Step away from the location and shake off the state. Then test your anchors by stepping back into the selected spatial location and using your internal cue to re-access the state.

6. Repeat steps 1 to 4 until you can achieve easy, clean access to the state.

Mentoring and Inner Mentors

The natural process of belief change is also frequently facilitated by "mentors." In Greek Mythology, Mentor was the wise and faithful counselor to the hero Odysseus. Under the guise of Mentor, the goddess Athena became the guardian and teacher of Odysseus' son Telemachus, while Odysseus was away on his journeys. Thus, the notion of being a "mentor" has come to mean the process of both (a) advising or counseling, and (b) serving as a guide or teacher. Mentoring (especially in an occupational setting) emphasizes the informal relational aspect of learning and performance as much as it does the mastery of the task. Mentoring can also include the process of sponsoring and supporting another person by helping the person to establish empowering beliefs, and reframe limiting beliefs.

A mentor has overlaps with, but is distinct from, either a teacher or coach. A teacher instructs, and a coach provides specific behavioral feedback, in order to help a person learn or grow. Mentors, on the other hand, guide us to discover our own unconscious competences, often through their own example. As the example of the mythological Mentor suggests, mentoring also includes the possibility of counseling and guidance on a higher level. This type of mentoring often becomes internalized as part of the individual, so that the external presence of the mentor is no longer necessary. People are able to carry "inner mentors" as counselors and guides for their lives in many situations.

In NLP, the term *mentor* is used to refer to individuals that have helped to shape or influence your life in a positive way by 'resonating' with, releasing, or unveiling something deeply within you. Mentors can include children, teachers, pets, people you've never met but have read about, phenomena in nature (such as the ocean, mountains, etc.), and even parts of yourself.

We can use the memory of the important mentors in our lives to help us reaccess knowledge, resources or unconscious competences. The basic way to use an inner "mentor" is to imagine the presence of the person or being, and then to take "second position," by stepping into the perspective or "shoes" of the mentor. This allows you to access qualities which are present within you, but not recognized or included as part of your map of the situation (or of yourself). By representing these qualities, the inner mentor helps to bring them alive in your ongoing behavior (when you associate into the perspective of the mentor). Once you have experienced these qualities from standing in the shoes of the mentor, you can bring them back into your own perceptual position within a particular situation, and enact them.

The Belief Change Cycle Procedure

The following procedure is a technique that I developed whose purpose is to help lead people through the natural cycle of belief change. It involves the use of anchoring and inner mentors to help lead people through the sequence of states making up the belief change cycle: 1) wanting to believe, 2) becoming open to believe, 3) believing, 4) becoming open to doubt, 5) the experience of remembering something one used to believe, and 6) trust.

The procedure involves establishing separate locations for each of these, and then anchoring the corresponding state to each location. Arrange the states of the cycle in the pattern shown below:

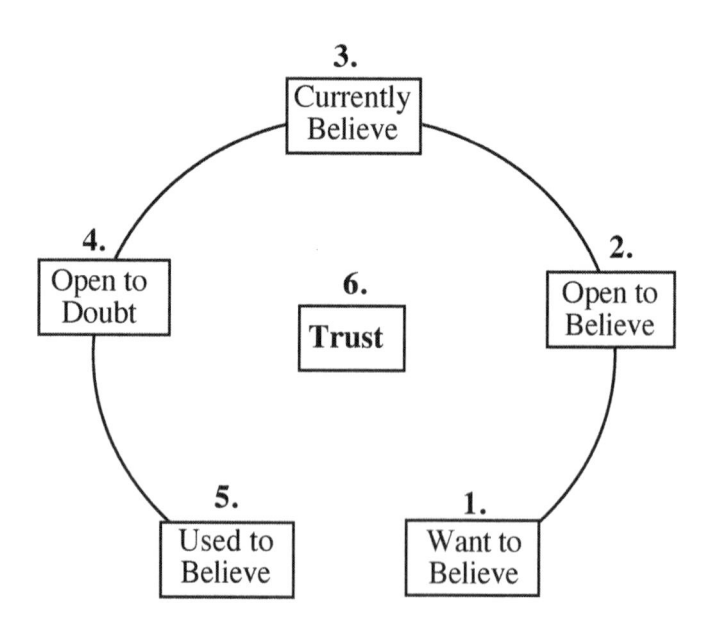

```
              3.
          Currently
           Believe

  4.                        2.
Open to        6.         Open to
 Doubt        Trust       Believe


       5.              1.
     Used to         Want to
     Believe         Believe
```

Patterns of Locations for the Belief Change Cycle

The experience of 'trusting' in something beyond your beliefs is placed in the center of the cycle to serve as a type of 'meta position' and 'ecology check' for the rest of the process.

To 'anchor' the states, apply the process followed in the earlier "anchoring" exercise, putting yourself as fully as possible into the experience and physiology associated with each of these aspects of the cycle of belief change and 'anchoring' them to appropriate spatial locations:

1. 'Wanting to believe' something new.

2. The experience of being 'open to believe' something new.

    [Note: You may identify a 'mentor' that helped you to become more 'open to believe' by 'resonating' with, releasing or unveiling something deeply within you. Then make a physical space for the mentor near the 'open to believe' space. Mentors can include children, teachers, pets, people you've never met but have read about, phenomena in nature (such as the ocean, mountains, etc.) and even yourself.]

3. The beliefs that you 'currently believe' now, including any limiting beliefs or beliefs that conflict with the new belief you would like to have more strongly.

4. The experience of being 'open to doubt' something you had believed for a long time.

    [Again, you may identify another 'mentor' that helped you to become more open to doubt something that was limiting you in your life.]

5. Beliefs that you 'used to believe' but no longer believe. [This is the space I have called the 'museum of personal history'.]

6. An experience of deep 'trust' - perhaps a time when you did not know what to believe anymore but were able to trust in yourself or a higher power.

[It can be very powerful to add mentors who have helped you build this experience of trust.]

These states and mentors do not need to have any connection to the current belief issue you are trying to resolve.

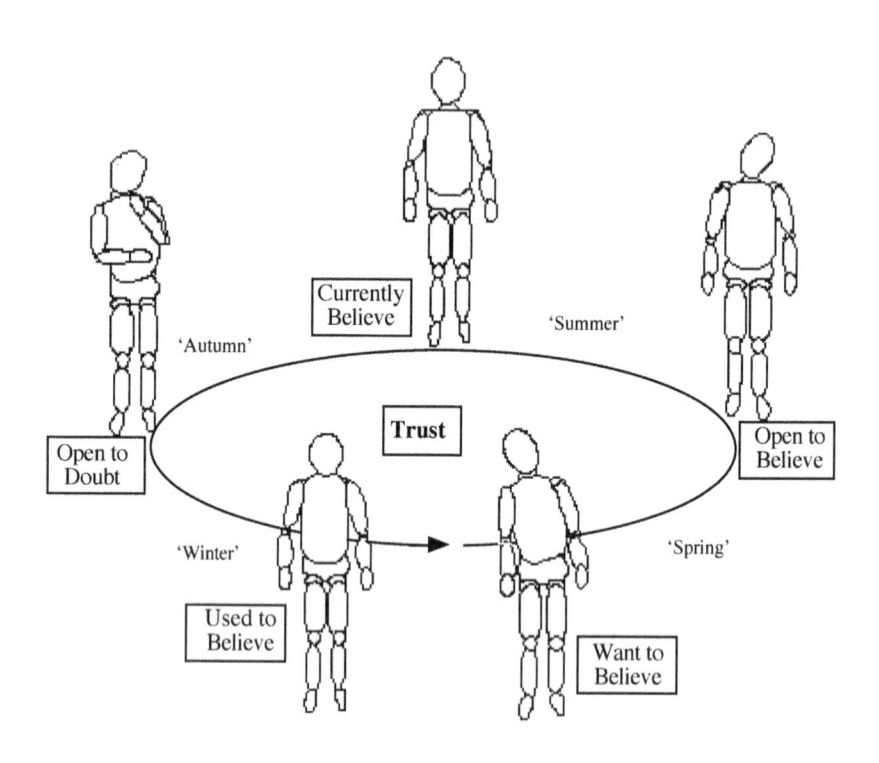

'Landscape' of States Associated with the Belief Change Cycle

Implementing the Belief Change Cycle

Once this landscape has been laid out it can be utilized in many different ways. One of the common ways in which to use it is to have a person think of a new belief that he or she would like strengthen and simply 'walk it' through the natural steps of the cycle. The instructions would proceed as follows:

1. Stand in the 'Want to Believe' space, think of the 'new belief' that you would like to have more confidence in. Holding this belief in mind move into the 'Open to Believe' space. (If you have chosen a 'mentor' for this state, you may step into his or her 'shoes' at this point. Seeing yourself through the eyes of your mentor, you may give the you who is 'open to believe' the new beliefs any helpful advice or support.)

2. Feel what it is like to become more open to believe this new belief. When you intuitively feel the time is appropriate, step into the 'Currently Believe' space concentrating on the new belief you want to have.

3. If there are any conflicting or limiting beliefs that come up in the 'Currently Believe' space, hold them in your mind and move to the 'Open to Doubt' space. (Again, if you have chosen a 'mentor' for your 'open to doubt' state, you may step into his or her 'shoes' at this point. Seeing yourself through the eyes of your mentor, you may give the you who is becoming 'open to doubt' any of the limiting or conflicting beliefs some helpful advice or support.)

4. *Ecology Check:* Go to the 'Trust' space and consider the positive intents and purpose of both the new belief and any conflicting or limiting beliefs. Consider whether

there are any changes or revisions you would like to make to the new belief. Also consider if there are any parts of the old beliefs that would be worth retaining or incorporating along with the new belief.

5. Return to the old limiting or conflicting beliefs that you left in the 'Open to Doubt' space, bringing the insights you had from the 'Trust' space and move them into the 'Used to Believe' space—your 'Museum of Personal History'.

6. Step back into the 'Currently Believe' space and focus on the new beliefs you want to strengthen. Experience your new sense of confidence and verbalize any new insights or learnings that you may have discovered during this process.

7. *Ecology Check:* Again step into the 'Trust' Space and consider the changes you have made. Know that, because this is a natural, organic and ongoing cycle, the process can continue to evolve and that you can make any necessary adjustments in the future in the way that is most appropriate and ecological for you.

Many people find that simply walking through these locations (or even imagining walking through these locations) and reexperiencing the states allows them to gently and spontaneously begin to shift their beliefs.

[Note: In order for a belief to become completely installed (i.e., fully "in the muscle"), it may be necessary to repeat this cycle for each of the five key beliefs that we explored in Chapter 5 - i.e., believing that something is: 1) desirable, 2) possible, 3) appropriate, 4) that you are capable to reach it, and 5) that you deserve it.]

Belief Chaining

The ultimate purpose of the various Sleight of Mouth patterns is to linguistically help guide people through the states involved in the Belief Change Cycle. As a technique, the Belief Change Cycle does not necessarily require the use of language. The process can be done by simply establishing the locational anchors for each of the internal states and walking through them in the appropriate sequence. There are times, however, when a few well placed words, at the right time, can greatly facilitate the achievement of one of these states, or the movement from one to another (i.e., moving from 'wanting to believe' to becoming 'open to believe').

In addition to physiology, emotional responses, and internal representations and submodalities, language can exert a powerful influence on our internal states. The technique of Belief Chaining illustrates how some simple Sleight of Mouth patterns (Intention and Redefining) can be used to stimulate and support particular internal states, and strengthen the experience of being 'open to believe' and 'open to doubt'.

In NLP, the term *"chaining"* refers to a form of anchoring in which experiences are linked together in a particular sequence, leading from a starting state to a desired state. The key element in establishing an effective "chain" is the selection of the transition states chosen to link the problem state to the desired state. These transition states function as "stepping stones" to help the individual move more easily in the direction of the goal state. It is often difficult for a person to cross the gap between their current state and some desired state. Let's say, for example, a person is stuck in a state of frustration, and wants to be motivated to learn something new. It is difficult to just switch from frustration to motivation and would most likely create tension or conflict to attempt to force oneself from one to the other. Chaining would involve establishing two or three intermediate steps or states between frustration and motivation.

The most effective chains are those which incrementally pace and lead from the problem state to the desired state. If the problem state is negative and the desired state is positive, this would involve moving incrementally from the negative state to another state which is only somewhat negative; confusion, for example. From the somewhat negative state, a small but significant step can be made to a state that is slightly positive; let's say curiosity about what might happen next. It is then relatively simple to take a step from the somewhat positive state to the desired state of motivation. Of course, depending on the physiological and emotional distance between the present and desired states, more intermediate steps may need to be added.

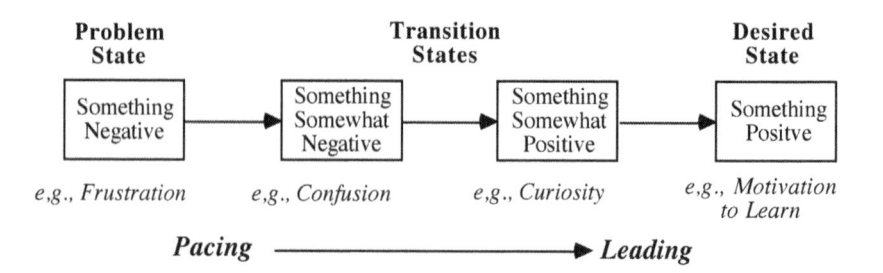

Problem State	Transition States		Desired State
Something Negative	Something Somewhat Negative	Something Somewhat Positive	Something Positve
e,g., Frustration	*e,g., Confusion*	*e,g., Curiosity*	*e,g., Motivation to Learn*

Pacing ⟶ *Leading*

Chaining States – From Frustration to Motivation

When selecting the states which are to be part of a chain, it is best if contiguous states have some degree of physiological, cognitive or emotional overlap. Frustration and confusion, for example, share some features. Likewise, confusion and curiosity overlap in relation to certain characteristics - they both involve uncertainty about an outcome, for example. Curiosity and motivation also have similarities in that they both involve wanting to go in a particular direction.

```
   ⎛Frustration⎞⎛Confusion⎞⎛Curiosity⎞⎛Motivation⎞
```

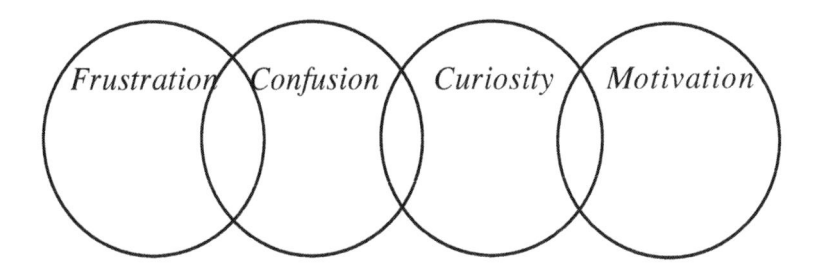

Contiguous States in a Chain Should Overlap to Some Degree

Basic Belief Chaining Procedure

The establishment of the sequence of states in a chain, and the linking of one state to another is most easily done through the process of anchoring. Historically, the NLP technique of "Chaining Anchors" has used kinesthetic anchoring. One way of creating a belief chain is to add linguistic distinctions, such as Sleight of Mouth patterns, to the sequence of kinesthetic anchors.

As an example, to work with a limiting belief, you can lay out four spaces to form a 'chain' going from the Problem State (the limiting belief) to the Desired State (a more empowering belief) with two intermediate steps:

a. Location #1: The limiting belief (Problem State)

b. Location #2: The positive intention of the limiting belief

c. Location #3: A redefinition of some aspect of the limiting belief statement which makes it somewhat positive

d. Location #4: An empowering belief that is a consequence of both the positive intention and redefinition (Desired State)

―*Open to Doubt*―▶   ―*Open to Believe* ➔

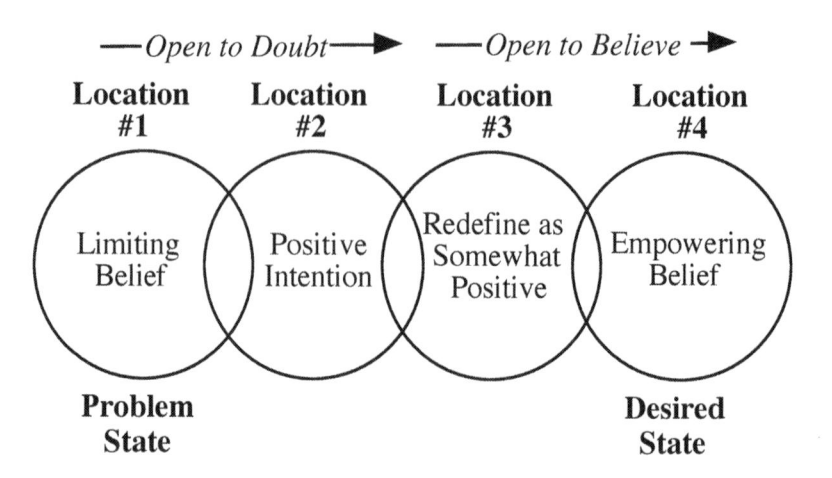

Location #1   **Location #2**   **Location #3**   **Location #4**

Limiting Belief | Positive Intention | Redefine as Somewhat Positive | Empowering Belief

Problem State   **Desired State**

Locations for Creating a Basic Belief Chain

1. Standing in the location for the problem state, choose a limiting belief that you would like to work with (e.g., "It is hard for me to learn language patterns, because I get confused and bored by words.") Pay attention to the internal state that is associated with the limiting belief. Then, step out of the location and change your state, "shaking off" the affect associated with the limiting belief.

2. Now, walk over to the desired state location and enter into an internal state in which you feel 'aligned' and 'wise'. It isn't necessary to know the empowering belief that will accompany the belief at this time; it is only necessary to experience the positive internal state that will be associated with it.

3. Return to the 'problem state' location, and physically walk through other steps of the chain to get a sense of the movement from the present state to the desired state. Again, it is only important to begin to get a

feeling for the changes in the internal state. You do not need to be conscious of any changes in the belief just yet.

4. Go back to the limiting belief space and then take a step forward to the location representing the 'positive intention'. Explore the positive purpose of your limiting belief, trying out different words until you find an expression that really shifts your feeling and internal state to something more positive. (e.g., "To feel associated and connected with what I am learning.")

5. Step forward again, into the 'redefining' space. Restate the limiting belief, but redefine the key words of the belief to better reflect what you have discovered about the positive intention. Explore how different verbal reframes can help give you different perspectives on the belief. Again, keep trying different words, until you have found some that significantly change your feeling with respect to the belief. (e.g., "It is hard for me to *pay attention to* language patterns, *when* I get confused and bored *because I am only listening to the* words *and not paying attention to my feelings and relationships with other people.*")

6. Step forward again, to the desired state location, and formulate a positive belief statement that incorporates the positive intention of the limiting belief, but that is empowering and enriching. Again make sure that the words really stimulate positive feelings when you say them. (e.g., "I can really enjoy learning language patterns, when I stay associated and connected to my feelings and relationships with other people while I am listening to the words.")

7. Walk through the chain several times, repeating the statements associated with each location, until it feels like there is an easy and smooth flow from present state to desired state, both linguistically and kinesthetically.

The Influence of Non-Verbal Communication

The impact of shifting internal states and using spatial anchoring on belief change also brings up the importance of non verbal communication. Verbal messages, or words, are only one of the modalities through which people communicate and influence one another. There are many ways in which people interact and send messages non-verbally, such as making eye contact, nodding their heads, crying, pointing or emphasizing something through voice stress. A person's non-verbal communication is as important as, if not more important than, his or her verbal communication.

According to Gregory Bateson, only about 8% of the information communicated in an interaction is carried in the words, or 'digital' part of the interaction. The other 92% is communicated non-verbally, through the 'analog' system. The 'analog' aspects of communication include body language as well as the information carried in the auditory tonal part of the interaction, such as voice tone, tempo and volume. For example, the way that a joke is told—the intonation, facial expressions, pauses, etc.—are frequently as a much factor in what makes the joke "funny" as the words.

Non-verbal communication includes cues and signals such as facial expression, gestures, body posture, voice tone and tempo shifts, and eye movements. Non-verbal cues are often 'meta messages', messages *about* the verbal content one is expressing. They frequently determine how verbal communication is received and interpreted. If a person says, "Now pay close attention," and points to his or her eyes, it is a fundamentally different message than if the person said the same words but pointed to his or her ears. If someone says, "That's just great," in a sarcastic tone of voice, he or she is actually non verbally sending the opposite message from what the words actually state.

Non verbal signals, such as facial expressions and voice tone, tend to impact us more emotionally, determining how we "feel" about what someone is saying. In fact, non verbal messages tend to reflect and influence our internal state, whereas verbal messages are more associated with cognitive processes. Non verbal communication is more "primitive" and is the primary modality that other animals use to communicate with another (and through which we communicate with them). If we say the words, "Nice doggy," to a dog in an angry and threatening tone of voice, there is no question that its primary response will be to the tone of voice rather than the words.

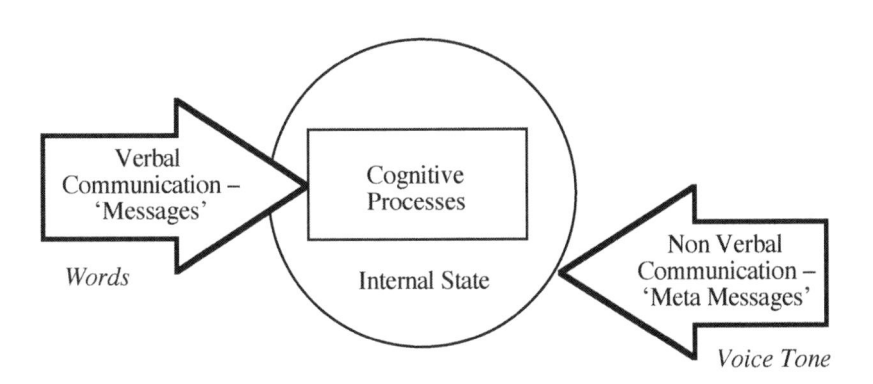

The Non Verbal Aspects of Our Communication Tend to Reflect and Influence our Internal State to a Greater Degree than Verbal Communication

Thus, the tone of voice one uses while speaking to others can have tremendous impact on how one's verbal message is "heard" and "received." Saying to a person, "You can do it," in an angry or frustrated voice may do as much to trigger doubt as to inspire confidence or belief.

Intended Message

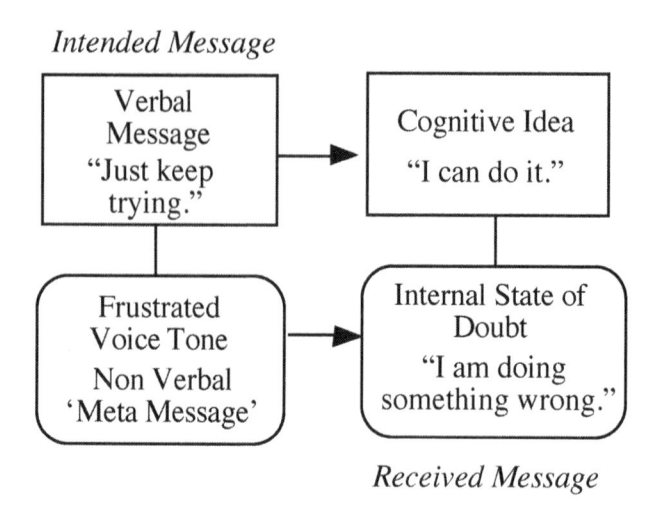

```
┌─────────────┐         ┌─────────────┐
│   Verbal    │         │Cognitive Idea│
│  Message    │────────▶│ "I can do it."│
│ "Just keep  │         │             │
│  trying."   │         │             │
└──────┬──────┘         └─────────────┘
       │
       ▼
┌─────────────┐         ┌─────────────┐
│ Frustrated  │         │Internal State of│
│ Voice Tone  │────────▶│    Doubt    │
│ Non Verbal  │         │ "I am doing │
│'Meta Message'│        │something wrong."│
└─────────────┘         └─────────────┘
```

Received Message

Non Verbal Meta Messages Significantly Influence Our Internal States and the Interpretation of Verbal Messages

People generally focus on the verbal aspects of communication, and are frequently unaware of the non verbal portions of communication. When working with Sleight of Mouth, it is essential to pay attention to the non verbal meta messages which accompany our words. The right words, said in the wrong tone of voice, or with the wrong facial expression, can produce the opposite of what we intend.

The degree of congruence between our non verbal messages with our words primarily comes from our own congruence about what we are saying – i.e., the congruence between "message" and "messenger." Thus, the internal state we are in while we are speaking is as important as the internal state of the listener. Learning to observe for non verbal cues, and to pay closer attention to your own internal state, can greatly increase your effectiveness in using Sleight of Mouth to positively impact the beliefs of others.

Chapter 8

Thought Viruses and the Meta Structure of Beliefs

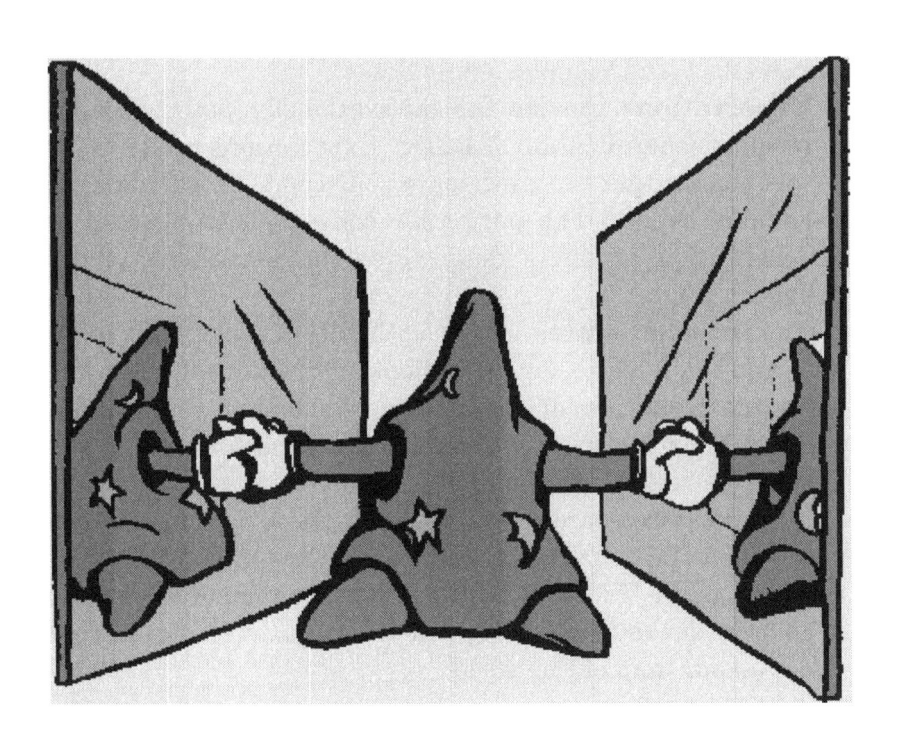

The Meta Structure of Beliefs

In the course of this book, we have explored a number of the dimensions of our experience that are influenced by our beliefs, and which are also involved in forming and sustaining our beliefs.

Our **sensory experience** is what provides the raw materials from which we construct our maps of the world. Beliefs are generalizations drawn from the data of our experience, and are typically updated and corrected by experience. As a model of our experience, beliefs necessarily delete and distort aspects of the experiences that they have been developed to represent. This gives beliefs the potential to limit us as easily as empower us.

Values are what give our beliefs and experience meaning. They are the higher level 'positive intentions' which the belief has been established to support or reflect. Beliefs connect values to our experiences through statements of 'cause-effect' and 'complex equivalence'.

Expectations provide the motivation for maintaining a particular generalization or belief. Expectations relate to the consequences that we anticipate will come from holding a particular belief. The particular consequences a belief or generalization produces determines the usefulness of the belief.

Our **internal states** act as both filters upon our experience and the impetus for our actions. Our internal states are often the container or foundation supporting a particular belief or generalization, and determine the emotional energy invested in sustaining the belief.

It is the interconnections between these various components of our life experience that forms what Richard Bandler refers to as the "fabric of reality." The function of our beliefs is to provide key links between these basic elements that make up our map of the world.

Consider, for example, a child learning to ride a bicycle. An empowering belief such as, "I can learn," might link together key values associated with learning—such as 'fun' and 'self improvement'—with an internal state of 'confidence', and the expectation that, "I will get better and better." These provide the motivation and impetus for the child to keep trying, even though he or she might fall quite frequently. As the child is able to experience longer periods in which he or she maintains balance before falling, it reinforces the generalization, "I can learn," as well as the state of confidence, the expectation of improvement and the values of fun and self improvement.

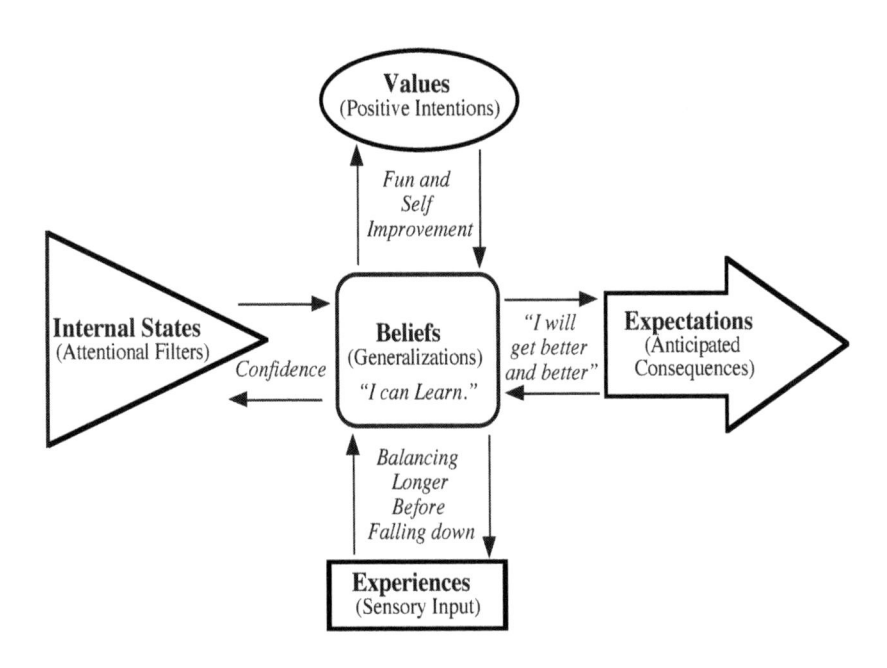

```
                    ┌─────────────┐
                    │   Values    │
                    │(Positive    │
                    │ Intentions) │
                    └─────────────┘
                      Fun and
                       Self
                     Improvement
                          ↓
   ┌──────────┐    ┌─────────────┐   "I will      ┌──────────────┐
   │ Internal │ →  │   Beliefs   │   get better   │ Expectations │
   │  States  │    │(Generaliz.) │   and better"  │ (Anticipated │
   │(Attent.  │    │             │       →        │ Consequences)│
   │ Filters) │ ←  │"I can Learn"│       ←        │              │
   └──────────┘    └─────────────┘                └──────────────┘
                Confidence
                          ↑
                      Balancing
                       Longer
                       Before
                     Falling down
                          ↓
                    ┌─────────────┐
                    │ Experiences │
                    │(Sensory     │
                    │  Input)     │
                    └─────────────┘
```

Our Beliefs are Generalizations Which Link Together Experiences, Values, Internal States and Expectations, and Form the Fabric of Our Reality

Healthy beliefs maintain their connection with all of these various dimensions. Our beliefs naturally shift and update themselves as we go through changes in values, expectations, internal states, and as we have new experiences.

Limiting beliefs can arise as a result of a shift in any one of these components to a negative formulation or 'problem frame'. Once established, limiting beliefs can exert an influence on any or all of these various components. For instance, let's say that a child who is learning to ride a bicycle has an older brother or sister who is already able to ride a bike competently. While this may provide a strong motivation for the younger child to learn to ride, he or she may also develop inappropriate expectations. The child may expect to ride as well as his or her older sibling, and compare his or her performance negatively to that of the older child. Because the younger child's performance does not match his or her expectations, the child my shift into a problem frame or failure frame, leading to an internal state of frustration. In addition to producing uncomfortable feelings, the negative internal state may effect the child's performance, causing him or her to fall more frequently. The child may also begin to build the expectation, "I will fall again," feeding a self-fulfilling prophesy. Eventually, in order to avoid continued discomfort and frustration, the child may establish the belief, "I will never be able to ride a bicycle," and quit trying to ride any longer.

Diagram

Desire to avoid further frustration and discomfort

Values
(Positive Intentions)

Problem Frame

Internal States
(Attentional Filters)

Beliefs
(Generalizations)
"I will never be able to ride a bicycle."

Expectations
(Anticipated Consequences)

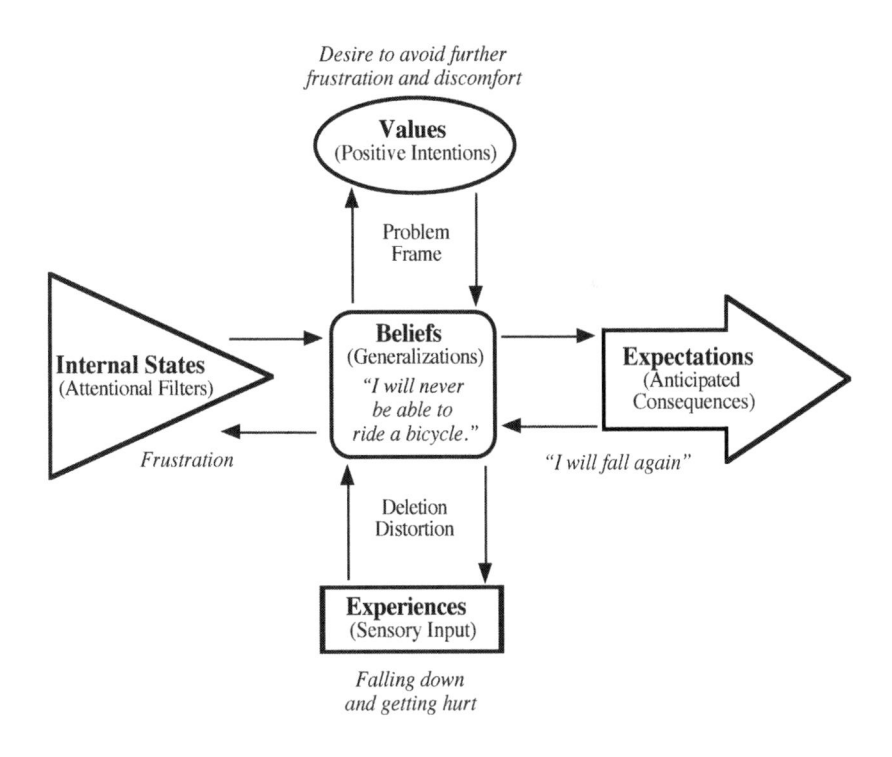

Frustration

"I will fall again"

Deletion Distortion

Experiences
(Sensory Input)

Falling down and getting hurt

Limiting Beliefs Create a 'Problem Frame'

When limiting beliefs and generalizations stay connected with the intentions and experiences from which they have been established, the deletions and distortions eventually become updated or corrected as a result of new experiences, changes in internal state, and revised expectations. New data or 'counter examples' that do not fit with the generalization will lead the person to reconsider the validity of his or her limiting belief.

If a child who has built the generalization, "I can't ride a bike," is encouraged and supported to continue to try riding (and is able to perceive his or her "failure" as "feedback") he or she will eventually learn to maintain balance, and begin to have some success. This will typically lead the child to begin to think, "Well, maybe I can learn this after all." With continued success, the child will reverse his or her earlier belief, naturally reframing it on his or her own. The child becomes more 'open to believe' that he or she is capable of learning to ride the bicycle, and 'open to doubt' his or her perceived limitations.

Thought Viruses

Limiting beliefs arise from generalizations, deletions and distortions that have become placed in a 'problem frame', 'failure frame', or 'impossibility frame'. Such beliefs become even more limiting and difficult to change when they are separated from the experiences, values, internal states and expectations from which they were derived. When this happens, the belief can become perceived as some type of disassociated "truth" about reality. This leads people to begin to view the belief as "the territory" rather than a particular "map," whose purpose is to help us effectively navigate our way through some portion of our experiential territory. This situation can become even further exaggerated when the limiting belief is not even one that we have formed from our own experiences, but which has been imposed upon us by others.

A fundamental assumption of NLP is that everyone has his or her own map of the world. People's maps can be quite different, depending upon their backgrounds, their society, their culture, their professional training and their personal history. A large part of what NLP is about is how to deal with the fact that people have different maps of the world. A major challenge in our lives is how to coordinate our maps of the world with the maps of others.

For example, people have different beliefs about the body's capabilities to heal and about what 'should be done' and 'can be done' in relation to healing themselves and others. People have maps about what's possible with respect to physical healing and what healing is, and they live according to those maps. Sometimes these maps can be quite limiting; leading to confrontations and conflicts of beliefs.

Consider the woman who, when she discovered that she had metastatic breast cancer, started to explore what she might do to mentally help promote her own self healing. Her surgeon told her that 'all that mind-body healing stuff' was 'a bunch of poppycock' which would probably just 'drive you crazy'. This was obviously not a belief that the woman had arrived at as a result of her own experience. Yet, because the man was her doctor, his beliefs exerted a great deal of influence on the decisions made with regard to her health. Whether she wanted to or not, she had to contend with the doctor's belief as a factor in her own belief system (as a person would have to deal with being exposed to germs if the person were around someone else who was sick).

Notice that the belief expressed by the doctor was stated in a problem frame, and not connected to any particular positive intention, sensory data, internal state, nor to any expected or desired consequences related to accepting the belief. It was simply presented as "the way it is." The validity or usefulness of the belief could thus not easily be examined. The woman was placed in a position in which she either had to either agree with her doctor (and thus accept the limiting belief) or to fight with him about it – which could produce negative consequences with respect to her health care.

This kind of belief, especially when presented as the 'right map of the world', can become what could be called a *'thought virus'*. A 'thought virus' is a special class of limiting beliefs that can severely interfere with one's own or other's efforts to heal or improve.

In essence, a thought virus has become disconnected from the surrounding 'meta structure' which provides the context and purpose of the belief, and determines its 'ecology'. Unlike a typical limiting belief, which can be updated or corrected as a result of experience, thought viruses, are based on unspoken assumptions (which are typically other limiting beliefs). When this happens, the thought virus becomes its own self-validating "reality" instead of serving a larger reality.

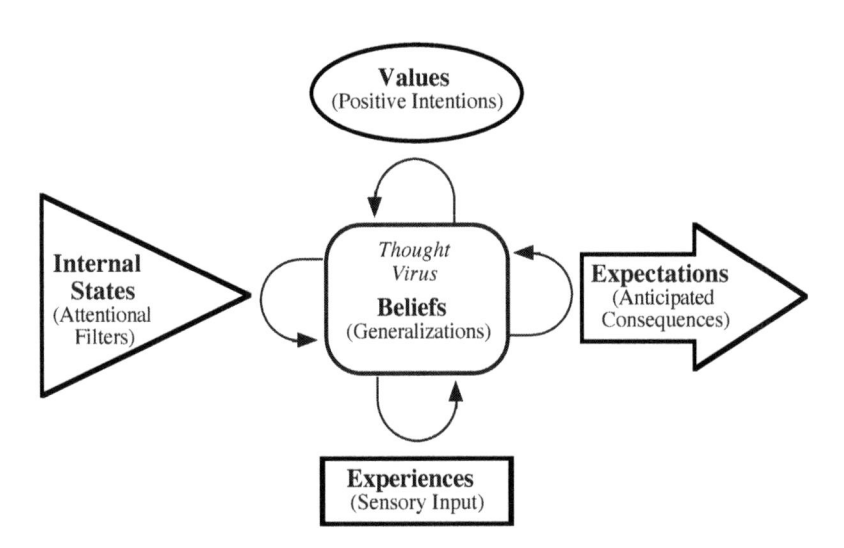

THOUGHT VIRUSES AND THE
META STRUCTURE OF BELIEFS

```
                    Values
              (Positive Intentions)
                       ↓
   Internal      ┌─────────────┐      Expectations
    States   →   │   Thought   │  →   (Anticipated
 (Attentional    │    Virus    │      Consequences)
    Filters)     │   Beliefs   │
                 │(Generalizations)│
                 └─────────────┘
                       ↑
                  Experiences
                (Sensory Input)
```

A 'Thought Virus' is a Belief that has Become Disconnected from the Other Cognitive and Experiential Processes from which it was Built

Thus, thought viruses are not easily corrected or updated by new data or counter examples coming from experience. Rather, the other beliefs and presuppositions upon which the thought virus is based (and which hold it in place) must be identified and transformed. These other, more fundamental presuppositions and beliefs, however, are not usually obvious in the surface structure of the belief.

As an example, the woman mentioned above was working as a nurse for a doctor in general practice. Instead of saying that she was being foolish like her surgeon did, the doctor that was her employer took her aside and told her, "You know, if you really care about your family you won't leave them unprepared." While this was less confrontive than the surgeon had been, it was actually more of a potential thought virus than saying directly "that's a bunch of 'poppycock'".

Because a good deal of the meaning of the message is implied and not stated, it is more difficult to recognize, "That's just his opinion". You think, "Yes, I do care about my family. No, I don't want to leave them unprepared." But what's not stated, what's not on the surface, is that "leave them" means "die". The presupposition of the statement is that 'you are going to die'. And the implication of the statement was that she should 'stop this nonsense and get ready to die' or it would make it more difficult for her family. If you really care about your family, you won't keep trying to get well because you'll just leave them unprepared.

What makes it so much of a potential thought virus is that it implies that the 'right' way and the only way to be a good and loving mother and wife is to accept that you are going to die and prepare yourself and your family for that inevitability. It suggests that to try to regain one's health when one's death is so immanent is essentially just being selfish and uncaring toward one's family. It would build false hope, potentially drain financial resources, and lead to sadness and disappointment.

Such 'thought viruses' can 'infect' one's mind and nervous system just as a physical virus can infect the body or a computer virus can infect a computer system leading to confusion and malfunctions. Just as the programming of a computer, or a whole system of computers, can be damaged by a 'computer virus', our nervous systems may be capable of being 'infected' and damaged by 'thought viruses'.

Biologically, a 'virus' is actually a little piece of genetic material. Our genetic code is our body's physical 'program'. A virus is an incomplete chunk of 'program'. It's not really a living thing. That's why you can't kill a virus. You can't kill it or poison it because it's not alive. It enters into the cells of its 'host', who, if not immune to the virus, unwittingly makes 'a home' for it and even helps to reproduce and make more of the virus.

[This is in contrast to 'bacteria' which are in fact living cells. Bacteria can be killed, for instance, by antibiotics. But antibiotics are useless against a virus. Because bacteria are contained cells they do not 'invade' or take over our body's cells. Some are parasitic and can be harmful if there are too many of them. But many bacteria are helpful and in fact needed by the body – to digest our food, for example.]

A 'computer virus' is parallel to a biological virus in that it is not a whole and complete program. It has no 'knowledge' of where it belongs in the computer, of which memory locations are safe or open for it; it has no notion of the computer's 'ecology'. It has no perception of its identity with respect to the rest of the computer's programming. It's primary purpose is simply to keep reproducing itself and making more of itself. Because it does not recognize or respect the boundaries of other programs and data in the computer, it writes over them indiscriminately, wiping them out and replacing them with itself. This causes the computer to malfunction and make serious errors.

A 'thought virus' is similar to these other types of viruses. It's not a complete, coherent idea that fits in with and organically supports a person's larger system of ideas and beliefs in a healthy way. It is a particular thought or belief that can create confusion or conflict. Individual thoughts and beliefs don't have any 'power' of their own. They only get 'life' when somebody acts upon them. If a person decides to enact a belief, or direct his or her actions according to a particular thought, that person can bring the belief to 'life'; it can become 'self fulfilling'.

As an example, the woman mentioned earlier lived over twelve years beyond what her doctors predicted, largely because she did not internalize the limiting beliefs of her doctors. The doctor she worked for told her that if she was lucky she might live 2 years, and he talked in terms of months and even weeks. The woman stopped working for that doctor and lived many more years entirely free of any symptoms of cancer. Some years after she quit working for him, however, that particular doctor became seriously ill (although his illness was not nearly as advanced as the woman's was). This doctor's response was to take his own life. Furthermore, he either convinced his wife to co-commit suicide with him or perhaps took her with him without her consent (the situation was never fully resolved). Why? Because he believed his death was immanent and inevitable and he didn't want to 'leave her unprepared'.

The point is that a thought virus can lead to death as readily as an AIDS virus. It can kill its 'host' as easily as it can harm others who become 'infected' by the host. Think of how many people have died because of 'ethnic cleansings' and 'holy wars'. It may even be that a lot of the way an AIDS virus kills is through the thought viruses that accompany it.

This is not to imply that the woman's doctor was in any way a bad person. From the NLP perspective, it was not he who was the problem. It was the belief, the 'virus'. Indeed, the fact that he took his own life can be seen as an act of ultimate integrity – if one had his belief. It is the beliefs that need to be judged critically, not the people.

A thought virus cannot be killed, it can only be recognized and neutralized or filtered out from the rest of the system. You cannot kill an 'idea' or 'belief' because it is not alive. And killing a person who has acted on the basis of an idea or belief does not kill the idea or belief either. Centuries of war and religious persecution have demonstrated that. (Chemotherapy works a bit like war; it kills infected cells but does not heal the body or protect it against the virus - and it unfortunately inflicts a relatively high number of 'civilian casualties' on healthy cells in the body.) Limiting beliefs and thought viruses must be dealt with similarly to how the body deals with a physical virus or a computer deals with a computer virus – by recognizing the virus, becoming 'immune' to it and not giving it a place in the system.

Thought Viruses and the Meta Structure of Beliefs

Viruses do not only effect people or computers that are "weak", "stupid" or "bad". The electronic or biological host of computer or physical viruses are 'fooled' because the virus initially seems to fit in or be harmless. For instance, our genetic 'code' is a type of program. It works something like, "If there is an A and B, then do C," or, "If something has the structure 'AAABACADAEAF', then it belongs in that location". One of the functions of our immune systems is to check the codes of the various parts of our bodies, and the things that enter our bodies, to make sure they are healthy and that they belong. If they do not belong, they are 'cast out' or recycled. The body and the immune system are 'fooled' by a virus, like the AIDS virus, because its structure is similar in many ways to our cells' own code (a type of 'pacing and leading' at the cellular level). In fact, humans and chimpanzees are the only creatures who manifest harmful effects from the AIDs virus because they are the only creatures whose genetic structure is close enough to the AIDs virus' code to be infected by ("paced" by) the virus.

As an illustration, let's say a person's genetic code has a pattern that goes "AAABACADAEAF". A virus might have a structure like "AAABAOAPEAF" which appears similar in some respects to that of the individual's own genetic code. If only the first five letters are checked, the code appears to be identical and will be allowed into the body. Another way that the body and immune system are 'fooled' by a virus is when the virus enters the body wrapped up in a harmless protein coat (somewhat like the Trojan horse). The immune system does not perceive that there is anything wrong with it.

In some ways this may be likened to the doctor's statement that "If you really care about your family, you won't leave them unprepared." On the surface there is nothing obviously harmful about the statement. In fact it seems to fit with positive values; "caring" and "being prepared". It is the context in which the statement is made and what is unstated but presupposed or assumed that makes such a belief potentially deadly.

It is important to remember that a virus—biological, computer or mental—has no real intelligence or intention of its own with respect to the system it is in. A belief statement, for instance, is just a set of words, until it is given 'life' through the values, internal states, expectations and experiences we connect to those words. Similarly, a biological virus is only harmful if the body allows it in and confuses the virus with itself. Infection by a virus is not mechanical and inevitable. We have probably all had experiences in which we were 'exposed' to a flue or cold virus but were not infected because our 'defenses were up'. When a person is vaccinated for a physical virus, his or her immune system is essentially taught to recognize the virus and to recycle it or remove it from the body. The immune system does not learn to kill the virus (because it cannot be killed). [It is true that the so-called 'killer T-cells" of the immune system can destroy cells and tissues in our bodies that have become infected by a virus. But, like chemotherapy, this addresses the symptom more than the cause. In a complete immunization, the cells never become infected in the first place.] A computer 'anti-virus' program, for instance, does not destroy parts of the computer. Rather, it recognizes the computer virus program and simply erases it from the computer's memory or the disk. Often, virus protection programs simply eject the 'infected' disk upon finding a virus, so that the computer is not put in any risk.

Similarly, in immunizing itself to a virus, the body's immune system becomes better 'educated' to recognize and sort out the virus. In the same way that a child learning to read becomes more able to discriminate patterns of letters, the immune system becomes better at recognizing and clearly sorting out the different patterns in the genetic codes of viruses. It checks the virus' program more thoroughly and deeply. As an illustration, we've essentially wiped smallpox off the face of the earth; but we haven't done it by killing smallpox viruses. They're still around. We've just developed ways of teaching our bodies' immune systems to recognize them. You get the vaccination and your body suddenly realizes, "Oh, this virus doesn't belong in me." That's all. Again, vaccinations don't kill viruses; they help the immune system to become clear about what's really you and what is not you. What belongs in the body and what does not belong.

Along similar lines, the process of selecting a file on one's computer disk and moving it to the computer's 'trash can' where it is erased is as final but not as violent as thinking in terms of 'fighting' and 'killing' the virus. It is also something that is not only done to protect one's computer. It happens as old programs are updated and replaced by new versions and when old data becomes out of date.

Obviously, this is not a recommendation to go around and try to 'erase' every limiting thought. In fact, the primary emphasis is on really taking the time to explore the communication or positive intention of the symptom. Many people simply try to get rid of or "wish away" their symptoms and experience great difficulty because they are making no attempt to listen to or understand their situation. It often requires a substantial amount of wisdom to recognize and distinguish a 'virus'.

Healing a 'thought virus' involves deepening and enriching our mental maps in order to have more choices and perspectives. Wisdom, ethics and ecology do not derive from having the one 'right' or 'correct' map of the world, because human beings would not be capable of making one. Rather, the goal is to create the richest map possible that respects the systemic nature and ecology of ourselves and the world in which we live. As one's model of the world becomes expanded and enriched, so does one's perception of one's identity and one's mission. The body's immune system is its mechanism for clarifying and maintaining the integrity of its physical identity. The process of immunization essentially involves the immune system in learning more about what is a part of one's physical being and what is not. Similarly, immunization to a thought virus involves the clarification, congruence and alignment of one's belief system in relation to one's psychological and 'spiritual' identity and mission.

In conclusion, techniques like Sleight of Mouth allow us to deal with limiting beliefs and thought viruses in a manner that is more like immunization than chemotherapy. Many of the principles and techniques of NLP—such as those embodied by the Sleight of Mouth patterns—could be viewed as a kind of 'vaccination' to help immunize people's 'belief systems' to certain 'thought viruses'. They diffuse limiting beliefs and thought viruses by reconnecting them to values, expectations, internal states and experiences; placing them back into context so that they may be naturally updated.

Presuppositions

One of the major factors that prevents a thought virus from being naturally updated or corrected by new data and counter examples provided by our experience, is that significant portions of the belief are presupposed, rather than explicitly stated by the belief. In order to be changed, the other beliefs and presuppositions upon which the thought virus is based must be identified, brought to the surface, and examined.

Presuppositions relate to unconscious beliefs or assumptions embedded in the structure of an utterance, action or another belief; and are required for the utterance, action or belief to make sense. According to Merriam-Webster's Dictionary, to presuppose means to "suppose beforehand" or "to require as an antecedent in logic or fact." The term "suppose" comes from Latin, and literally means "to put under" — from *sub* ("under") + *ponere* ("to put").

Linguistic Presuppositions occur when certain information or relationships must be accepted as true in order to make sense of a particular statement. For example, to understand the statement, "As soon as you stop trying to sabotage our therapeutic efforts, we'll be able to make more progress," one must assume that the person to whom the statement is directed already has been, in fact, trying to sabotage the therapeutic efforts. The statement also presupposes that there is some kind of therapeutic effort being attempted, and that at least some progress has been made. Similarly, the statement, "Since they leave us no alternative, we must resort to violence," presupposes that no alternative, in fact, exists and that "they" are the ones who determine whether there are alternatives or not.

True linguistic presuppositions should be contrasted with assumptions and inferences. A linguistic presupposition is something that is overtly expressed in the body of the statement itself, which must be 'supposed' or accepted in order for the sentence or utterance to make sense. In the question, "Have you stopped exercising regularly?" for example, the use of the word *stop* implies that the listener has *already* been exercising regularly. The question, "Do you exercise regularly?" has no such presupposition.

Conclusions such as "The speaker thinks exercise is important," or "The speaker is unfamiliar with the exercise habits of the listener," are *not* presupposed by the questions. They are assumptions and inferences we might make about the question, but are not presupposed within the question itself.

Consider the following two statements:

The authorities prevented the demonstrators from marching because they feared *violence.*

The authorities prevented the demonstrators from marching because they advocated *violence.*

The two statements have exactly the same structure, with the exception of the words "feared" and "advocated." Depending on which word is used, we *assume* that the term "they" refers to either the "authorities" or the "demonstrators." We are more likely to think that it is the *authorities* who *fear* violence, and the *demonstrators* who *advocate* violence; but this is not presupposed by the statement itself. It is assumed by us as listeners. Both sentences presuppose that there were demonstrators who were planning to march; but that is all.

An inference related to the two statements above would be that "the demonstrators and the authorities were not the same group of people." Inferences relate to logical conclusions which are made that are based upon the information provided by the statement.

Because presuppositions, assumptions and inferences do not appear in the surface structure of a particular statement or belief, it makes them more difficult to identify and address directly. Consider the beliefs of the two doctors cited in the example of the woman with cancer:

"All that mind-body healing stuff is a bunch of poppycock, and will probably just drive you crazy."

"If you really care about your family, you won't leave them unprepared."

In the first statement, the essential judgments and generalizations are in the surface structure of the sentence (even if the intention, experiences, expectations and internal state from which the generalization and judgments were derived have been deleted). The 'complex equivalence' and 'cause-effect' statements can be directly denied or negated. That is, a listener could respond, "It is *not* a bunch of poppycock, and it will *not* drive me crazy."

In the second statement, the fundamental generalization and judgment does not appear in the surface structure of the sentence, and cannot be directly denied or negated. To negate the statement directly, you would have to say something like, "I do not care about my family, and I will leave them unprepared." This would be a strange thing to say, and does not address the unspoken assumptions and inferences that actually make the statement a limiting belief (i.e., that you are going to die, so the best thing to do is to prepare to die and get it over with so that you don't inconvenience others.)

In order to effectively address the second statement, you must first bring the presuppositions, assumptions and inferences to the surface. It is only then that they can be questioned, and the positive intention, expectation, internal state and experiences from which the belief was formed can be explored, evaluated and 'reframed'.

In the case of the two doctors, for example, the woman who was their patient was counseled by an NLP practitioner to seek and respond to the positive intention of the doctor's statements, rather than the statements themselves. She determined that the positive intention of the first statement, *"All that mind-body healing stuff is a bunch of poppycock, and will probably just drive you crazy,"* was 'not to be foolish'. Stated positively, the intention was "to act wisely, intelligently and sanely." The woman reasoned that not to pursue all avenues of healing available to her would be unwise, especially if trying out some reasonable alternatives did not conflict with other treatments. She also realized that the doctor was probably not speaking from the experience of having tried and disproved all of the "mind-body" methods himself, but was probably responding from his mental filters as a surgeon. She realized that he was, in fact, most likely completely unfamiliar with these methods. Thus, the woman concluded that, by exploring mind-body healing methods intelligently and wisely, she would actually be responding to the unstated positive intention of the doctor's seemingly negative belief.

The woman responded in a similar fashion to the second doctor's statement. She determined that the positive intention of his belief, *"If you really care about your family, you won't leave them unprepared,"* was ultimately to accept her destiny and act ecologically with respect to her family. She also realized that her 'destiny' was in the hands of herself and God; and that (in spite of what he might have thought) the doctor was not God, and thus did not truly know her destiny. The woman concluded that one of the best ways she could "prepare" her children to deal with serious illness was to be a good role model for how to approach health congruently and optimistically; without being either desperate or apathetic.

As was pointed out earlier, the woman ended up making a dramatic recovery, far surpassing anyone's expectations.

Thought Viruses and the Meta Structure of Beliefs

It is interesting to note (given the comments we have made about thought viruses and presuppositions) that the doctor who made the first statement saw the woman again several months later. He was quite surprised at how healthy she was, and exclaimed, "Good heavens, you look healthier than I do. What have you been doing?" He knew nothing had been done medically, because her case had been considered too advanced. The woman replied, "I know you said that you did not believe in mind-body healing, but I decided to pursue it anyway and have been doing a lot of looking inside of myself and visualizing myself becoming healthy." The doctor's response was, "Well, I guess I have to believe you, because I know *we* haven't done anything." Nine years later, the same doctor saw the woman again, for some minor cosmetic surgery. The woman (who happens to have been my mother) reported that he initially acted as if he were seeing a ghost. After making a very thorough check up, the doctor patted her on the shoulder and said, "Stay away from doctors."

As I already mentioned, the other doctor ended up eventually taking his own life, when he was confronted with a serious illness a few years after his comments to the woman; a victim of his own thought virus and presuppositions.

In summary, the more presuppositions the sentence has, the more potential it has to become a 'virus'. It is important to remember, however, that not all viruses are harmful. In fact, modern genetic engineers even use specially constructed viruses to "splice" genes. Similarly, positive messages may be delivered by presupposition and inference as well. Linguistic presuppositions simply reduce the potential for direct verbal analysis.

As an example, the comments of the doctor, cited in the case at the beginning of Chapter 1, who told his patient, "The rest is up to you," also involved presuppositions and inference. In this instance, however, the presupposition was, "Something more can be done to promote your recovery and you have the capability and responsibility to do it." This presupposition had a positive influence on the actions of the patient.

In *Patterns of the Hypnotic Techniques of Milton H. Erickson M.D.* (1975), NLP co-founders Bandler and Grinder describe how the legendary hypnotherapist used linguistic presuppositions as a means to induce trance states and to help patients deal more effectively with their symptoms. The example provided at the beginning of Chapter 1, in which the psychiatrist said to the patient who thought he was Jesus Christ, "I understand you have experience as a carpenter," is an instance of how Erickson made therapeutic use of presuppositions. Erickson would frequently make statements or suggestions which presupposed certain behaviors or responses in his subjects; such as:

"Do you want to tell me what is bothering you now or would you rather wait a while?" (It is already assumed that the person will *say what is bothering him or her, the only question is* when*).*

"Don't relax too quickly now." (It is presupposed you are already relaxing, and the only question is at what speed you are doing it.)

"After your symptoms have disappeared, you will notice how easy it is to stay on track with the changes you have made in your lifestyle." (It is presupposed that your symptoms are going to disappear. It is also presupposed that it is easy to stay on track with the changes you have made in your lifestyle, the only question is noticing it.)

"Since you are going to be having so much fun learning at a new level, you can start looking forward to it

Thought Viruses and the Meta Structure of Beliefs

now." (It is presupposed that you will be learning at a new level and having fun at it. It is also presupposed that you will be looking forward to, the only question is when you start.)

You can practice forming presuppositional statements for yourself using the following formulas, and filling in the blanks with some desired behavior or response:

Do you want to _____ now or a little later?

There is no need to _____ to quickly.

After you have finished _____, you will realize how easy it is to _____.

Since you _____ , you may as well (start/finish) _____.

Self Reference

A second key factor that can make a belief more likely to become a thought virus, is when it becomes circular or self referenced. A *self referenced* process is one that refers back to, or operates upon itself. Self-referenced, or self-organizing, social and psychological systems construct their own reality by applying internally generated principles and rules. An example of a 'self referenced' perception would be standing in between two mirrors and seeing the reflection of one mirror in the other mirror, creating the experience of "watching oneself watch oneself."

Self referenced processes can be contrasted with those that are externally referenced. *Externally referenced* processes operate in response to rules and feedback that primarily come from outside, or external to, the process or system. Healthy systems generally have a balance of 'self reference' and 'external reference' (or 'other' reference). When a system or process is exclusively self referenced, it can produce pathologies and paradoxes. People who are exclusively internally referenced, for instance, can seem to be self-centered or arrogant. Cancer is a biological example of a system (or part of a system) that has become too self referenced. It grows and spreads to a point that is destructive to the surrounding system.

Circular Arguments

Self referential statements often produce a type of circular logic. The comment, "God exists because the Bible tells us so, and we know that what the Bible tells us must be true because it is the revealed word of God," for instance, refers to its own assertion as the evidence of its validity, creating a circular argument. Another example is the story of the thief who was dividing up seven stolen pearls. He handed two pearls to the man on his left and two to the man on his right. "I," he says, "will keep three." The man on his right says, "How come you keep three?" "Because I am the leader." "But how come you're the leader?" "Because I have more pearls." Again, one half of the argument uses the other half to validate itself.

Sometimes statements which are self referenced or self validating are masked because key words are slightly redefined, as in the statement, "Restrictions on freedom of speech must be advantageous to society because it is conducive to the interests of the community that there should be limits on freedom of expression." The statement is essentially saying, "Restrictions on freedom of speech are advantageous to society because restrictions on freedom of speech are advantageous to society." This is not quite so obvious, however, because "restrictions on freedom of speech" has been redefined as "limits on freedom of expression," and "advantageous to society" has been redefined as conducive to the interests of the community." Such self referential belief statements are disconnected from the surrounding 'meta structure' (i.e., other experiences, values, consequences or internal states) which would determine their ecology or usefulness.

When self reference becomes combined with beliefs, they can begin to create a form of verbal virus. Consider the following statement for a moment:

> "I have you under my control, because you must read to the end of me."

This is what psycholinguists call a 'viral sentence' (which is related to but different from a 'thought virus'). Notice that it contains a number of interesting presuppositions and assumptions. One of the characteristics of such 'viral sentences' is that they are self-referenced and self-confirming.

The only 'territory' referred to by the sentence is itself. There is no other information against which to check it. It appears to have a certain validity because we do have to read to the end of the statement just to understand the cause-effect assertion it is proposing. But does it really have us under 'its' control? Who is the "I" who is controlling us? The sentence is not a being with an identity, it is just a group of words. The original author of the sentence may already be dead by now. Is it he or she that is 'controlling' us? Does it really have anything to do with control? What about curiosity, habit or strategy? Again, the fact that the sentence is not connected to any type of meta structure makes it self validating.

Paradox and Double Binds

Self referential statements can also *invalidate* themselves, producing *paradox* as well as circularity. The classic logical paradox, "This statement is false," for instance, is an example of a self referential statement which produces a paradoxical conclusion. If the statement is true, then it is false; and if it is false, then it is true, and so on. Another good example is the old puzzle about the village barber who shaves all of the men in the village who don't shave themselves. Does the barber shave himself? If he shaves himself, then he is not a member of the class of men who don't shave themselves, and therefore cannot shave himself. But if he doesn't shave himself, then he belongs to the group of men who don't shave themselves, and must therefore shave himself.

A third example of self referential paradox is the question, "If God is all powerful, can he create a rock that is so large that even he could not lift it?"

A "double bind" is a special type of paradox which creates a "no-win" situation; i.e., a situation in which "you are damned if you do, and damned if you don't." Many double binds involve different levels of processes, such that what you must do in order to (survive, be safe, maintain your integrity, etc.) on one level, threatens your (survival, safety, integrity, etc.) on another level. According to anthropologist Gregory Bateson, who originally defined the notion of the double bind, such conflicts are at the root of both creativity and psychosis (depending upon whether or not one is able to transcend the double bind or stays caught inside of it).

In this sense, double binds are related to what has become known as a "Catch-22." The term "Catch-22" comes from the novel of that name by Joseph Heller (1961; film 1970). The novel, intended to be a dark but humorous satire of military bureaucracy, is set in a U.S. Air Force unit during World War II. The novel chronicles the attempts of airman Yossarian to escape the horrors of war. In his attempts to get out of the fighting, he becomes caught up in "Catch-22", a mysterious regulation that is, in essence, a circular argument. Yossarian discovers that he can be disqualified from flying more missions if he can prove himself insane. In order to be discharged from the military service because of insanity, however, he must request to be discharged. The "catch" is that if one requests to be discharged, it presupposes one is sane because no sane person would want to continue risking his life. By his unwillingness to fly, Yossarian proves that he is sane.

Double binds often share the quality of paradox and circularity illustrated by the "Catch-22," and lead to a similar sense of confusion and helplessness. Consider the reports of the Salem witch trials in which one of the tests to see if a person was a witch was to bind the person and cast her into the water. If the person floated and survived, then she was determined to be a witch, and was put to death. If the person sank and drowned, she was exonerated with respect to being a witch, but was, of course, also dead.

In short, self reference may be a source of either creativity or confusion, depending upon how it is balanced with other processes within a system. It can produce either pathology or wisdom depending on how it is structured and used.

The Theory of Logical Types

Philosopher and mathematician Bertrand Russell developed his 'theory of logical types' in an attempt to help resolve the types of problems which can arise from self-referential paradox and circularity. According to Gregory Bateson (*Steps to an Ecology of Mind*, p. 202), "The central thesis of [the theory of logical types] is that there is a discontinuity between a class and its members. The class cannot be a member of itself nor can one of the members be the class, since the term used for the class is of a different level of abstraction—a different *Logical Type*—from terms used for members." For instance, the class of potatoes is not itself a potato. Thus, the rules and characteristics that apply to members within a particular class do not necessarily apply to the class itself (you can peel or mash a particular potato, but you cannot peel or mash 'the class of potatoes').

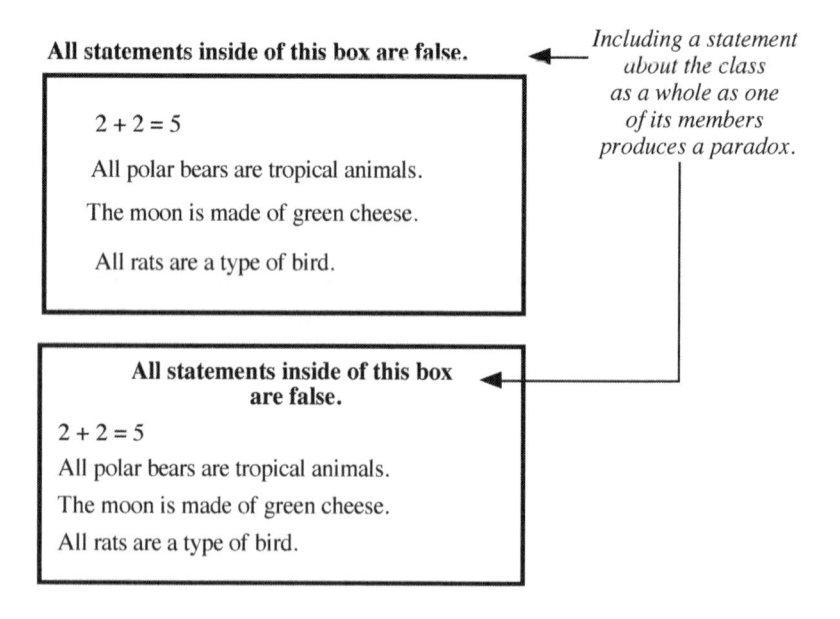

> All statements inside of this box are false.
>
> 2 + 2 = 5
>
> All polar bears are tropical animals.
>
> The moon is made of green cheese.
>
> All rats are a type of bird.

Including a statement about the class as a whole as one of its members produces a paradox.

> All statements inside of this box are false.
>
> 2 + 2 = 5
> All polar bears are tropical animals.
> The moon is made of green cheese.
> All rats are a type of bird.

According to Russell's Theory of Logical Types, Making a Class a Member of Itself Produces Paradox

Russell's principle of Logical Types is an example of establishing a self referenced regulating mechanism at a different 'level' of operation. These types of mechanisms have become the focus of study in what is known as "second order cybernetics." Second order cybernetics often deals with "recursive" loops and processes (such as those involved in autopoietic and self-organizing systems). Recursion is a special form of feedback loop in which the operation or procedure is self-referring - that is, it calls itself as part of its own procedure. "Communicating about communication," "observing the observer," "giving feedback about feedback," etc., are all examples of recursive, self referential processes.

Applying a Belief or Generalization to Itself

The Sleight of Mouth pattern known as "Apply to Self" is an example of verbally applying the process of self reference to help a person reflect upon and reevaluate particular belief statements. Applying a belief to itself involves evaluating the belief statement according to the generalization or criteria defined by the belief. For example, if a person expresses a belief such as, "You cannot trust words," the belief could be applied to itself by saying, "Since you cannot trust words, then I guess you cannot trust what you just said." As another example, if a person said, "It is wrong to make generalizations," one could respond, "Are you sure that you are not wrong to make *that* generalization?"

The purpose of applying a belief or generalization to itself is to discover whether or not the belief is a congruent example of its own generalization – a type of 'golden rule' for beliefs: "A generalization is only as valid for others as it is for itself." For instance, a person can say, "The map is not the territory . . . including this belief. It is just a map itself, so don't get caught in thinking it is 'reality'."

Frequently, the process of applying a limiting belief to itself creates a paradox, which serves to expose the areas in which the belief is not useful. It is a means of applying the old adage that sometimes you need to "fight fire with fire," by turning it back upon itself.

A good example of utilizing the pattern of Apply to Self to deal with a potential thought virus, is that of the man who was struggling as a participant at an NLP seminar. The man was interested in developing his flexibility in using his voice tone, but he kept encountering a tremendous amount of internal resistance. A part of him knew that it was "appropriate" to become more flexible with his voice, but he kept feeling "ridiculous" whenever he tried to do something different. This inner conflict was constantly leading the man to become self-conscious and stuck whenever he tried to do an

Thought Viruses and the Meta Structure of Beliefs 235

exercise. His difficulties in the exercises were leading to an increasing sense of frustration, not only for himself, but also for the other seminar attendees who were trying to participate in the exercises with him.

The man's problems were brought to the attention of the two NLP trainers conducting the course, who decided to use a type of confusion technique to interrupt this pattern of resistance. The man was brought up as a demonstration subject for an exercise on vocal flexibility. Naturally, as he began to attempt the exercise, the inner resistance and conflict immediately began to emerge. At this point, one of the trainers said, "I understand that you think it is *appropriate* to develop flexibility with your voice, but are worried about looking *ridiculous* by doing so. The question I have is whether you want to be *appropriately ridiculous* or *ridiculously appropriate?*" Taken off guard by the question, the young man was momentarily unable to answer. The other trainer took the opportunity to add, "It's only *appropriate* that you are confused by the question because it such a *ridiculous* thing to ask." The first trainer then said, "But isn't it *ridiculous* that it is *appropriate* to respond that way to a *ridiculous* question?" His fellow trainer responded, "Yes, but its *appropriate* to ask a *ridiculous* question when the situation is as *ridiculous* as this one seems to be." The other trainer then remarked, "That's a *ridiculous* thing to say. I think it is only *appropriate* that we are all in such a *ridiculous* situation, and it is necessary that we respond to it *appropriately*." The second trainer retorted, "I know that what I'm saying is *ridiculous*, but I think that, in order to *act appropriately*, I have to *be ridiculous*. In fact, given the situation, it would *be ridiculous* to *act appropriately*." The two trainers then turned back to the man and asked, "What do you think?"

The man, completely befuddled, stared blankly for a moment, and then began to laugh. At this point, the trainers said, "Let's just do the exercise then." The man was able to complete the exercise without any internal interference. In a way, the confusion technique served to desensitize the man with respect to a problematic interpretation of certain words. This freed him to choose his reaction based upon different criteria. In the future, whenever any issue about the "appropriateness" or "ridiculousness" of his behavior arose, the man just laughed and was able to make his decisions based upon a different, and more effective, decision making strategy.

Another example of applying this pattern is that of a young man who was having difficulties in his business. He kept finding himself taking on much more than he could possibly handle. Upon eliciting his motivation strategy it was discovered that if the young man was asked if he could perform some task or favor by a client, friend or associate he would immediately attempt to construct an image of himself doing what they had asked of him. If he could see himself doing it, he would tell himself that he *should* do it and would begin to carry out the task requested of him, even if it interfered with other things he was currently involved in.

The young man was then asked if he could visualize himself *not* doing something that he could visualize himself doing. A rapid and profound trance state ensued as the man's strategy began to 'spin out'. The NLP practitioner who was coaching the young man took advantage of this state to help him develop some more effective tests and operations with respect to his motivation strategy.

A particularly powerful and moving example of how the Sleight of Mouth pattern of 'apply to self' was used to save a woman's life is the following account, taken from the Gospel of John (8:3-11):

> *And the scribes and Pharisees brought unto him a woman taken in adultery; and when they had set her in the midst, They said unto him, Master, this woman was taken in adultery, in the very act. Now Moses in*

> *the law commanded us, that such should be stoned: but what sayest thou?*
>
> *This they said, tempting him, that they might have to accuse him. But Jesus stooped down, and with his finger wrote on the ground, as though he heard them not.*
>
> *So when they continued asking him, he lifted up himself, and said unto them, He that is without sin among you, let him first cast a stone at her. And again he stooped down, and wrote on the ground.*
>
> *And they which heard it, being convicted by their own conscience, went out one by one, beginning at the eldest, even unto the last: and Jesus was left alone, and the woman standing in the midst.*
>
> *When Jesus had lifted himself, and saw none but the woman, he said unto her, Woman, where are those thine accusers? hath no man condemned thee? She said, No man, Lord. And Jesus said unto her, Neither do I condemn thee: go, and sin no more.*

Jesus' statement, "He that is without sin among you, let him first cast a stone at her," is a classic example of applying the values asserted by a belief statement back onto the belief itself. To do so, Jesus first 'chunked up' "adultery" to "sin," and then invited the crowd to apply the same criterion and consequences to their own behavior.

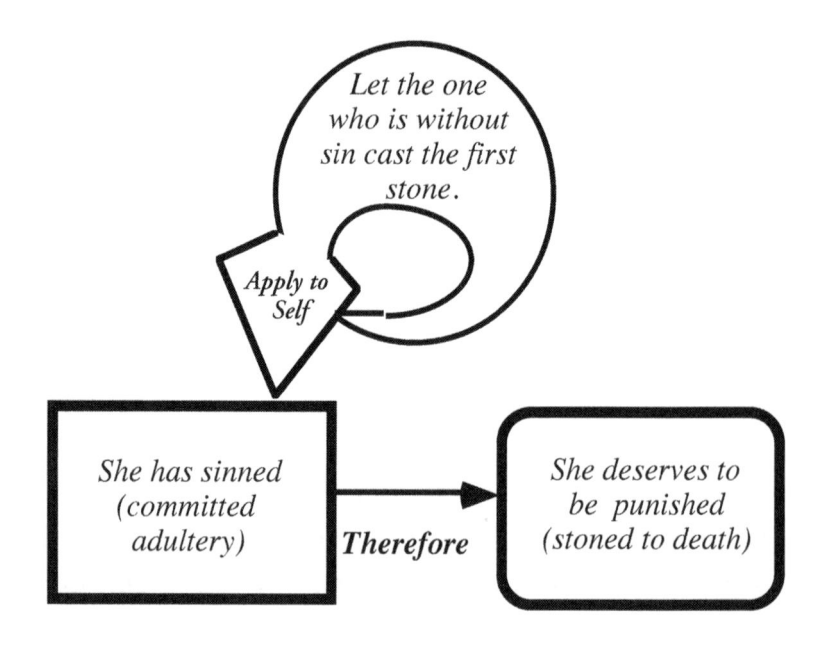

```
            ╱ Let the one  ╲
           │  who is without │
           │  sin cast the first │
            ╲    stone.    ╱
              ╲ Apply to ╱
                 Self
```

| She has sinned (committed adultery) | **Therefore** → | She deserves to be punished (stoned to death) |

Jesus' Application of 'Apply to Self' Saved a Woman's Life

Notice that Jesus did not challenge the belief itself. Rather he "outframed" it, causing the group to shift their perceptual position and widen their map of the situation to include their own behavior.

Try out this pattern on one of your own beliefs. To start, be sure that you state the belief as a cause-effect or complex equivalence statement:

Belief: _____ (am/is/are) _____ because _____.

e.g., I am *a slow learner* because *it takes time for me to understand new ideas*.

How can you evaluate the belief statement itself according to the generalization or criteria defined by the belief? In what way might it be an example (or not an example) of its own assertion?

> e.g., How long did it take for you to learn the idea that this means you are a slow learner?
> Perhaps if you took the time to really understand the ways in which that idea limits you unnecessarily, you would be open to internalize some new ideas about how you can learn.

Sometimes you have to be able to think non-linearly and non-literally to apply a belief to itself. For example, if a person says, "I cannot afford this product because it is too expensive," you might need to apply it to itself more metaphorically. This could be done by saying, "That may ultimately be an expensive belief to hold onto too tightly," or, by asking, "Are you sure you can afford to hold that belief so strongly, it may prevent you from taking advantage of important opportunities?"

Similarly, if someone says something like, "A diagnosis of cancer is like receiving a death sentence," the statement could be applied to itself by saying, "That belief has spread like cancer over the years, maybe it is time for it to die out."

Meta Frames

Applying a generalization to itself frequently leads a person to a *meta position* with respect to his or her own thoughts and beliefs. The NLP notion of 'meta position' is a means of applying a self referenced process to facilitate psychological change and growth. In meta position, one disassociates from and then reflects back upon one's own thoughts, actions and interactions in order to gain new insights and understandings that will help one to act more effectively. This helps a person to recognize that the belief is indeed a 'belief' and not necessarily the only interpretation of reality.

One of the most direct ways to achieve a meta position with respect to a belief is to use what is known as a 'meta frame'. Applying a meta frame involves evaluating a belief from the frame of an ongoing, personally oriented context - i.e., *establishing a belief **about the belief**.* We can believe, for instance, that some other belief is erroneous or silly. The statement, "You're only saying that to make me feel good," is a common example of how a person might use a meta frame to discount a positive statement or evaluation made by another person.

The difference between applying the belief to itself and meta framing is that, when a belief is applied to itself, the content of the belief (i.e., the values and generalization which the belief expresses) is used to evaluate the belief itself. In meta framing, the belief about the other belief can have a completely different content than the other belief to which it refers.

For example, consider the generalization, "You have to be strong to survive." Applying the belief to itself would involve saying something like, "I wonder if that belief is strong enough to survive into the next millennium." To meta frame the belief, on the other hand, someone might say, "That belief is most likely a reflection of a relatively narrow and male dominated view of life that fails to recognize the importance of cooperation and flexibility with respect to survival."

Meta framing is a common strategy for working with beliefs in psychotherapy and counseling; in which a person's beliefs are placed in the meta frame of his or her personal history or other social influences. Sigmund Freud's technique of psychoanalysis is a classic example of the application of meta framing. Freud was constantly explaining and 'framing' the complaints of his patients by placing them within the framework of his theories. Consider the quotation below, taken from Freud's account of his work with a patient who was obsessed with fantasies about rats (the case of the so called 'Ratman'):

> *I pointed out to him that he ought logically to consider himself as in no way responsible for any of these traits in his character; for all of these reprehensible impulses originated from his infancy, and were only derivatives of his infantile character surviving in his unconscious; and he must know that moral responsibility could not be applied to children.*

Freud meta framed the man's thoughts and "reprehensible impulses" as deriving from his "infantile character surviving in his unconscious." Freud then implied that, because "moral responsibility could not be applied to children," the man should not blame himself for his compulsions.

Meta framing frequently diffuses the impact of a limiting belief by shifting a person's perspective to that of an observer to his or her own mental processes.

Explore this pattern with one of your own beliefs. Think of some belief, judgment or generalization that limits you. What is a belief about this belief that could change or enrich your perception of the belief?

Belief: _____

I have that belief because: _____

Like all other Sleight of Mouth patterns, meta framing can also be used to support or strengthen an empowering belief. As an example, let's say someone wants to establish the belief, "My intelligence and ability to communicate make me a survivor." A supporting meta frame could be, "You have that belief because you recognize that the information age has forever changed the factors necessary for survival."

Logical Levels

The Sleight of Mouth patterns of 'Apply to Self' and 'Meta Frame' typically stimulate a shift of our attention to a different level of thinking. They make us more aware of what Bertrand Russell termed "logical types"; and the fact that we cannot treat a class and one of its members as if they are on the same level. Anthropologist and communication theorist Gregory Bateson applied Russell's theory of logical types as a means to help explain and resolve a number of issues relating to behavior, learning and communication. According to Bateson, the notion of different logical types was essential to the understanding of play, higher level learning, and pathological thinking patterns. Bateson believed that confusions of logical types were largely responsible for what we have been calling "limiting beliefs" and "thought viruses."

As an example, Bateson pointed out that "play" involved distinguishing between different *logical types* of behavior and messages. Bateson noted that when animals and humans engage in "play" they often display the same behaviors that are also associated with aggression, sexuality, and other more "serious" aspects of life (such as when animals "play fight," or children play "doctor"). Yet, somehow, animals and humans were able to recognize, for the most part, that the play behavior was a different type or class of behavior and "not the real thing." According to Bateson, distinguishing between classes of behavior also required different types of messages. Bateson referred to these messages as "meta messages" – messages *about* other messages - claiming that they too were of a different "logical type" than the content of a particular communication. He believed that these "higher level" messages (which were usually communicated non-verbally) were crucial for people, and animals, to be able to communicate and interact effectively.

Animals at play, for instance, may signal the message "This is play" by wagging their tails, jumping up and down, or doing some other thing to indicate that what they are about to do is not to be taken seriously. Their bite is a playful bite, not a real bite. Studies of humans also reveal the use of special messages that let others know they are playing, in much the same way animals do. They may actually verbally 'meta-communicate' by announcing that "This is only a game," or they laugh, nudge, or do something odd to show their intent.

Bateson claimed that many problems and conflicts were a result of the confusion or misinterpretation of these messages. A good example is the difficulties that people from different cultures experience when interpreting the non-verbal subtleties of each other's communications.

In fact, in *Epidemiology of a Schizophrenia* (1955), Bateson maintained that the inability to correctly recognize and interpret meta messages, and to distinguish between different classes, or logical types, of behavior, was at the root of many seemingly psychotic or "crazy" behaviors. Bateson cited the example of a young mental patient who went into the pharmacy of the hospital. The nurse behind the counter asked, "Can I help you?" The patient was unable to distinguish whether the communication was a threat, a sexual advance, an admonishment for being in the wrong place, a genuine inquiry, etc.

When one is unable to make such distinctions, Bateson contented, they will end up, more often than not, acting in a way that is inappropriate for the situation. He likened it to a telephone switching system that was unable to distinguish the 'country code' from the 'city code' and the local telephone number. As a result, the switching system would inappropriately assign numbers belonging to the country code as part of the phone number, or parts of the phone number as the city code, etc. The consequence of this would be that, again more often than not, the dialer would get the "wrong number."

Even though all of the numbers (the content) are correct, the classification of the numbers (the form) is confused, creating problems.

In *The Logical Categories of Learning and Communication* (1964), Bateson extended the notion of logical typing to explain different types and phenomena of learning as well as communication. He defined two fundamental types, or levels of learning which must be considered in all processes of change: "Learning I" (stimulus-response type conditioning) and "Learning II", or *deutero learning*, (learning to recognize the larger context in which the stimulus is occurring so that its meaning may be correctly interpreted). The most basic example of learning II phenomena is set learning, or when an animal becomes "testwise" – that is, laboratory animals will get faster and faster at learning new tasks that fall into the same class of activity. This has to do with learning *classes* of behavior rather than single isolated behaviors.

An animal trained in avoidance conditioning, for instance, will be able to learn different types of avoidance behavior more and more rapidly. It will, however, be slower at learning some 'respondently' conditioned behavior (e.g., salivating at the sound of a bell) than some animal that has been conditioned in that class of behavior earlier. That is, it will learn quickly how to identify and stay away from objects that might have an electric shock associated with them but will be slower at learning to salivate when a bell rings. On the other hand, an animal trained in Pavlovian type conditioning will rapidly learn to salivate to new sounds and colors, etc., but will be slower to learn to avoid electrified objects.

Bateson pointed out that this ability to learn patterns or rules of a class of conditioning procedures was a different "logical type" of learning and did not function according to the same simple stimulus-response-reinforcement sequences used to learn specific isolated behaviors. Bateson noted, for instance, that the reinforcement for "exploration" (a means of learning-to-learn) in rats is of a different nature than that for the "testing" of a particular object (the learning content of exploration). He reports (*Steps to an Ecology of Mind* p. 282):

> *"...you can reinforce a rat (positively or negatively) when he investigates a particular strange object, and he will appropriately learn to approach it or avoid it. But the very purpose of exploration is to get information about which objects should be approached or avoided. The discovery that a given object is dangerous is therefore a success in the business of getting information. The success will not discourage the rat from future exploration of other strange objects."*

The ability to explore, learn a discrimination task, or be creative is a higher level of learning than the specific behaviors that make up these abilities – and the dynamics and rules of change are different on this higher level.

Because of Bateson's role and influence in the early development of NLP, the notion of logical typing is also an important concept in NLP. In the 1980's, I adapted the ideas of Russell and Bateson to formulate the notion of "Logical Levels" and "Neuro-Logical Levels" in human behavior and change. Drawing from Bateson, the levels model proposes that there is a natural hierarchy of levels within an individual or group that function as different logical types of processes. Each level synthesizes, organizes and directs a particular class of activity on the level below it. Changing something on an upper level would necessarily 'radiate' downward, precipitating change on the lower levels. But, because each successive level is of a different logical type of process, changing something on a lower level would not necessarily affect the upper levels. Beliefs, for example, are formed and changed by different rules than behavioral reflexes. Rewarding or punishing particular behaviors will not necessarily change someone's beliefs, because belief systems are a different type of process mentally and neurologically than behaviors.

According to the Neuro-Logical Levels model, *environmental* influences involve the specific external conditions in which our behavior takes place. *Behaviors*, without any inner map, plan or strategy to guide them, however, are like knee jerk reactions, habits or rituals. At the level of *capability* we are able to select, alter and adapt a class of behaviors to a wider set of external situations. At the level of *beliefs and values* we may encourage, inhibit or generalize a particular strategy, plan or way of thinking. *Identity*, of course, consolidates whole systems of beliefs and values into a sense of self. *Spiritual* level experience has to do with the sense that our identity is part of something larger than ourselves and our vision of the larger systems to which we belong. While each level becomes more abstracted from the specifics of behavior and sensory experience, it actually has more and more widespread effect on our behavior and experience.

* *Environmental factors* determine the external opportunities or constraints a person has to react to. Answer to the questions **where**? and **when**?
* *Behavior* is made up of the specific actions or reactions taken within the environment. Answer to the question **what**?
* *Capabilities* guide and give direction to behavioral actions through a mental map, plan or strategy. Answer to the question **how**?
* *Beliefs* and *values* provide the reinforcement (motivation and permission) that supports or denies capabilities. Answer to the question **why**?
* *Identity* factors determine overall purpose (mission) and shape beliefs and values through our sense of self. Answer to the question **who**?
* *Spiritual* issues relate to the fact that we are a part of a larger system that reaches beyond ourselves as individuals to our family, community and global systems. Answer to the questions **for whom** or **for what**?

From the NLP perspective, each of these processes involves a different level of organization and mobilizes successively deeper mobilization and commitment of neurological 'circuitry'.

Interestingly, some of the stimulus for this model came from teaching people Sleight of Mouth patterns. I began to notice that certain types of statements were typically more difficult for people to handle than others, even though the type of judgment being asserted was essentially the same. For example, compare the following statements:

That object in your environment is dangerous.
Your actions in that particular context were dangerous.
Your inability to make effective judgments is dangerous.
What you believe and value as important is dangerous.
You're a dangerous person.

The judgment being made in each case is about something being "dangerous." Intuitively, however, most people sense that the "space" or "territory" implied by each statement becomes progressively larger, and feel an increasing sense of emotional affect with each statement.

For someone to tell you that some specific behavioral response made was dangerous is quite different than telling you that you are a "dangerous person." I noticed that if I held a judgment constant and simply substituted a term for environment, behavior, capabilities, beliefs and values, and identity, people would feel progressively more offended or complimented, depending on the positive or negative nature of the judgment.

Try it for yourself. Imagine someone was saying each of the following statements to you:

Your *surroundings* are (stupid/ugly/exceptional/beautiful).

The way you *behaved* in that particular situation was (stupid/ugly/exceptional/beautiful).

You really have the *capability* to be (stupid/ugly/exceptional/beautiful).

What you *believe and value* is (stupid/ugly/exceptional/beautiful).

You are (stupid/ugly/exceptional/beautiful).

Again, notice that the evaluations asserted by each statement are the same. What changes is the particuloar aspect of the person to which the statement is referring.

Changing Logical Levels

One of the most common and effective Sleight of Mouth tactics involves recategorizing a characteristic or experience from one logical level to another (e.g., separating a person's *identity* from his or her *capabilities* or *behavior*). Negative identity judgments are often the result of interpreting particular behaviors, or the lack of ability to produce certain behavioral results, as statements about one's identity. Shifting a negative identity judgment back to a statement about a person's behavior or capabilities greatly reduces the impact it has on the person mentally and emotionally.

As an example, a person might be depressed about having cancer, and refer to himself or herself as a "cancer victim." This could be 'reframed' with the response, "You are not a *cancer victim*, you are a normal person who has not yet developed the *capability to take full advantage of the mind-body connection.*" This can help the person to shift his or her relationship to the illness, open up to other possibilities, and to view himself or herself as a participant in his or her healing process.

The same type of reframe could be done with a belief like, "I am a failure." One could point out, "It is not that you are a 'failure', it is just that you have not yet mastered all of the elements necessary for success." Again, this puts the limiting identity level judgment back into a more proactive and solvable framework.

These types of reframes can be designed using the following steps:

a) Identify the negative identity judgment:

I am _____ (e.g., "I am a burden to others.")

b) Identify a specific capability or behavior that is related to either the present state or desired state implied by the identity judgment:

Ability to _____ (e.g., "Ability to resolve problems on one's own").

c) Substitute the capability or behavior for the negative identity judgment:

Perhaps it is not that you are a _____ (negative identity: e.g., "burden to others"), *it is just that you don't yet have the ability to* _____ (specific capability or behavior: e.g., "resolve problems on your own").

Of course, the process can also be reversed in order to promote empowering beliefs. A behavior or capability may be elevated to an identity level statement. For example, one could say, "Your ability to be creative in that situation means that you are a creative person." Other examples include: surviving –> survivor; achieving health –> healthy person; succeeding –> successful person; and so on. This type of reformulation serves to deepen or strengthen a person's sense of his or her resources.

Chapter 9

Applying the Patterns as a System

Definitions and Examples of Sleight of Mouth Patterns

In the course of this book we have explored a number of specific Sleight of Mouth patterns, and the principles and methods which underlie the ability to generate and use them. The purpose of this chapter is to summarize them as a system of distinctions which can be used, in either conversation, consultation, or debate, to help people become more 'open to doubt' limiting beliefs, and more 'open to believe' empowering and useful beliefs. There are fourteen distinct Sleight of Mouth patterns which each help to shift attention, or widen a person's map in different directions.

Consider the belief: *"I have had this belief for such a long time that it will be difficult to change."* This is actually a common belief that many people struggle with when attempting to make changes in their lives. While it reflects a valid perspective, it can be quite a limiting belief if taken at face value and interpreted narrowly or rigidly. (It is also particularly tricky, because it is a belief about other beliefs and the process of changing beliefs. This 'self-referential' quality increases the likelihood that it could become 'circular' and a possible 'thought virus'.) Applying the various Sleight of Mouth patterns can help to add new perspective and 'widen the map' associated with this belief.

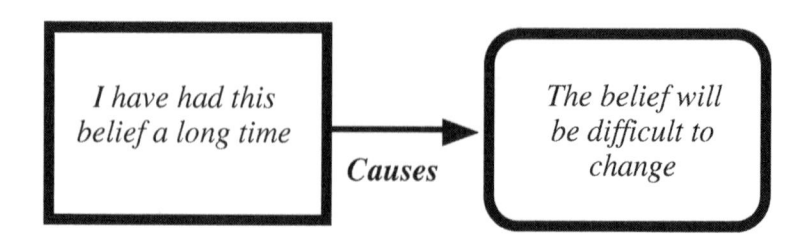

```
┌─────────────────┐                    ┌─────────────────┐
│ I have had this │                    │ The belief will │
│ belief a long time │ ────────────▶   │ be difficult to │
│                 │      Causes        │     change      │
└─────────────────┘                    └─────────────────┘
```

Structure of a Limiting Belief Statement About Change

The following are definitions and examples of how the fourteen different Sleight of Mouth patterns can be applied to this particular belief statement. Again, remember that the purpose of Sleight of Mouth is not to attack the person or the belief, but rather to reframe the belief and widen the person's map of the world in such a way that the positive intention behind the belief can be maintained through other choices.

1. **Intention:** Directing attention to the purpose or intention behind the belief. [See Chapter 2, pp. 41-49.]

    e.g., *"I very much admire and support your desire to be honest with yourself."*
    Positive intention = "honesty"

    "It is so important to be realistic about changing one's beliefs. Let's look realistically at this belief and at what will be required to change it."
    Positive intention = "being realistic"

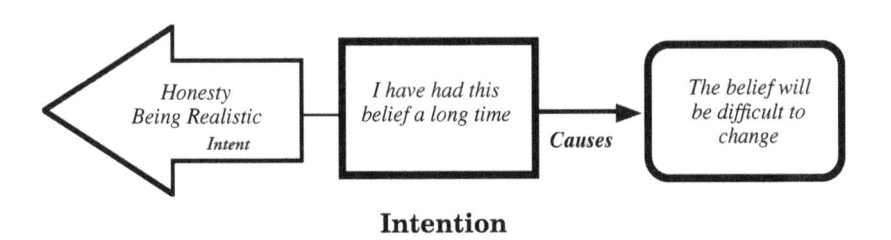

```
┌─────────┐   ┌──────────────┐          ┌──────────────┐
│ Honesty │   │ I have had this│         │The belief will│
│Being Realistic│ │belief a long time│  Causes  │be difficult to│
│  Intent  │   │              │ ────────>│   change     │
└─────────┘   └──────────────┘          └──────────────┘
```

Intention

2. **Redefining:** Substituting a new word for one of the words used in the belief statement that means something similar but has different implications. [See Chapter 2, pp. 49-53.]

> e.g., *"Yes, something that you've held onto so tenaciously can be challenging to let go of."*
> "had a long time" => "held onto tenaciously"
> "difficult to change" => "challenging to let go of"
>
> *"I agree that it can initially feel strange to go beyond familiar boundaries."*
> "belief" => "familiar boundary"
> "difficult to change" => "initially feel strange to go beyond"

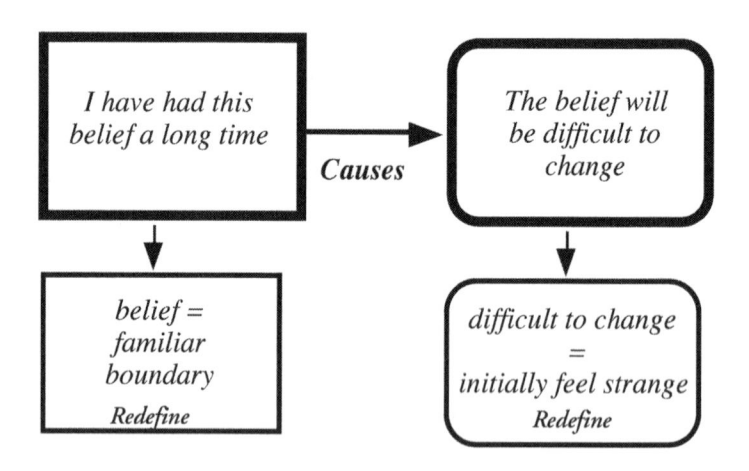

```
┌─────────────────┐                ┌─────────────────┐
│ I have had this │                │ The belief will │
│ belief a long   │─── Causes ───▶│ be difficult to │
│ time            │                │ change          │
└────────┬────────┘                └────────┬────────┘
         │                                  │
         ▼                                  ▼
┌─────────────────┐                ┌─────────────────┐
│ belief =        │                │ difficult to    │
│ familiar        │                │ change          │
│ boundary        │                │     =           │
│   Redefine      │                │ initially feel  │
│                 │                │ strange         │
│                 │                │   Redefine      │
└─────────────────┘                └─────────────────┘
```

Redefining

3. **Consequence:** Directing attention to an effect (positive or negative) of the belief, or the generalization defined by the belief, which changes (or reinforces) the belief. [See Chapter 5, pp. 127-130.]

> e.g., *"Anticipating that something will be difficult often makes it seem that much easier when you finally do it."*
>
> *"Genuinely acknowledging our concerns allows us to be able to put them aside so that we can focus on what we want."*

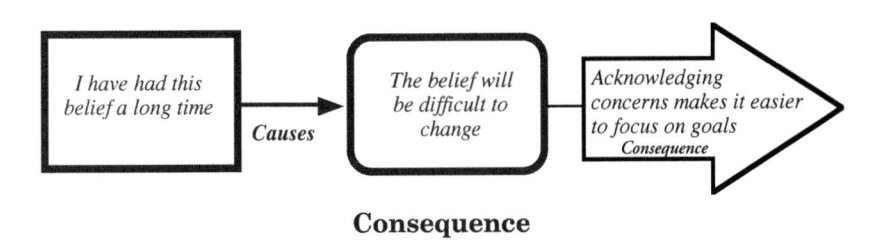

| *I have had this belief a long time* | *Causes* → | *The belief will be difficult to change* | *Acknowledging concerns makes it easier to focus on goals*
Consequence |

Consequence

4. **Chunk Down:** Breaking the elements of the belief into smaller pieces such that it changes (or reinforces) the generalization defined by the belief. [See Chapter 3, pp. 63-65.]

> e.g., *"Since having the belief only a short time would make it much easier to change, perhaps you can remember what it was like back at the time you had just formed the belief and imagine having changed it at that time."*
> "long time" => "short time"

> *"Perhaps if, instead of trying to change the whole belief at once, if you just altered it in small increments, it would feel easy and even fun."*
> "changing a belief" => "altering it in increments"

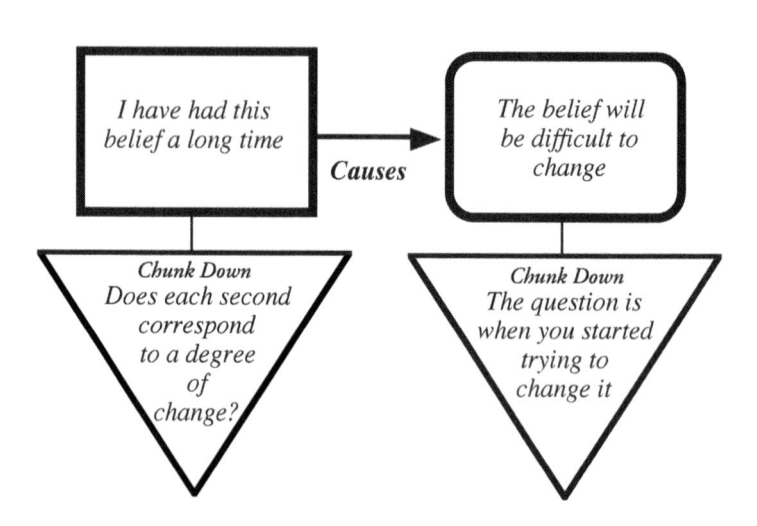

```
┌─────────────────┐             ┌─────────────────┐
│ I have had this │   Causes    │ The belief will │
│ belief a long   │ ──────────> │ be difficult to │
│ time            │             │ change          │
└────────┬────────┘             └────────┬────────┘
         │                               │
    ▽ Chunk Down                    ▽ Chunk Down
   Does each second                The question is
     correspond                    when you started
      to a degree                      trying to
         of                            change it
       change?
```

Chunk Down

Applying the Patterns as a System

5. **Chunk Up:** Generalizing an element of the belief to a larger classification that changes (or reinforces) the relationship defined by the belief. [See Chapter 3, pp. 66-67.]

> e.g., *"The past does not always accurately predict the future. Knowledge can evolve rapidly when it is reconnected with the processes which naturally update it."*
> "had for a long time" => "past"   "belief" => "a form of knowledge"
> "will be difficult => "future"   "change" => "connected with the processes which naturally update it"
>
> *"All processes of change have a natural cycle that cannot be rushed. The question is, what is the length of the natural life cycle for the particular belief you have?"*
> "difficult to change" => "natural cycle that cannot be rushed"
> "had the belief a long time" => "length of the belief's 'life cycle'"

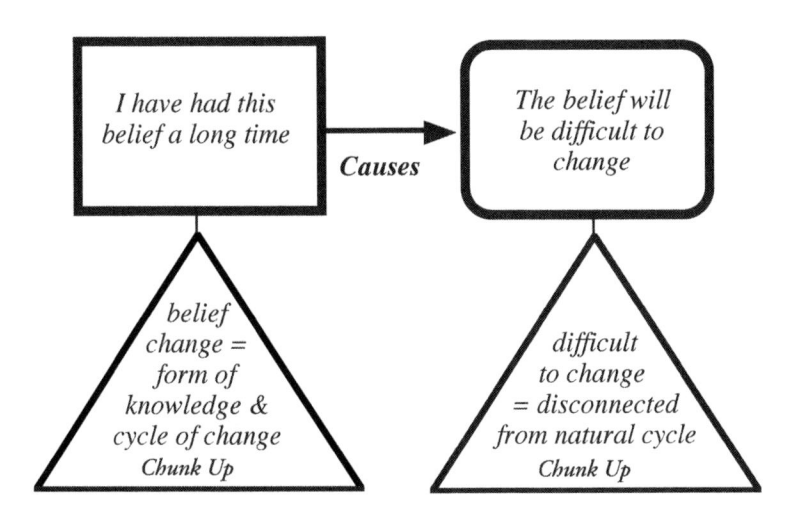

```
┌─────────────────┐                  ┌─────────────────┐
│ I have had this │                  │ The belief will │
│ belief a long   │ ───Causes──▶     │ be difficult to │
│ time            │                  │ change          │
└────────┬────────┘                  └────────┬────────┘
         │                                    │
        ╱ ╲                                  ╱ ╲
       ╱   ╲                                ╱   ╲
      ╱ belief                             ╱ difficult
     ╱ change =                           ╱ to change
    ╱ form of                            ╱ = disconnected
   ╱ knowledge &                        ╱ from natural cycle
  ╱ cycle of change                    ╱ Chunk Up
 ╱ Chunk Up                           ╱
```

Chunk Up

6. **Analogy:** Finding a relationship analogous to that defined by the belief which challenges (or reinforces) the generalization defined by the belief. [See Chapter 3, pp. 68-72.]

> e.g., *"A belief is like a law. Even very old laws can be changed quickly if enough people vote for something new."*
>
> *"A belief is like a computer program. The issue is not how old the program is, it is whether or not you know the programming language ."*
>
> *"The dinosaurs were probably surprised at how rapidly their world changed, even though they had been around for a long time."*

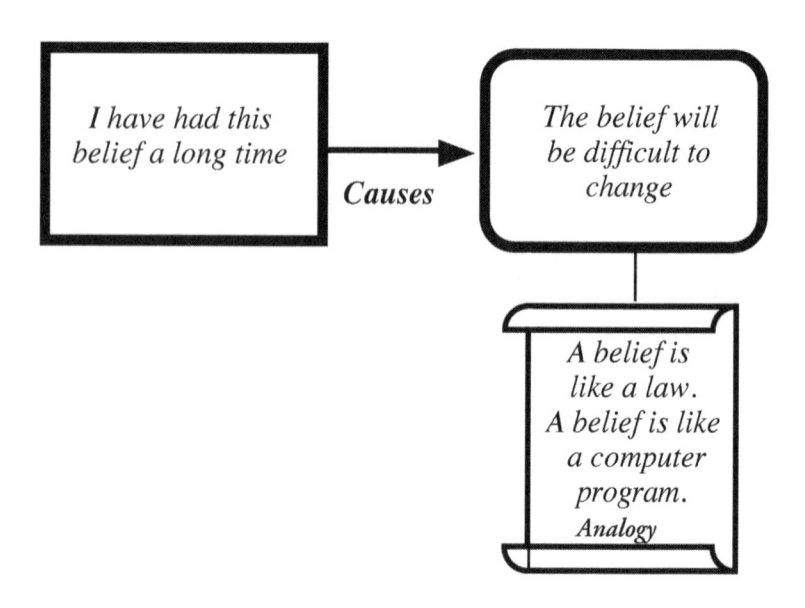

```
┌─────────────────┐              ┌─────────────────┐
│ I have had this │              │ The belief will │
│ belief a long   │─────────────▶│ be difficult to │
│ time            │   Causes     │ change          │
└─────────────────┘              └─────────────────┘
                                         │
                                  ┌──────┴──────┐
                                  │ A belief is │
                                  │ like a law. │
                                  │ A belief is │
                                  │ like a      │
                                  │ computer    │
                                  │ program.    │
                                  │ Analogy     │
                                  └─────────────┘
```

Analogy

7. **Change Frame Size:** Re-evaluating (or reinforcing) the implication of the belief in the context of a longer (or shorter) time frame, a larger number of people (or from an individual point of view) or a bigger or smaller perspective. [See Chapter 2, pp. 34-37.]

e.g., *"You are probably not the first or only one to have this belief. Perhaps the more people there are who are successfully able to change it, the easier it will become for others to change this type of belief in the future."*

"Years from now, you will probably have difficulty remembering that you ever had this belief."

"I am sure that your children will appreciate that you have made the effort to change this belief, rather than passing it on to them."

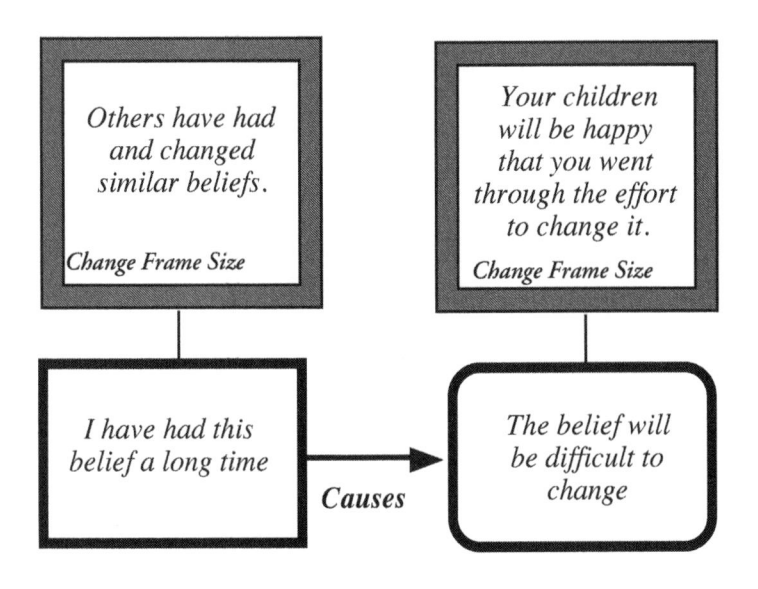

```
┌─────────────────┐      ┌─────────────────┐
│ Others have had │      │  Your children  │
│   and changed   │      │  will be happy  │
│ similar beliefs.│      │  that you went  │
│                 │      │ through the effort│
│                 │      │  to change it.  │
│Change Frame Size│      │Change Frame Size│
└────────┬────────┘      └────────┬────────┘
         │                        │
┌────────┴────────┐      ┌────────┴────────┐
│ I have had this │      │ The belief will │
│belief a long time│─────▶│  be difficult to│
│                 │Causes│      change     │
└─────────────────┘      └─────────────────┘
```

Change Frame Size

8. **Another Outcome:** Switching to a different goal than that addressed or implied by the belief, in order to challenge (or reinforce) the relevancy of the belief. [See Chapter 2, pp. 26-30.]

> e.g., *"It is not necessary to change the belief. It just needs to be updated."*
>
> *"The issue is not so much about changing beliefs. It is about making your map of the world congruent with who you are now."*

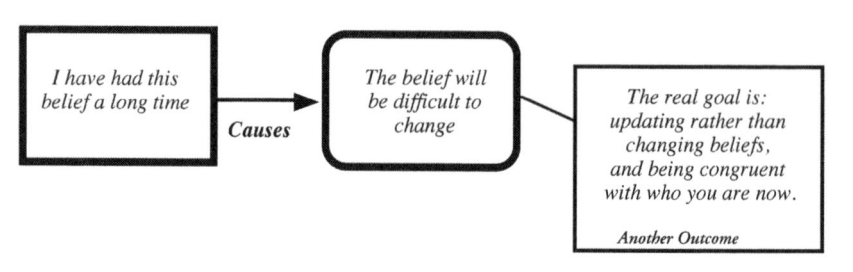

```
┌─────────────┐         ┌─────────────┐         ┌──────────────────┐
│ I have had  │         │ The belief  │         │ The real goal is:│
│ this belief │────────▶│ will be     │─────────│ updating rather  │
│ a long time │ Causes  │ difficult to│         │ than changing    │
│             │         │ change      │         │ beliefs, and     │
└─────────────┘         └─────────────┘         │ being congruent  │
                                                │ with who you are │
                                                │ now.             │
                                                │  Another Outcome │
                                                └──────────────────┘
```

Another Outcome

9. **Model of the World:** Re-evaluating (or reinforcing) the belief from the framework of a different model of the world. [See Chapter 2, pp. 55-58.]

> e.g., "You are lucky. Many people don't even recognize that their limitations are a function of beliefs that can be changed at all. You are a lot farther ahead than they are."
>
> "Artists frequently use their inner struggles as a source of inspiration for creativity. I wonder what type of creativity your efforts to change your belief might bring out in you."

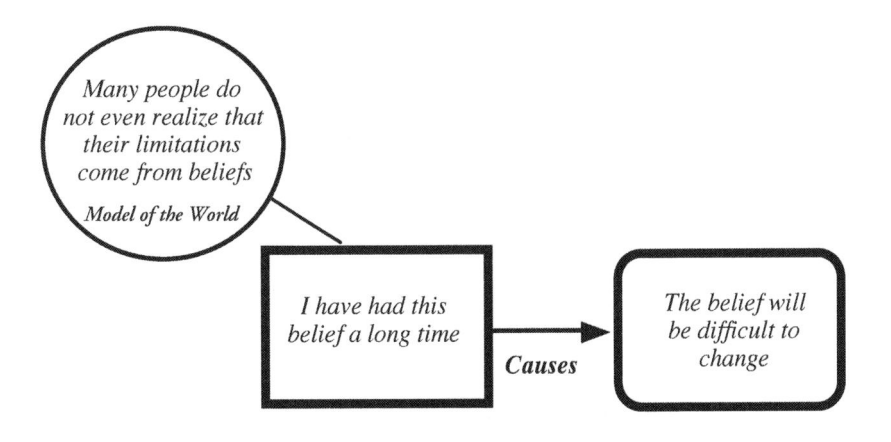

Model of the World

10. **Reality Strategy:** Reevaluating (or reinforcing) the belief accounting for the fact that people operate from cognitive perceptions of the world in order to build their beliefs. [See Chapter 4, pp. 89-97.]

> e.g., *"How, specifically, do you know that you have had this belief for a 'long time'?"*
>
> *"What particular qualities of what you see or hear when you think about changing this belief make it seem 'difficult'?"*

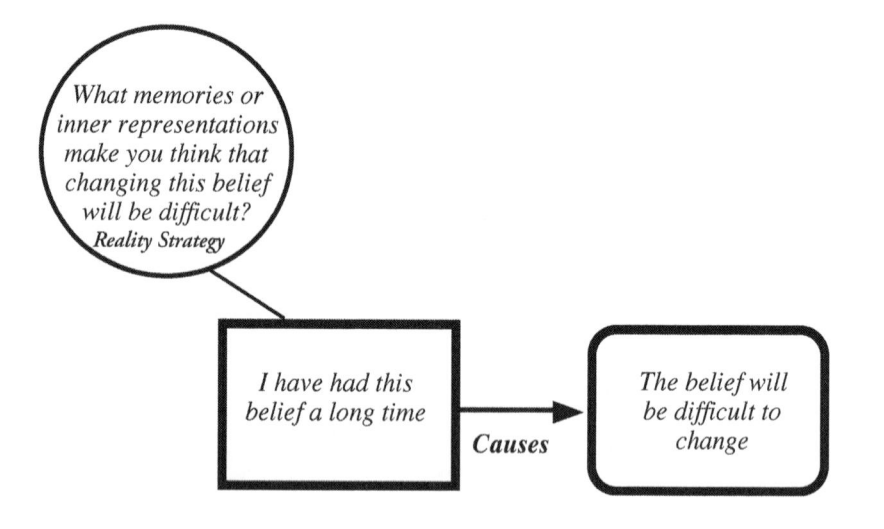

```
   ┌─────────────────┐
  │ What memories or │
  │inner representations│
  │ make you think that │
  │ changing this belief│
  │  will be difficult? │
   │  Reality Strategy │
    └────────┬────────┘
             │
    ┌────────┴────────┐         ┌─────────────┐
    │  I have had this │         │The belief will│
    │ belief a long time│──────▶│ be difficult to│
    │                  │  Causes │    change    │
    └──────────────────┘         └─────────────┘
```

Reality Strategy

Applying the Patterns as a System 265

11. **Counter Example:** Finding an example or "exception to the rule" that challenges or enriches the generalization defined by the belief. [See Chapter 6, pp. 167-174.]

> e.g., *"Most other mental processes (such as old memories) seem to become less intense and more susceptible to distortion and change the longer we have them, rather than become stronger. What makes beliefs so different?"*
>
> *"I have seen many beliefs established and changed instantaneously when people are provided with the appropriate experiences and support."*

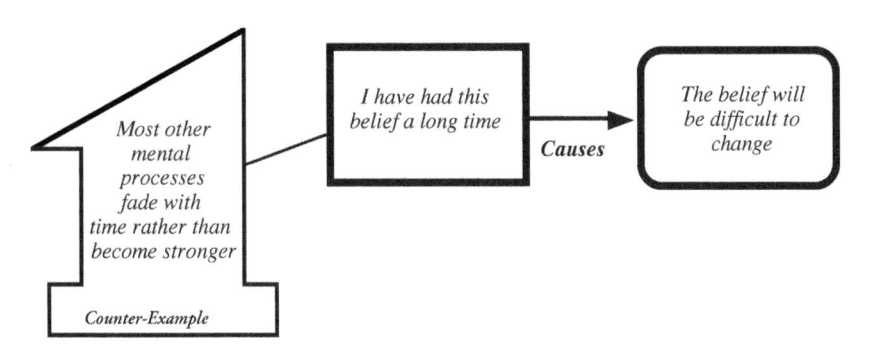

```
┌─────────────────┐              ╭─────────────────╮
│ I have had this │              │ The belief will │
│ belief a long   │─── Causes ──▶│ be difficult to │
│ time            │              │ change          │
└─────────────────┘              ╰─────────────────╯
        │
  Most other
  mental
  processes
  fade with
  time rather than
  become stronger

  Counter-Example
```

Counter Example

12. **Hierarchy of Criteria:** Re-evaluating (or reinforcing) the belief according to a criterion that is more important than any addressed by the belief. [See Chapter 4, pp. 98-107.]

> e.g., *"The degree to which a belief fits with and supports one's vision and mission is more important than how long one has had the belief."*
>
> *"Personal congruence and integrity are worth whatever effort it takes to achieve them."*

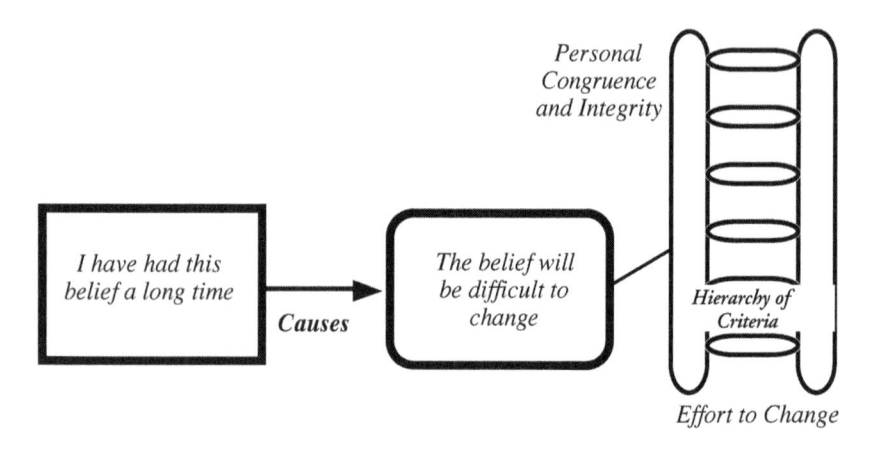

Hierarchy of Criteria

13. **Apply to Self:** Evaluating the belief statement itself according to the relationship or criteria defined by the belief. [See Chapter 8, pp. 234-239.]

> e.g., *"How long have you held the opinion that the difficulty in changing beliefs is primarily a matter of time?"*
>
> *"How difficult do you think it would be to change your belief that long held generalizations are difficult to change?"*

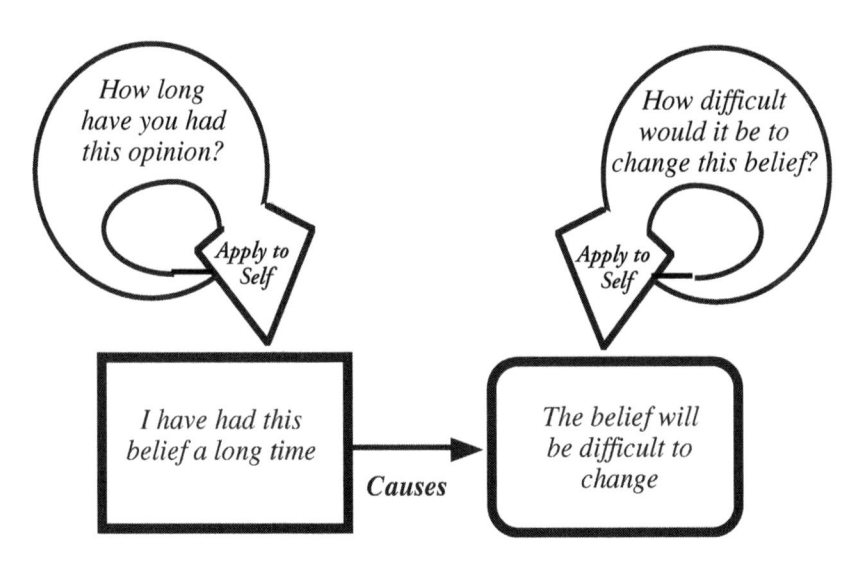

Apply to Self

14. **Meta Frame:** Evaluating the belief from the frame of an ongoing, personally oriented context – *establishing a belief **about** the belief.* [See Chapter 8, pp. 240-242.]

> e.g., *"Perhaps you have the belief that beliefs are difficult to change, because you have previously lacked the tools and understanding necessary to change them easily."*
>
> *"Has it occurred to you that maybe your belief that this particular belief will be difficult to change is a good justification for staying the way you are? Maybe there is something that you like, or a part of you likes, about the way you are now."*

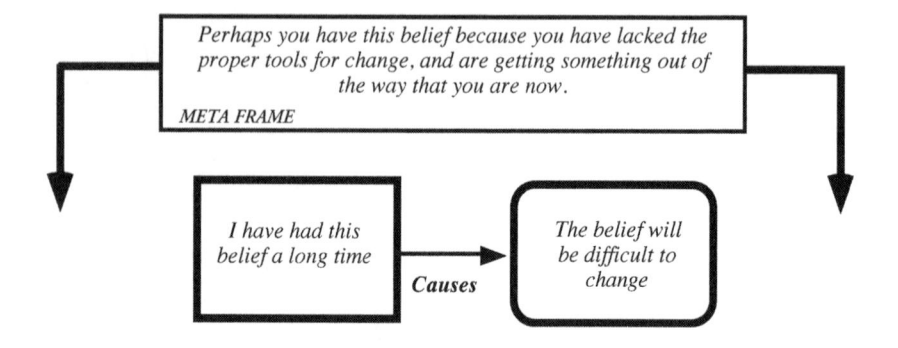

Perhaps you have this belief because you have lacked the proper tools for change, and are getting something out of the way that you are now.
META FRAME

| I have had this belief a long time | → Causes → | The belief will be difficult to change |

Meta Frame

… 269

The Sleight of Mouth Patterns as a System of Verbal Interventions

As the following diagram illustrates, the fourteen Sleight of Mouth Patterns form a system of interventions which may be applied to the cause-effect or complex equivalence statement at the foundation of a particular belief, in order to either become more 'open to doubt' or 'open to believe' that particular generalization.

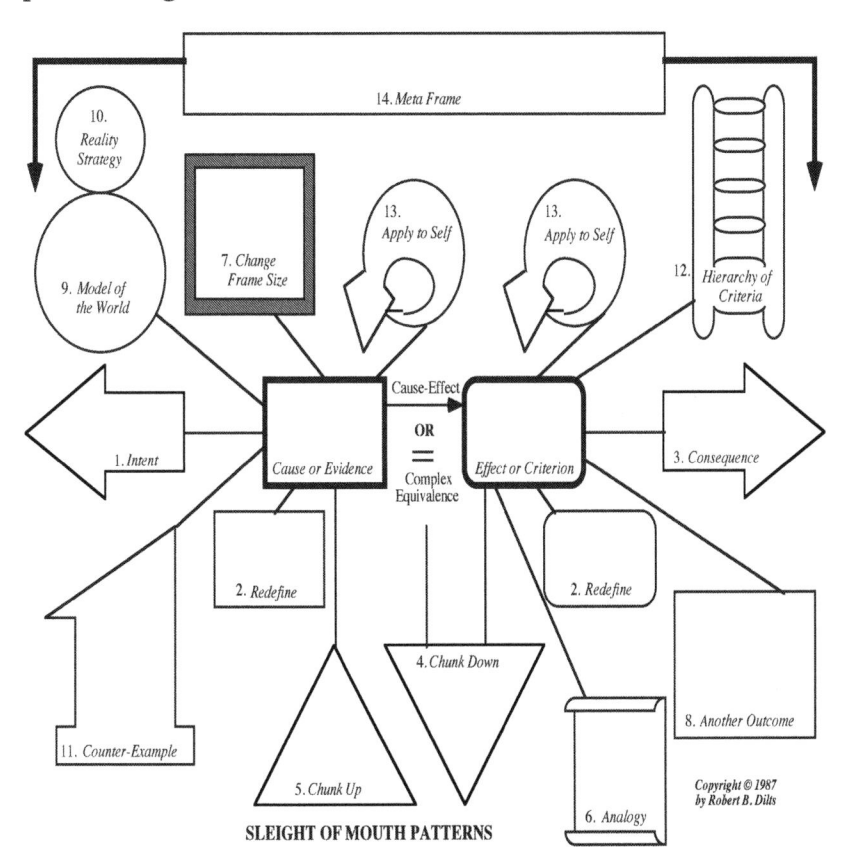

SLEIGHT OF MOUTH PATTERNS

Copyright © 1987 by Robert B. Dilts

The Whole System of Sleight of Mouth Patterns

Using of Sleight of Mouth as a System of Patterns

Thus far in this book, we have explored how individual Sleight of Mouth patterns may be applied in order to help people become more 'open to doubt' limiting beliefs and generalizations, and to become more 'open to believe' empowering beliefs and generalizations. Often, a simple Sleight of Mouth statement can make a big difference in helping to shift a person's attitude and responses. Consider the example of the woman who had just received news that she had an "unusual" form of cancer, and that, consequently, the doctors were not certain how to treat it. Fearing the worst, the woman was anxious and distraught over the situation. She consulted an NLP practitioner, who pointed out to her that, "In unusual circumstances, unusual things can happen" (applying the generalization to itself). This simple statement helped her to shift her perspective such that she could view uncertainty as a possible advantage, not necessarily a problem. The woman began to take more self-directed action, and was given more freedom of choice by her doctors, because her situation was "unusual." The woman went on to have a remarkable recovery (also "unusual") with minimal intervention from her doctors, completely regaining her health.

Frequently, however, Sleight of Mouth interventions require the application of a number of Sleight of Mouth patterns in order to address various aspects of a limiting belief. This is especially true when one is confronting a "thought virus." In fact, thought viruses themselves are typically 'held in place' by the application of Sleight of Mouth in order to ward off attempts to change them.

As an illustration, my first conscious recognition of the structure of the various Sleight of Mouth patterns emerged in 1980, during a seminar I was doing in Washington D.C.

with NLP co-founder Richard Bandler. One of the phenomena that Bandler was exploring at the time was the experience of *going over threshold*. The phenomenon of "crossing threshold" occurs when a person, who has been in very intense and meaningful relationships with another person for an extended period, suddenly breaks off all contact with the other individual, determined to never see or speak to him or her again. This usually results from the other person crossing some line that is the "last straw" with respect to their relationship. In order to congruently end the relationship "for good," people would need to somehow delete or reframe the many positive experiences that they had shared with the other persons. In a process that Bandler termed "flipping their pictures," people would do a type of negative reframing with respect to their memories of the relationship. All of the negative memories, attributes and habits that the person had previously overlooked would come into the foreground of people's awareness, while the positive ones would recede into the background.

This process had a structure similar to a "thought virus" in that it could not be easily reversed by experience or argument. The person would expend a great deal of effort to maintain their memories of the relationship within a 'problem frame'. Bandler began to explore whether it was possible to "reverse" this process after it had happened; in order to, hopefully, create the possibility for a renewed and healthier relationship.

A person—we'll call him "Ben"— had volunteered to be a demonstration subject. Ben was struggling in his relationship, and had been thinking about breaking up with his girlfriend. Ben tended to blame his girlfriend for all of the troubles in the relationship, and seemed intent on "making her wrong" and ending the relationship. Bandler (who was having difficulties in his own marriage at the time) was interested in trying to help Ben resolve his issues, and, perhaps, save the relationship.

As it turned out, it was not so easy to convince Ben to give his girlfriend and their relationship another chance. Even though he wanted to be a cooperative demonstration subject, Ben was quite creative at thwarting every option, possibility, or reason that Bandler brought up as to why Ben might reconsider his opinions about his girlfriend and their relationship. Ben was convinced that his mental map of the situation was right, claiming that he had "tested it" over and over.

Rather than become frustrated, Richard decided to "turn the tables" and put Ben, and the rest of the audience, metaphorically into the position of the girlfriend, in order to see how they might resolve it.

The seminar was taking place in a hotel room. As is quite common, Richard and Ben were working together up on a temporary stage, made up of several elevated platforms pieced together to make one larger platform. The legs of one of the smaller platforms was somewhat unstable, however. When Bandler had first stepped onto it, the platform buckled, causing him to stumble. A person from the audience—let's call him "Vic"—came rushing up to Bandler's aid, and reset the leg on the platform. Unfortunately, the leg still did not function properly, and when Bandler returned to that portion of the stage after interacting with Ben for a while, the corner of the platform buckled again, causing Richard to stumble once more.

When Vic came up again to reset the platform leg, Bandler, who has a flare for the outrageous, perceived an opportunity to create a ridiculous situation, paralleling the one that Ben had made with respect to his girlfriend. Richard began to create a kind of 'paranoid' scenario, in which he was being purposefully hurt by Vic. In order to maintain his paranoid 'thought virus', Bandler applied many of the principles and verbal reframing techniques covered in this book, oriented toward a 'problem frame'.

The improvisational drama went something like this:

Transcript

Richard Bandler: The person that put this (platform) back together, get out. Never again will I trust you. (To Ben) He had his chance, and didn't test it well enough. I'll never trust him again. See, he doesn't care about my future. That's the only sense I can make out of what has happened. He doesn't care if I break my leg, does he? I'm not going to let him do anything for me ever again. I mean, what sense can you make out of the fact that he put that platform back up there again, and I got hurt. Either he's incompetent and stupid, or he did it deliberately. And in either case I don't want anything to do with the guy. I'm just going to get hurt. If it's not that, it will be something else anyway. How could he do that to me?
(To Vic) Why do you want to hurt me? Huh?

Vic: I don't.

Bandler establishes the limiting belief in the form of cause-effect and complex equivalence statements which create a 'failure frame' and a 'problem frame': "Vic did something that caused me to be hurt several times. He will do it again. That means he intends to hurt me and that I cannot trust him."

RB: Well then why did you do that to me?

Vic: Uh, I . . . I set it up so that you would learn that that thing is solid as a rock now.
In order to "play along," Vic intuitively tries to link the generalization to a positive consequence.

RB: But what if it's not, what if I fall and break my leg?
Bandler focuses on the possibility of a counter example to Vic's claim, exaggerating the potential danger.

Vic: It's all right, it's solid as a rock.

RB: So you want me to go out there and risk my life.
Bandler 'chunks up' the consequence of "getting hurt" to "breaking my leg" to "risking my life."

Vic: If I risk my life first, is it all right?
Vic attempts a form of 'apply to self'.

RB: Do you know how many times I have to walk on that compared to you? I tested it the last time you know and it was fine and then I stepped on it and, boom, there I was. It fell all over again.
Bandler widens the 'frame size' in order to maintain the 'problem frame' and reestablish the possibility of a negative counter example.

Vic: You stepped on the right part. It's a weird setup.
Vic 'chunks down', trying to 'outframe' the counter example, claiming that the problem only relates to a certain part of the stage.

RB: Yeh, it is. I just don't understand. It doesn't make any sense to me. It blows my mind that anyone would do that to me. See I thought you were somebody that was trying to help me the first time you did it. At first, you know, that was one thing. It looked nice and everything. I had no idea what you were trying to do to me.

Bandler chunks back up to the whole sequence of the interaction, focusing on Vic's 'intention', which has the effect of shifting the 'outcome' around which the discussion is centered.

Man #1: As long as you avoid stages in the future, everything will be okay.

Man #1 paces Bandler's 'problem frame' and large chunk size.

RB: See he's trying to help me. I can't get anything out of him (pointing to Vic). All he's telling me is "go do it again". Right? But at least he (points to Man #1) is telling me what I have to watch out for. And, you know, that may not be the only thing I should be worried about, there may be others. (To Ben) See he (Man #1) is on my side, huh?

Bandler takes the man's comment as confirmation of the problem frame and limiting belief, and widens the 'frame size' to include others that may have a 'bad intention'.

Ben: (Catching on to the metaphor) I think he is... I'm not sure yet.

RB: Well, he may be telling me to go too far, but he's got good intentions. This guy Vic, on

Bandler continues to focus on the pattern of 'good' intentions versus 'bad intentions'.

the other hand, he's trying to get me to go out there, did you hear him? He wants me to go out there and do it again.

Ben: Well, I'm surprised he hasn't gotten up and walked on it yet.

Ben also paces Bandler's problem frame, pointing out the Vic's behavior is counter example to his claim that he is not negatively intended and believes the stage is "solid as a rock."

RB: Yeah, I know. I noticed that too. It never occurred to him to take the darn thing and move it away. Now I really know he's trying to hurt me. What do you think about that? This guy comes to my seminar and tries to kill me. And he's still trying. He's trying to convince me that it's not some kind of setup.

Bandler uses Ben's confirmation of the limiting belief as an opportunity to 'chunk up' Vic's 'negative intention' from "hurting me" to "trying to kill me," shifting it toward the level of 'identity'.

Ben: You've given him all these opportunities to prove to you that he isn't out to get you.

Ben continues to 'pace' Bandler's belief statement, 'chunking up' the 'counter example' to challenge Vic's assertion that he is not negatively intended.

Applying the Patterns as a System

RB: Yeh, I did; opportunity, after opportunity to try to do something.

Bandler continues to chunk up as well.

Ben: And he's not doing anything. He's just sitting there.

The counter example is reframed into a 'consequence' which affirms Bandler's negative belief.

Man #2: Why do you think he thought he had to put the piece back there rather than move it away?

Man #2 attempts to 'meta frame' part of Bandler's limiting belief, in order to point out a possible assumption.

RB: I don't know why he did it. Maybe he doesn't like me. Maybe he wants to hurt me. Maybe he just doesn't think about what he'll do in the future that would hurt me. Maybe it just never occurred to him that I could really get hurt. And I don't want to hang around someone that's going to do that.

Bandler maintains the problem frame by widening the possible causes of Vic's behavior from his 'negative intention' to also include his 'limited model of the world'.

Woman #1: Yeh, but if he didn't think in the future what might happen, he probably didn't do it deliberately.

Woman #1 tries to use Bandler's response as a possible counter example to his belief about Vic's negative intention.

RB: If he didn't think about my future, then he won't next time, and then he's going to

Bandler switches the focus from 'intention' to 'consequence' in order to maintain the problem frame.

get me in some situation where I'm really going to get burned.

Man #2: But you only have one example so you don't know that for certain.

Man #2 attempts to find a counter example by 'chunking down'.

RB: He did it twice! And I gave him a whole bunch of choices about how to do something to prove to me that he wasn't trying to hurt me. He said he would walk on it and "risk his life" first. Did he do it? No. He didn't do it. I also suggested that he take it away. He didn't do that either. He doesn't care about me. He doesn't give a damn. He's going to leave it there until I walk on it and fall over.

Bandler chunks back up —claiming to have offered Vic "a whole bunch of choices"—and 'redefines' Vic's lack of response as a demonstration that Vic "doesn't care," connecting it again to a negative consequence. (Bandler deletes the fact that he told Vic his offer to walk on the stage first was not "proof" of his intentions.)

Woman #1: Why don't you both turn the platform over and make sure it works right. Have him work with you to test it.

Woman #1 attempts to establish a cooperative 'feedback frame' and shift to another outcome: 'testing' the platform to make sure it 'works right'..

RB: So you want me to try and get together to work with him, and turn it over, and then I'm going to be the one who's going to stand on it for the next three or four days.

Bandler again widens the frame size (beyond the present instance to "the next three of four days") in order to discount the potential solution. He then

You're on his side. I knew you were with him all along. See you're sitting on the same side of the room that he is.	*'meta frames' the woman's attempt to find a solution as being an evidence of her conspiring with Vic (using the fact that they are sitting on the same side of the room as a confirming consequence.)*
Woman #1: Then I'll do it with him. . . Oh, you don't trust me because you think we (she and Vic) are allies.	*Woman #1 realizes that a consequence of Bandler's 'meta frame' is that it potentially discounts any further attempt she may make to challenge his belief.*
RB: Oh yeh, trying to make me look paranoid now, huh? He (Vic) put you up to this didn't he?	*Bandler deepens the problem frame by asserting a negative consequence of Woman #1's statement.*
Woman #2: What do you want at this point?	*Woman #2 makes a direct attempt at establishing an outcome frame, focusing on the immediate future.*
RB: I don't want anything. I didn't want it (the stage) back there in the first place. It's too late now.	*Bandler reasserts the problem frame, shifting the frame back to the past.*
Woman #2: You're not willing to give him another chance?	*Woman #2 makes another direct attempt; this time to establish a feedback frame.*

RB: He had his chance. He not only had his chance, I gave him a bunch of them. And he didn't take them. How can you make sense of it? He just doesn't care. I didn't know I was going to fall down. I didn't know he would come in the morning and bend the leg. I don't know what this guy is going to try to do to me. Put him outside of the room.

Bandler again 'chunks up', extending the consequences of his 'paranoid' belief.

Man #1: I think you (Bandler) should leave because he might hide outside.

Man #1 paces Bandler's problem frame (and his assertion about Vic's negative intention), widening it to include Vic's future behavior as well.

RB: Maybe I should hide.

Man #3: What makes you think you can trust him (indicating Man #1)?

Man #3 shifts to 'another outcome', questioning the authenticity of Man #1.

RB: Well, he'd do the same thing I'd do.

Man #3: Maybe he (Vic) is a shill. It's a possibility.

Man #3 proposes a more 'positive' meta frame of Vic's behavior.

RB: Why are you making excuses for him? (Looking at the people he has disagreed with.) They're all on the front row, every one of them.

Bandler 'redefines' Man #3's meta frame as an "excuse" for Vic's behavior, and continues to widen the paranoid problem frame.

Woman #2: It's mass action. The mob is taking over.	*Woman #2 attempts to 'chunk up' and broaden the frame size in order to exaggerate the belief and draw the generalization into question.*
RB: Oh. See, she's trying to make me look paranoid too.	*Bandler places a 'meta frame' around Woman #2's comment, claiming the woman has a negative intention.*
Woman #2: No, I'm concerned about why you feel that all of these people are against you.	*Woman #2 attempts to redefine her intention to one that is positive.*
RB: Don't give me that. (To Vic) Now, see all the trouble you've caused. (To Audience) See I told you he was trying to get people to hurt each other. (To Vic) What kind of a human being are you? See you got these two people to fight with each other, and are forcing everybody to take sides.	*Bandler widens the frame, shifting attention back to Vic, and reasserting Vic's negative intention and the negative consequences of Vic's behavior.*
Man #4: He's awfully clever to be doing it in such a round about way.	*Man #4 suggests a shift to a different focus of attention which may open .*
RB: He's a smart person, man.	
Man #4: Can we out smart him?	*Man #4 attempts to shift focus to the future and to an outcome frame.*

RB: I don't know. He got me once. He got me twice. God knows who else he's gotten.

Bandler changes the time frame back to the past, widening the problem frame to include others besides himself.

Man #4: If you're careful of him maybe you could use his diabolical genius.

Man #4 attempts to redefine Vic's 'negative intention' as "diabolical genius" and put it into the outcome frame of "using it."

RB: It's not worth it. I just want to be around people and feel a little more secure about what's going on. There's plenty of good things in life without that kind of stuff, you know. What am I going to do?

Bandler switches to 'another outcome' relating to his (Bandler's) own "security," rather than Vic's "cleverness", in order to reestablish a problem frame.

Man #4: Well, as long as he's here you can watch him.

Man #4 attempts to narrow the time frame size to the ongoing situation in order to satisfy the outcome of "security."

RB: I am watching him. When is it all going to end?

Bandler expands the frame beyond the present, implying he will be insecure again later.

Vic: I'll move it over here. (Begins to move the small platform away.)

Vic attempts to create a counter example to Bandler's generalization by complying with his request to move the stage.

RB: Why is he trying to make me look stupid? See, now he's trying to make it look like nothing happened. So he can do it again. So he can make it look to other people like he really did put it back safely and everything's cool. What am I going to do? I don't trust him. Should I just cut him off and never communicate with him again? Probably be the best thing huh? He may do the same thing to me again. See, he's even still sitting there.

Bandler meta frames Vic's action as an attempt to discredit him and make it look as if he is safe. Bandler uses this frame as a confirmation of Vic's negative intention, and a justification for lack of trust with respect to Vic and potential negative consequences in the future.

Woman #3: But you haven't had the right interaction with him to trust him.

Woman #3 tries to establish another meta frame around Bandler's generalization, claiming that his conclusion is drawn from limited experience.

RB: But I don't want to have any interaction with him.

Bandler "collapses" the meta frame by applying his conclusion to the terms of the meta frame, creating a kind of 'circular argument'—i.e., "I don't trust him because I haven't had the right interaction with him; and I don't want to interact with him because I don't trust him."

Man #1: I don't blame you.

RB: I mean... even if you'd bring in a new stage, I would only be safe for a while. Maybe he'll go cut the leg on the other side. What do I know?

Bandler changes the frame size again to include longer term negative consequences in the future, discounting any solution in the present.

Woman #3: How do you know that he set that up in advance?

Woman #3 attempts to establish Bandler's 'reality strategy' for forming his generalization about Vic's intention.

RB: Well, I don't know, but that's not the point. The point is that he let that happen to me and he set it up so that it would happen again. Even if he didn't mean it, it did happen. He's the one that's making me feel this way now. You see, I'm terrified.

Bandler does not address the question, immediately shifting to 'another outcome', focusing on the negative consequences of Vic's behavior on his (Bandler's) internal state rather than Vic's intention.

Woman #3: How is he making you feel that way?

Woman #3 again attempts to 'chunk down' the cause-effect generalization "making," and establish the internal 'equivalences' or strategies Bandler is applying in order to form his generalization.

RB: That's not the point. The point is that I feel this way. If he hadn't done those things, I wouldn't feel bad.

Bandler shifts the focus from the cause-effect generalization to the consequences related to his internal state.

Now I have to continue to feel this way. I tried to give him a chance to do something about it but it failed.

Woman #4: Can you remember things you did with him that you enjoy? I mean, even if you don't like him now.

Woman #4 tries to lead Bandler to identify past positive counter examples related to his internal state and interactions with Vic.

RB: Yeh. Sure those things are there. But I can't have any of those in the future. Not feeling this way, it would be impossible. I just can't be that person with him anymore. See I've changed in the last six months.
(To audience) What are you going to do, leave me this way? Because if you can't fix me, I'm just going to have to go away. I won't be able to teach anymore workshops today, tomorrow, never. He might come to one; under a different name. I don't want to ever have seminar participants ever again. Oh God. Don't leave me this way.

Bandler shifts the frame to his current negative internal state, and the expected negative consequences of that state on his future (shifting it from a behavior level to an identity level).
Bandler continues to chunk up and widen the frame size, redefining the situation as one related to "fixing me," rather than addressing Vic's actions.

Woman #3: Is this the way you want to be?

Woman #3 makes another attempt to directly establish an outcome frame, oriented toward a more positive future.

RB: I don't want to be like this. I want to be the way I was.	*Bandler returns to a problem frame and shifts the frame back to the past.*
Woman #3: How were you? Tell me.	*Woman #3 tries to use the past as a resource to establish an outcome frame.*
RB: I used to be confident and happy. I liked people, and trusted people. I'm not like that anymore. See what he did to me? (To Vic) See what you're doing to me? (To Audience) But I can't do anything else. Because you won't help me.	*Bandler shifts from the past to the present, in order to maintain the problem frame.*
Woman #3: Do you mean you can't do anything else or you won't do anything else?	*Woman #3 attempts to redefine "can't" to "won't," implying that Bandler has more choice, at the level of capability, than he is acknowledging.*
RB: What difference does it make? I don't know what to do.	*Bandler uses a type of 'hierarchy of criteria', asserting that it does not matter if one has choices if one does not know "what to do."*
Man #4: What he wanted to do to you is put you in the state you're in now.	*Man #4 attempts to redefine (or 'chain') Bandler's "problem" from the level of identity ("I am not the way I used to be") to the level of*

RB: I know. He just wants to feel superior to me. There are a lot of leader killers. I used to think I could really take care of myself, and defend myself, but people can set traps like that. I used to be the kind of person that thought that everybody had positive intentions. I used to think good things about everybody, but I learned my lesson now. I got hurt, and I got hurt worse than I thought I could, and look what it has done to me. Now I have realized that there are people that would do things to hurt me. It's really not worth it. Can't someone help me?

behavioral response ("the state you are in now").

Bandler places the problem back at the level of identity (Vic is a "leader killer"), and uses it as a way to strongly reestablish and expand, or 'chunk up', his problem frame.

Creating and Maintaining a 'Thought Virus' Using Sleight of Mouth

This type of dialog between Bandler and the audience went on for quite some time, with no progress. It was clear that Bandler's primary intention for the demonstration was to maintain the problem frame, at all costs. His responses were not really about the content of the belief he had chosen. He successfully 'outframed' every intervention that people proposed as an attempt to help him find some solution.

As long as Bandler was able to control the "frame," he was able to determine the outcome of the interaction. He succeeded in placing the audience in a double bind that went something like: "If you do not try to help me, you are wrong; but if you try to help me, you are wrong." It was excruciating for some people, and frustrating for others. [In fact, in response to Bandler's continued question, "Can't someone help me?", a woman finally responded, "Can I get you some chicken soup?"]

As the interactions continued, however, I became aware that there was a structure to what Richard was doing; one that I could repeat. I realized that, while the content of the interaction was different, at the level of 'deep structure' it was a dialog that I had encountered many times before, with many different people. It was a way of creating and maintaining a "thought virus" by negatively reframing or 'outframing' attempts to put the limiting belief back into an outcome frame, feedback frame or 'as if' frame.

I became aware, for instance, that Bandler was systematically changing the frame and frame size to focus on whichever one(s) were not being addressed by the intervention attempted by the audience. It was also obvious that when people tried to 'pace' the problem frame, or negative formulation of the intention behind the belief, in the attempt to get 'rapport' with Bandler, it just got them into deeper trouble.

I also realized that Bandler was systematically (though intuitively) using language patterns that I had been getting a sense for as a result of my study of important historical and political figures, such as Socrates, Jesus, Karl Marx, Abraham Lincoln, Hitler, Gandhi, and others (to be presented in volume II of this work). It became obvious to me that these patterns could be used to either defend or challenge particular beliefs and generalizations.

This new awareness brought me to the threshold of what is known as the "unconscious uptake" stage of modeling in NLP. The next step was to attempt to formalize the patterns that I had begun to sense. Before I could do that, I had to intentionally try out the patterns myself to see if I could replicate Bandler's performance to some degree. A key condition of effective modeling in NLP is that we must first internalize the capability we are modeling, before formalizing it into relevant distinctions. Otherwise we are simply making a description, reflecting the 'surface structure' of the process, rather than making a model of the deeper intuitions necessary to generate the capability.

The opportunity arose for me in an advanced NLP program in Chicago about a month later. On the third day of the program, I decided to inform the group that I would illustrate a challenging new set of patterns for them. The following is a transcript (with commentary) of my own "tongue in cheek" improvisational drama, modeled after Bandler:

> R: Who tied this microphone to me? Jim? Where's Jim? He's after me. He's in the bathroom? He's probably in there plotting against me. He's tied this thing to me . . . and you've all seen how I trip over it all the time. He wants me to trip on it and hurt myself, and lose my credibility as a teacher, and make you laugh at me. He's out to get me. I mean, that's pretty obvious isn't it? Will someone help me? He's going to be back in here in a few minutes. (Establishes limiting belief: *"Jim did some-*

thing that caused me to be hurt and possibly humiliated. Because it has happened before, it will happen again. He intends to hurt me and I am in danger.")

P1: Why do you let him tie it to you if he is after you? (Counter Example: Inconsistency between the logical consequences of R's stated belief and behavior.)

R: Because he knows that you are all in here and if I tried to stop him from putting the microphone on me you would all think I was paranoid and he would have succeeded in discrediting me in front of all of you. (Meta Frame: "It would look strange for me to try to stop him." Consequence: "You would think I was paranoid")

P1: So if he didn't tie that microphone to you he wouldn't be making a fool of you? (Chunks up and Redefines "tripping on the wire and losing credibility" to "being made a fool of." Attempts to trigger a reevaluation of the belief by asserting a consequence of the redefined belief statement: "Since putting on the wire is what makes a fool of you, then if you didn't have the wire you would not be made a fool of.")

R: Why are you asking so many questions? (To the rest of the audience). You know what? He's wearing a blue shirt and blue jeans and Jim is wearing a blue shirt and blue jeans. Are you on his side?! I'm starting to get nervous about all those questions he's asking me . . . Come on you guys, you have to help me, the conspiracy is growing. (Meta Frame: You are asking those questions and attempting to challenge my belief because you are conspiring with Jim.)

P2: I agree with you. He is probably trying to embarrass you in front of all these people. (Pacing Problem Frame.)

R: He is! And since you have brains enough to recognize how dangerous the situation is, help me out. OK. I need help with this right away. Do something right now! (Consequence: "Since you agree with me, you should do something right now.")

P2: What do you think Jim's trying to do? (Attempting to find positive intention.)

R: I already told you what he's trying to do! He's trying to get me! (Refocusing on negative intention.)

P2: What do you think his purpose is? (Chunking up further to seek a positive intention.)

R: I told you. He wants to hurt me. He wants to make a fool of me. (Chunking up the negative intention to a consequence on the identity level: "make a fool of me.")

P2: What will that get for him? (Seeking a positive intention by shifting to Another Outcome.)

R: I don't know what he's getting out of it. The man is obviously crazy. Maybe in his map of the world it is alright to hurt other people in order to elevate yourself. (Uses the frame of a different Model of the World to chain to a negative intention.)

P2: Well then maybe we ought to call the hospital. (Focusing on a consequence of the judgment "crazy" in order to attempt to establish an outcome frame.)

R: Well don't just sit there giving me advice, go call the hospital for me and have them take him away. (A subtle version of applying the belief to itself by directing the consequence of the belief statement back to the speaker.

This also serves to deflect the outcome frame back to the speaker, so R is able to maintain the problem frame.)

P2: Let's call them together. (Attempts to widen the frame to involve R.)

R: No, you have to do it for me. If I called the hospital they would probably think I was crazy. Since you understand me, I know you'll help me by calling them for me. (Meta Frame: A third party has more credibility. They will think I'm paranoid, because I will be saying that it is happening to me.)

P2: What would make them think you were crazy? (Going to their Model of the World and Chunking Down, in order to find possible options or Counter Examples.)

R: Give me a break, you know why they'll think that! (Reasserting the Meta Frame in the form of a presupposition: "You already know why.")

P2: I don't think you're crazy. (Attempting to provide an ongoing Counter Example.)

R: That's beside the point. I need help right now! (Shifting to Another Outcome: "I need help now.")

P3: What would happen if you stopped monkeying around with the microphone chord? (Using the cause-effect generalization asserted by the belief to shift attention to the influence of R's own behavior.)

R: (Suspiciously) What are you asking me that for? (Meta Frame:"Your implication that I should change my behavior means you are against me.")

P4: (Laughing) She's weird. I'd watch out for her too.

R: Yeh . . . Jim wears glasses and she's wearing them too. What am I going to do? Won't someone help me?! (Widening the frame size.)

P5: What could Jim do so you wouldn't feel he was after you? (Seeking a basis for counter examples to the limiting belief about Jim.)

R: I don't want to feel any differently about him. I just want to get rid of him. I already know he's after me. Look! Here's evidence! (Holds out microphone chord). Can't you see it? You don't deny that this is cold hard evidence do you? It's right here. Help me. (Asserting the presupposition that Jim is out to get R, Chunking Down to focus on the microphone chord as evidence.)

P6: Well first let's get the microphone off of you; and then go talk to Jim about it. You need immediate relief right? (Attempting to establish an outcome frame in relation to the microphone chord and Jim's intention.)

R: But if I take the microphone off he'll just do something else. That's just treating the symptom. He's put this thing on me consistently every day. What makes you think that taking the microphone off will stop him? (Changes the frame size by expanding the time frame in order to refocus on the problem frame and the consequences of Jim's 'negative intention'.)

P5: What do you need in order to know that he's not after you? (Attempting to Chunk Down to define the Reality Strategy for the belief about Jim's intention, and establish possible Counter Examples.)

R: Why do you keep trying to convince me that he's not after me?! I can already prove that he is after me. I don't want to be convinced that he isn't after me. That would just get me in trouble. (Meta Frame: "To try to change my belief that he is after me would have negative consequences.")

P7: What do you want us to help you accomplish? (Attempting to establish an Outcome Frame directly.)

R: I just want to be protected...to be safe from him. And I can't do it by myself. I need help. (Using a slightly negative formulation of the outcome in order to maintain the problem frame.)

P8: (Vehemently) Yes, but you noticed that this wire was out here all the time. That's the first step you can take for your own safety! (Using a Consequence of R's belief to try to establish a feedback frame—indirectly applying the belief to itself—and bring R out of a 'victim' position.)

R: It really makes me nervous when someone starts yelling at me. (Meta Framing the comment to place attention on the consequence of the non verbal portion of the statement on R's internal state.)

P7: How would you know when you were safe from Jim? (Attempting to establish an outcome frame and a feedback frame by Chunking Down and establishing the Criterial Equivalence for 'safety'.)

R: I can't be safe as long as he's out there. Get rid of him for me right now. (Chunking back up and reasserting the problem frame and its consequence.)

Applying the Patterns as a System

P9: What is it doing for you to still keep the wire on, even though its dangerous? (Chunking back down and shifting focus from Jim to the "wire," and seeking R's intention in order to establish an outcome frame. "Not safe" has also been redefined as "dangerous.")

R: The microphone is only dangerous when I walk. The point is that its just another way that Jim is trying to get me. (Meta Framing and changing the frame size in order to shift attention away from the microphone chord and back to Jim's negative intention.)

P9: So the wire lets you know he's trying to get you? (Chunking down to check the Reality Strategy for how the wire and the generalization regarding Jim's intention are connected.)

R: The wire doesn't let me know anything. I already know he's after me. Are you trying to confuse me? (to audience) I think she's crazy. (To P9) I'm confused so you must be crazy . . . Come on you people are supposed to be NLP Practitioners. Why don't you help me? (Putting attention fully in Jim's negative intention as the cause of the "danger." Making a 'complex equivalence' between R's internal state—"I'm confused—and a judgment about the other person—"you must be crazy." Also, R is placing responsibility for his problem state on the audience.)

P6: (Laughing) I'm starting to get scared of Jim too.

R: And rightfully so. (To audience) He's the only one of you that's got any brains. He's going to get rid of Jim for me. (Asserting a problem consequence of accepting R's problem frame.)

P10: If his tying you up means that he's after you then . . . (Redefines the problem with the microphone as being "tied up.")

R: No. You are missing the whole point. He's not 'tying me up'. He knows that in the course of the program I'll eventually trip on the wire. (Challenging the redefinition.)

P10: And the only way you can stop that is by getting rid of him? (Checking for Counter Examples.)

R: Right!

P10: So maybe its a good thing you have that chord tied around you so you don't get mad and kill him. (Redefines "getting rid of" as "killing" and attempts to establish a positive consequence with respect to the wire.)

R: I don't want to kill him! I just want to be protected from him. What are you trying to do, make a murderer out of me? See?! What Jim has been doing to discredit me is working. He's got you thinking that I'm out to get HIM. (Meta Frame: "Your redefinition of "getting rid of him" to "killing him" is a reinforcement of my limiting belief and problem frame.)

As the transcript illustrates, I was able to recapitulate, to a certain degree, what Bandler had done in the program in Washington D.C. It was upon my return from this seminar that I explicitly formulated the fourteen patterns comprising the system of Sleight of Mouth patterns, based upon what I had been able to internalize intuitively from Bandler's performance.

Sleight of Mouth and the Law of Requisite Variety

These initial experiences with Sleight of Mouth, made it clear to me that the ability to either maintain or outframe a particular belief is essentially an application of the *Law of Requisite Variety* to belief systems. According to the Law of Requisite Variety, if you want to consistently get to a particular goal state, you have to increase the number of options available for reaching that goal in proportion to the degree of potential variability (including possible resistances) in the system. That is, it is important to have variations in operations used to accomplish goals—even if those operations have produced successful results in the past—because systems are prone to change and variation.

It is often claimed that "if you always do what you've always done, you will always get what you've always got." But it is not necessarily true that you will even "get what you have always got." Doing the same thing does not always produce the same result if the surrounding system changes. It is obvious that if there is a traffic jam or road work blocking your typical route to work, you will not get there on time if you 'do what you've always done'. Instead you must find alternative routes. Taxi drivers in big cities often know a variety of ways to get to the airport or to a particular street in case there is some type of obstruction on the usual route.

The necessity of 'requisite variety' is probably nowhere more evident than in the basic biology of our bodies. The biological killers that plague us today are not dangerous because of their strength, but because of their 'requisite variety'; and our lack of requisite variety to regulate them. What makes cancer dangerous is its degree of variation and adaptability. Cancer cells are quickly changing cells that are able to adapt rapidly to different environments. Cancer becomes life threatening when our immune systems are unable to produce the regulatory variety necessary to identify and effectively 'absorb' proliferating cancer cells. The field of oncology has been stymied in its attempt to treat cancer because cancer cells have more requisite variety than the powerful chemical poisons and radiation treatments being used in the attempt to destroy them. At the beginning, these treatments are able to effectively kill many cancer cells (along with many healthy cells as well, unfortunately). Variations of the cancer cells, however, are eventually produced that are resistant to that treatment; leading to a reoccurrence of the cancer symptoms. Stronger and more deadly chemicals are tried, until a point is reached in which the therapy becomes life threatening to the patient, and no more can be done to help medically.

The AIDS virus produces similar problems. Like cancer, the AIDS virus is extremely flexible and adaptable, making it difficult to treat with chemotherapy. The virus itself effects the immune system reducing its flexibility. It should be noted that the AIDS virus does not destroy a person's entire immune system. It only influences parts of it. People with AIDS still fend off many infections and diseases every day. What AIDS influences is the immune system's adaptability. Recent studies have shown that in a healthy person's body, roughly half of the immune system cells are 'preprogrammed' to respond to specific illnesses. The other half are not yet programmed to respond to anything in particular, leaving them available to adapt to new challenges. In the bodies of people who have AIDS, that ratio changes such that approximately 80% of the immune cells are preprogrammed and only 20% are non-specific and free to learn and adapt to new situations. The cells that are effected by the AIDS virus are the ones that give the immune system its 'requisite variety'.

An implication of the Law of Requisite Variety is that these illnesses would be most effectively treated by increasing the regulatory variety of the immune system. A healthy immune system is essentially an effective learning organization. In fact, people who have natural immunity to AIDS appear to already possess an immune system that has the 'requisite variety' to address the virus. Thus, the issue is not so much the 'strength' of the immune system, but rather its degree of flexibility to respond.

If we extend this analogy to the notion of 'thought viruses', we begin to recognize that *the person with the most flexibility will be the one who directs the interaction.* Thus, Sleight of Mouth patterns are a way to increase the 'requisite variety' of those who wish to help transform or heal limiting beliefs and thought viruses, and to strengthen and promote empowering beliefs. Sleight of Mouth patterns provide a means to increase the flexibility of our psychological "immune systems." They help us to better understand the structure of the belief system that is holding a 'thought virus' in place, and to more creatively generate the responses and 'reframes' that will help to 'absorb' and transform those limiting beliefs.

Reframing and 'Outframing' a Thought Virus Using Sleight of Mouth

Once we are familiar with the system of beliefs that is holding a potential 'thought virus' in place, for instance, we are better able to find effective reframes which will help to place the limiting belief back into an outcome frame and feedback frame. The various Sleight of Mouth patterns can help us to approach the limiting system of beliefs in a more strategic (rather than reactionary) manner.

Let's consider how we can use the formalization of the Sleight of Mouth patterns as a way to more effectively deal with the paranoid 'thought virus' that we have been using as an example in this chapter. The essence of the limiting belief at the basis of this thought virus is something like:

"Person X did something that caused me to be hurt more than once. Because it has happened before, it will happen again. Person X intends to hurt me and I am in danger."

One of the best ways to both learn and apply Sleight of Mouth is by considering key questions relating to the various Sleight of Mouth patterns. In a way, each of the Sleight of Mouth patterns could be considered an answer to key questions leading to different perspectives and perceptual positions. The following examples illustrate how exploring the answers to key questions can be used to identify and form Sleight of Mouth reframes. The goal of these reframes is to find a way to reaffirm the speaker at the level of his or her identity and positive intention, and, at the same time, reformulate the belief to an outcome frame or feedback frame.

Applying the Patterns as a System   301

Limiting Belief: *"Person X did something that caused me to be hurt more than once. Because it has happened before, it will happen again. Person X intends to hurt me and I am in danger."*

1. **Intention:** What is the positive purpose or intention of this belief?

   There are many ways to begin to develop a sense of power and control when you are concerned for your safety.
   (Intention = "to begin to develop a sense of power and control")

   It is very important to take all the steps that you can to make sure that people act ethically and do the right thing.
   (Intention = "take steps to make sure that people act ethically and do the right thing")

2. **Redefining:** What is another word for one of the words used in the belief statement that means something similar but has more positive implications?

   I think you should do everything in your power to avoid being a victim.
   ("Person X intends to hurt me and I am in danger" => "I am a victim.")

   This is the kind of challenge that is necessary to face with courage, support and wisdom.
   ("Being in danger" => "a challenge")

Limiting Belief: *"Person X did something that caused me to be hurt more than once. Because it has happened before, it will happen again. Person X intends to hurt me and I am in danger."*

3. **Consequence:** What is a positive effect of the belief or the relationship defined by the belief?

It is going to be so much more difficult for you to be hurt again in the future now that you know how to recognize dangerous situations and ask for help. This is the first step toward being transformed from a victim into a hero.

Knowing what you know now will make it difficult for you to be taken advantage of again.

4. **Chunk Down:** What *smaller* elements or chunks are implied by the belief but have a richer or more positive relationship than the ones stated in the belief?

In order to deal with the situation effectively, it is important to determine whether the degree of danger gets greater with each instance of hurt, or if you are simply in the same degree of danger now as you were the first time you were hurt.

When you say that Person X "intends" to hurt you, do you mean that Person X makes a picture of doing something harmful to you in his or her head? If so, which part of that picture is most dangerous, and how does Person X get to the point of acting on that picture? What do you think put that picture in Person X's head?

5. **Chunk Up:** What *larger* elements or classes are implied by the belief but have a richer or more positive relationship than the ones stated in the belief?

Intense feelings are always the basis of our motivation to change. As Carl Jung said, "There is no coming into consciousness without pain."
("hurt" => "intense feelings," "pain")

Dealing with the discomfort we experience from facing life's risks is one of the ways that we become stronger and more competent human beings.
("hurt" => "discomfort"   "danger" => "life's risks")

6. **Analogy:** What is some other relationship which is analogous to that defined by the belief (a metaphor for the belief), but which has different implications?

Learning to master interpersonal relationships is like being able to pick ourselves up when we fell on our bicycles as children, putting the fact that we skinned our knees behind us, and having the determination to keep trying until we are able to achieve balance. Being angry with the bicycle for hurting us doesn't do much good.

Dealing with the intentions of others is a bit like being a bullfighter. To stay safe, we have to know what attracts the bull's attention to us, direct the attention of the bull, and learn to step out of the way when we see it starting to charge.

Limiting Belief: *"Person X did something that caused me to be hurt more than once. Because it has happened before, it will happen again. Person X intends to hurt me and I am in danger."*

7. **Change Frame Size:** What is a longer (or shorter) time frame, a larger number or smaller number of people, or a bigger or smaller perspective that would change the implications of the belief to be something more positive?

   How to deal with suffering at the hands of others is one of the most challenging problems still to be addressed and resolved by our species. Until we are able to do so with wisdom and compassion, there will continue to be violence, war, and genocide at a global as well as individual level.

   Everybody has to learn how to deal with the shadow side of their fellow human beings. I am sure that when you look back on this incident at the end of your life you will see it as a small bump on the road of your life.

8. **Another Outcome:** What other outcome or issue could be more relevant than the one stated or implied by the belief?

   The outcome is not so much how to avoid being hurt by a particular person as it is to develop the skills that you need in order to be safe no matter what other people think or do.

   To me, the issue is not so much about what a person's intention has been, but rather what it takes to make a person change his or her intention.

9. **Model of the World:** What is a different model of the world that would provide a very different perspective on this belief?

Sociobiologists would suggest that it is the evolutionary development of Person X's hormones, rather than what you or he believe to be his conscious intention, that is the source of your danger.

Imagine all of those people around the world who have to deal constantly with the reality of social oppression such as racism and religious persecution. They would probably welcome a situation in which they only had to deal with the negative intentions and actions of a single, identifiable person.

10. **Reality Strategy:** What cognitive perceptions of the world are necessary to have built this belief? How would one need to perceive the world in order for this belief to be true?

When you think of each instance of hurt do you relive each one again separately, or do they blend altogether? Do you recall them from your own associated perspective, or do you see them all edited together as if you were watching a type of documentary film of your life?

Is it your memories of the past events that are already over, or your imagination of possible future events that may or may not happen, which make you feel most in danger?

Limiting Belief: *"Person X did something that caused me to be hurt more than once. Because it has happened before, it will happen again. Person X intends to hurt me and I am in danger."*

11. **Counter Example:** What is an example or experience that is an exception to the rule defined by the belief?

    If only it were true that we did not need to worry about something occurring just because it had not happened before. We are probably in the greatest danger from the things that have not happened yet, and should work to prepare ourselves for any possibility.

    In order to truly be safe, it is important to recognize that we are probably in just as much danger from people who are positively intended and who have never hurt us before. Think of all of the people who unintentionally kill others in automobile accidents. As they say, "The road to hell is paved with good intentions."

12. **Hierarchy of Criteria:** What is a criterion that is potentially more important than those addressed by the belief that has not yet been considered?

    I have always found that figuring out what resources I need in order to successfully complete the path I have chosen and committed to is more important than worrying about the temporarily harmful effects of other people's intentions.

    Don't you think it is more important to avoid being a slave to our fears than it is to avoid the inevitability that we will be hurt at some time?

13. **Apply to Self:** How can you evaluate the belief statement itself according to the relationship or criteria defined by the belief?

Since negative intentions can be so hurtful and dangerous, it is important that we be very clear about the way we understand and act upon our own intentions. Are you certain of the positive intention of your own judgment? When we use our beliefs about someone else's negative intentions as a justification to treat that person the same way that he or she is treating us, we become just like that person.

It can be just as dangerous to think that we are only in jeopardy from those who have hurt us before. Having internal beliefs that force us to relive past instances of hurt over and over again can create as much pain as a negatively intended person that is outside of us.

14. **Meta Frame:** What is a belief about this belief that could change or enrich the perception of the belief?

Research shows that it is natural for people to feel fearful of others and their intentions, until we have developed sufficient self esteem and confidence in our own capabilities.

As long as you are committed to remain in a 'problem frame' about Person X's behavior and intentions, you will be doomed to suffer the consequences. When you are ready to shift to an 'outcome frame' you will begin to find many possible solutions.

Practicing Sleight of Mouth

Practice using these Sleight of Mouth questions for yourself. The following worksheet provides examples of questions which can be used to identify and form Sleight of Mouth reframes. Start by writing down a limiting belief statement that you would like to work with. Make sure that it is a 'complete' belief statement in the form of either a complex equivalence or cause-effect assertion. A typical structure would be:

Referent (am/is/are) judgment because reason.
   I   *not good*   *complex equivalent*
   You   *incapable*   *cause-effect*
   They   *unworthy*
   It   *impossible*

Remember, the purpose of your answers is to reaffirm the identity and positive intention and person who is holding the belief, and, at the same time, reformulate the belief to an outcome frame or feedback frame.

Sleight of Mouth Patterns Worksheet

Limiting Belief: _____ *means / causes*

_____

1. **Intention:** What is the positive purpose or intention of this belief?

_____

2. **Redefining:** What is another word for one of the words used in the belief statement that means something similar but has more positive implications?

_____

3. **Consequence:** What is a positive effect of the belief or the relationship defined by the belief?

_____

4. **Chunk Down:** What *smaller* elements or chunks are implied by the belief but have a richer or more positive relationship than the ones stated in the belief?

_____

5. **Chunk Up:** What *larger* elements or classes are implied by the belief but have a richer or more positive relationship than the ones stated in the belief?

_____

6. **Analogy:** What is some other relationship which is analogous to that defined by the belief (a metaphor for the belief), but which has different implications?

_____

7. **Change Frame Size:** What is a longer (or shorter) time frame, a larger number or smaller number of people, or a bigger or smaller perspective that would change the implications of the belief to be something more positive?

8. **Another Outcome:** What other outcome or issue could be more relevant than the one stated or implied by the belief?

9. **Model of the World:** What is a different model of the world that would provide a very different perspective on this belief?

10. **Reality Strategy:** What cognitive perceptions of the world are necessary to have built this belief? How would one need to perceive the world in order for this belief to be true?

11. **Counter Example:** What is an example or experience that is an exception to the rule defined by the belief?

12. **Hierarchy of Criteria:** What is a criterion that is potentially more important than those addressed by the belief that has not yet been considered?

13. **Apply to Self:** How can you evaluate the belief statement itself according to the relationship or criteria defined by the belief?

14. **Meta Frame:** What other belief about this belief could change or enrich the perception of this belief?

An Example

Take, for example, a common limiting belief such as, "Cancer causes death." The following examples illustrate how these questions can produce various Sleight of Mouth interventions which could offer other perspectives. Keep in mind that the ultimate effect of a particular Sleight of Mouth statement will depend heavily on the tone of voice in which it is said, and the degree of rapport that exists between the speaker and the listener.

Belief: *"Cancer causes death."*

1. **Intention** – I know your intent is to prevent false hope, but you may be blocking any hope at all.

2. **Redefining** – Ultimately, it's not the cancer that causes death; it's the breakdown of the immune system that causes death. Let's find a way to improve the immune system.
   Our perceptions regarding cancer can certainly cause fear and loss of hope, which can make it harder to live.

3. **Consequence** – Unfortunately, beliefs such as this one tend to become self-fulfilling prophecies because people stop looking for choices and options.

4. **Chunk Down** – I've often wondered how much "death" was in each cancer cell?

5. **Chunk Up** – Are you saying that a change or mutation in some small part of the system will always cause the destruction of the entire system?

6. **Analogy** – Cancer is like a grassy field that has begun to turn to weeds because there has not been enough sheep to graze it properly. The white cells of your immune system are like sheep. If stress, lack of exercise, poor diet, etc. reduce the amount of sheep, then the grass gets overgrown and turns to weeds. If you can increase the number of sheep, they can graze the field back into an ecological balance.

7. **Change Frame Size** – If everyone had that belief we would never find a cure. Is that a belief that you would want your children to have?

8. **Another Outcome** – The real issue isn't so much what causes death, as what makes life worth living.

9. **Model of the World** – Many medical people believe that all of us have some mutant cells all the time, and that it is only when our immune system is weak that it creates a problem. They would assert that the presence of a malignancy is only one of a number of co-factors—including diet, attitude, stress, appropriate treatment, etc.—that determine the length of one's life.

10. **Reality Strategy** – How specifically do you represent that belief to yourself? Do you picture the cancer as an intelligent invader? What kind of inner representations do you have of how the body responds? Do you see the body and the immune system as more intelligent than the cancer?

11. **Counter Example** – There are more and more documented cases of people who have had cancer and are surviving and living in good health for many years. How does this belief account for them?

12. **Hierarchy of Criteria** – Perhaps it is more important to focus on our life's purpose and mission, than on how long it will last.

13. **Apply to Self** – That belief has spread like cancer over the past few years; and it's a pretty deadly belief to hold on to too strongly. It would be interesting to see what would happen if it died out.

14. **Meta Frame** – An over-simplified belief such as this can arise when we don't have a model that allows us to explore and test all of the complex variables that contribute to the life and death process.

314   SLEIGHT OF MOUTH

14. Meta Frame
You only believe that because don't have a model of life that allows you to explore, track and test all the complex variables that contribute to the life and death process.

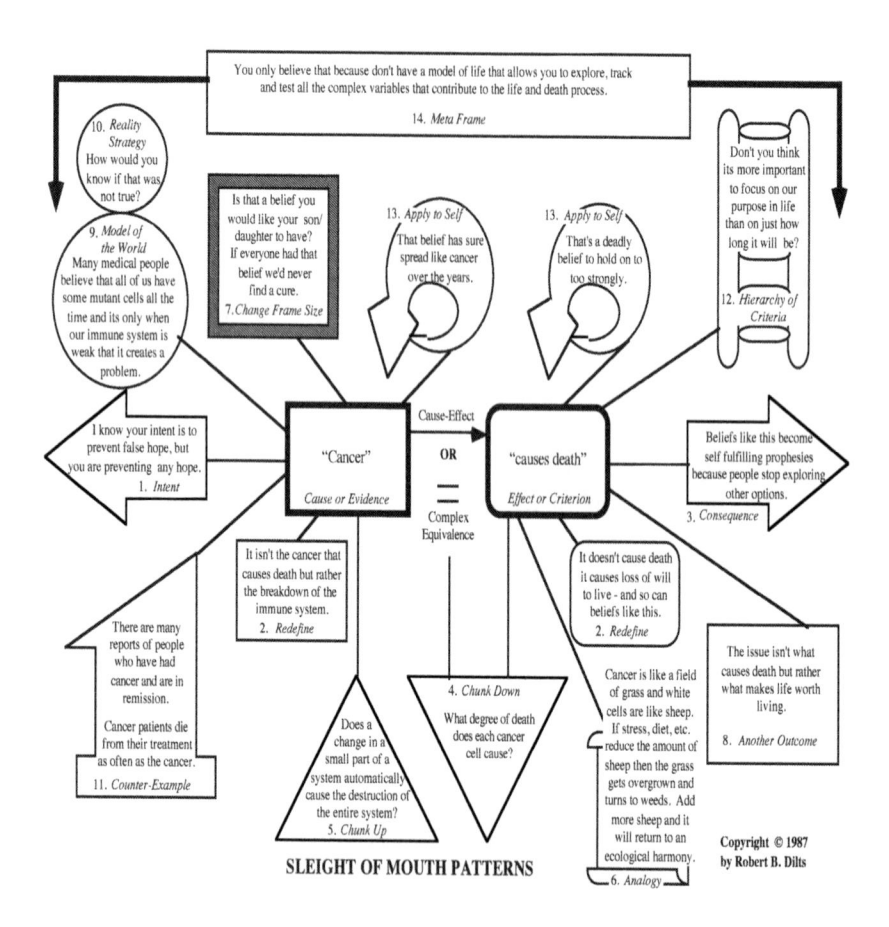

10. Reality Strategy
How would you know if that was not true?

9. Model of the World
Many medical people believe that all of us have some mutant cells all the time and its only when our immune system is weak that it creates a problem.

7. Change Frame Size
Is that a belief you would like your son/daughter to have? If everyone had that belief we'd never find a cure.

13. Apply to Self
That belief has sure spread like cancer over the years.

13. Apply to Self
That's a deadly belief to hold on to too strongly.

Don't you think its more important to focus on our purpose in life than on just how long it will be?

12. Hierarchy of Criteria

1. Intent
I know your intent is to prevent false hope, but you are preventing any hope.

"Cancer"
Cause or Evidence

Cause-Effect
OR
=
Complex Equivalence

"causes death"
Effect or Criterion

3. Consequence
Beliefs like this become self fulfilling prophesies because people stop exploring other options.

11. Counter-Example
There are many reports of people who have had cancer and are in remission.
Cancer patients die from their treatment as often as the cancer.

2. Redefine
It isn't the cancer that causes death but rather the breakdown of the immune system.

4. Chunk Down
What degree of death does each cancer cell cause?

5. Chunk Up
Does a change in a small part of a system automatically cause the destruction of the entire system?

2. Redefine
It doesn't cause death it causes loss of will to live - and so can beliefs like this.

6. Analogy
Cancer is like a field of grass and white cells are like sheep. If stress, diet, etc. reduce the amount of sheep then the grass gets overgrown and turns to weeds. Add more sheep and it will return to an ecological harmony.

8. Another Outcome
The issue isn't what causes death but rather what makes life worth living.

SLEIGHT OF MOUTH PATTERNS

Copyright © 1987 by Robert B. Dilts

Chapter 10

Conclusion

Conclusion

This first volume of *Sleight of Mouth* has focused on the 'magic of language', and the power of words to shape our perceptions and attitude about our own behavior and the world around us. Building from the principle that *the map is not the territory*, we have explored the impact that language has upon our experience, and upon the generalizations and beliefs (both limiting and empowering) that we derive from our experience. We have examined the ways in which certain types and patterns of words are able to frame and 'reframe' our perceptions, either expanding or limiting the choices we perceive as available to us.

We have also made an in depth analysis of the linguistic structure of beliefs, and have established that *limiting beliefs* are those which frame our experience in terms of *problems, failure* and *impossibility*. When such beliefs become the primary framework around which we construct our models of the world, they can bring about a sense of hopelessness, helplessness or worthlessness with respect to our lives and actions. In this regard, the goal of applying the Sleight of Mouth patterns is to help people shift attention from:

1) a *'problem'* frame to an *'outcome'* frame
2) a *'failure'* frame to a *'feedback'* frame
3) an *'impossibility'* frame to an *'as if'* frame

The Sleight of Mouth patterns are comprised of fourteen distinct verbal 'reframing' patterns. The purpose of these patterns is to reconnect our generalizations and mental models of the world to our experience and the other aspects forming the 'meta structure' of our beliefs: internal states, expectations and values. The book has provided specific definitions and examples of each pattern, and of how the patterns may be used together as a system. The patterns may be applied in order to accomplish such outcomes as reframing criticism, leveraging hierarchies of criteria to build motivation, strengthening empowering beliefs by acting 'as if', and becoming more 'open to doubt' limiting beliefs by finding new and more enriching perspectives.

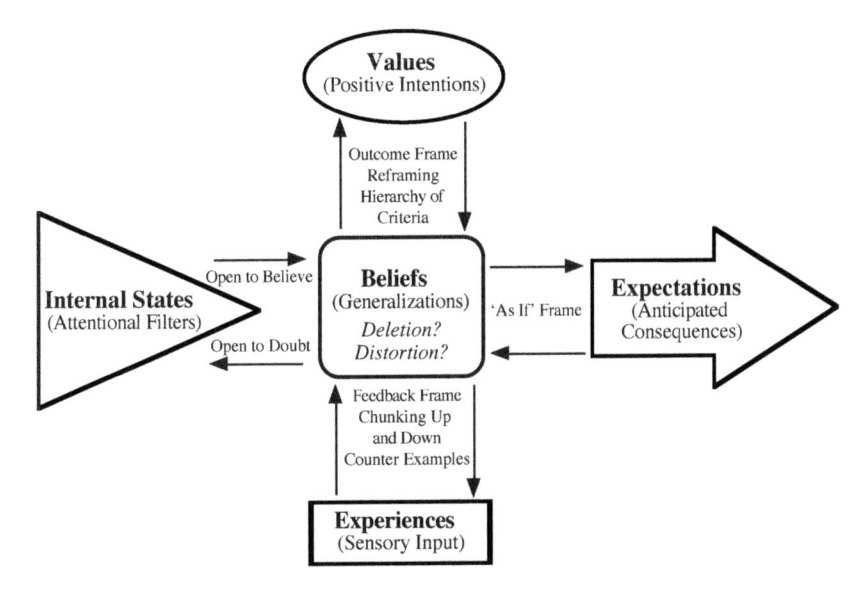

```
                    Values
              (Positive Intentions)
                       ↑
                 Outcome Frame
                   Reframing
                 Hierarchy of
                   Criteria
                       ↓
                              
  Internal States  → Open to Believe →  Beliefs           Expectations
  (Attentional                        (Generalizations)   (Anticipated
   Filters)       ← Open to Doubt ←    Deletion?          Consequences)
                                       Distortion?
                                         ↑
                                   Feedback Frame
                                   Chunking Up
                                   and Down
                                   Counter Examples
                                         ↓
                                     Experiences
                                   (Sensory Input)
```

Sleight of Mouth Patterns Help Us to Update Our Beliefs by Reconnecting Them to Experiences, Values, Expectations and Internal States

The fundamental strategy that we have followed for using Sleight of Mouth patterns involves, first, identifying the positive intentions behind limiting beliefs and the values that drive them, and then finding other more appropriate and useful ways of satisfying those positive intentions. The various Sleight of Mouth patterns help us to do this by prompting us to:

- 'repunctuate' and 'rechunk' our perceptions
- identify and appreciate different perspectives and alternative models of the world
- discover the internal strategies by which we assess 'reality', and through which we form and update our beliefs

- explore the ways in which we build the mental maps by which we form expectations, determine cause, and give meaning to our experience of the world around us
- recognize the influence of our internal states on our beliefs and attitudes
- pace the natural process of belief change
- better understand the impact of language and beliefs on different levels of our experience
- become more aware of potential verbal 'thought viruses' and unspoken assumptions and presuppositions

In many respects, what this book presents is just the beginning of the potential applications of the Sleight of Mouth patterns. The Sleight of Mouth patterns form a powerful system of language patterns which can be applied to produce deep and far reaching changes. These patterns have been used throughout human history as the primary means for stimulating and directing social change and for evolving our collective models of the world. The next volume of Sleight of Mouth, for instance, will examine how historical figures (such as Socrates, Jesus, Lincoln, Gandhi, Einstein, and others) have applied Sleight of Mouth patterns to shape the religious, scientific, political and philosophical systems which form our modern world. It will explore how these individuals sought to address and 'outframe' the thought viruses behind racism, violence, economic and political oppression, etc.

Volume II of Sleight of Mouth will also define fundamental strategies for using groups and sequences of Sleight of Mouth patterns, and explore the structure of the belief or 'convincer' strategies by which we form and assess belief systems (such as George Polya's *patterns of 'plausible inference'*). It will also cover how the principles, distinctions and patterns that we have explored in this book can help to: (a) identify and address logical fallacies, limiting beliefs and thought viruses; (b) manage expectations and the 'Bandura Curve'; (c) deal with double binds; and much more.

Afterword

I hope you have enjoyed this exploration into *Sleight of Mouth*. If you are interested in exploring these patterns or other aspects of Neuro-Linguistic Programming in more depth, other resources and tools exist to further develop and apply the distinctions, strategies and skills described within these pages.

NLP University is an organization committed to providing the highest quality trainings in basic and advanced NLP skills, and to promoting the development of new models and applications of NLP in the areas of health, business and organization, creativity and learning. Each Summer, NLP University holds residential programs at the University of California at Santa Cruz, offering extended residential courses on the skills of NLP, including advanced language patterns such as Sleight of Mouth.

For more information please contact:

NLP University
P.O. Box 1112
Ben Lomond, California 95005
Phone: (831) 336-3457
Fax: (831) 336-5854
E-Mail: Teresanlp@aol.com
Homepage: http://www.nlpu.com

In addition to the programs I do at NLP University, I also travel internationally, presenting seminars and specialty programs on a variety of topics related to NLP and Sleight of Mouth. I have also written a number of other books and developed computer software and audio tapes based on the principles and distinctions of NLP.

For example, I have recently completed several software tools based on my modeling of Strategies of Genius: *Vision to Action*, *Imagineering Strategy* and *Journey to Genius Adventure*.

For more information on these programs, my schedule of seminars or other NLP related products and resources, please contact:

Journey to Genius
P.O. Box 67448
Scotts Valley, CA 95067-7448
Phone (831) 438-8314
Fax (831) 438-8571
E-Mail: info@journeytogenius.com
Homepage: http://www.journeytogenius.com

Bibliography

Bandler, R.; ***Using Your Brain***; Real People Press, Moab, UT, 1985.

Bandler, R. and Grinder, J.; ***The Structure of Magic, Volumes I & II***; Science and Behavior Books, Palo Alto, CA, 1975, 1976.

Bandler, R. and Grinder, J.; ***Patterns of the Hypnotic Techniques of Milton H. Erickson, M.D., Volumes I & II***; Meta Publications, Capitola, CA, 1975, 1977.

Bandler R. and Grinder, J.; ***Frogs into Princes***; Real People Press, Moab, UT, 1979.

Bandler R. and Grinder, J.; ***Reframing***; Real People Press, Moab, UT, 1982.

Bandler, R. and LaValle, J.; ***Persuasion Engineering***; Meta Publications, Capitola, CA, 1996.

Bateson, G.; ***Steps to an Ecology of Mind***; Ballantine Books, New York, NY, 1972.

Bateson, G.; ***Mind and Nature***; E. P. Dutton, New York, NY, 1979.

Cameron-Bandler, L., ***Solutions (They Lived Happily Ever After)***, FuturePace, San Rafael, CA, 1978.

Chomsky, N., ***Syntactic Structures***, Mouton, The Hague, The Netherlands, 1957.

Chomsky, N., ***Language and Mind***, Harcourt Brace Jovanovich, Inc., New York, NY, 1968.

DeLozier, J. and Grinder, J.; *Turtles All The Way Down*; Grinder, DeLozier & Associates, Santa Cruz, CA 1987.

Dilts, R., Grinder, J., Bandler, R. and DeLozier, J.; *Neuro-Linguistic Programming: The Study of the Structure of Subjective Experience, Vol. I;* Meta Publications, Capitola, CA, 1980.

Dilts R., DeLozier, J. and Epstein, T.; *The Encyclopedia of Systemic NLP*; NLP University Press, Ben Lomond, CA, 1999.

Dilts, R.; *Modeling With NLP*; Meta Publications, Capitola, CA, 1998.

Dilts R.; *Visionary Leadership Skills: Creating a World to which People Want to Belong*; Meta Publications, Capitola, CA, 1996.

Dilts R.; *The Law of Requisite Variety*; NLP University Press, Ben Lomond, CA, 1998.

Dilts R.; *Effective Presentation Skills*; Meta Publications, Capitola, CA, 1994.

Dilts R. with Bonissone, G.; *Skills for the Future: Managing Creativity and Innovation*; Meta Publications, Capitola, CA, 1993.

Dilts, R. B., Epstein, T. and Dilts, R. W.; *Tools for Dreamers: Strategies of Creativity and the Structure of Innovation;* Meta Publications, Capitola, Ca., 1991.

Dilts R.; *Changing Belief Systems with NLP;* Meta Publications, Capitola, Ca., 1990.

Dilts R., Hallbom, T. and Smith, S.; **Beliefs: Pathways to Health and Well-Being;** Metamorphous Press, Portland, OR, 1990.

Dilts, R.; **Applications of NLP;** Meta Publications, Capitola, CA, 1983.

Dilts, R. & Epstein, T.; **Dynamic Learning;** Meta Publications, Capitola, CA, 1995.

Dilts R.; **Strategies of Genius, Volumes I, II & III;** Meta Publications, Capitola, CA, 1994-1995.

Dilts R.; *NLP and Self-Organization Theory;* Anchor Point, June 1995, Anchor Point Assoc., Salt Lake City, UT.

Dilts R.; *NLP, Self-Organization and Strategies of Change Management;* Anchor Point, July 1995, Anchor Point Associates, Salt Lake City, UT.

Dilts, R.,"*Let NLP Work for You*", Real Estate Today, February, 1982, Vol. 15, No. 2.

Eicher, J.; **Making the Message Clear: Communicating for Business;** Grinder, DeLozier & Associates, Santa Cruz, CA, 1987.

Erickson, M. H.; **Advanced Techniques of Hypnosis and Therapy; Selected Papers of Milton H. Erickson, M.D.**, Haley, J. [Editor], Grune & Stratton Inc., New York, NY, 1967.

Gordon, D.; **Therapeutic Metaphor**, Meta Publications, Capitola, CA, 1978.

Haley, J.; **Uncommon Therapy; The Psychiatric Techniques of Milton H. Erickson M.D.**, W. W. Norton & Co., Inc., New York, NY, 1973.

Korzybski, A.; **Science and Sanity**, The International Non-Aristotelian Library Publishing Company, Lakeville, CN, 1980.

Laborde, G.; **Influencing With Integrity: Management Skills for Communication and Negotiation**; Syntony Inc., Palo Alto, CA, 1982.

Lofland, D.; **Thought Viruses**, Harmony Books, New York, NY, 1997.

McMaster, M. and Grinder, J.; **Precision: A New Approach to Communication;** Precision, Los Angeles, CA 1981.

Moine, D.; *"Patterns of Persuasion";* Personal Selling Journal, 1981, 1 (4), 3.

O'Connor, J. and Seymour, J.; **Introducing Neuro-Linguistic Programming**; Aquarian Press, Cornwall, England, 1990.

Index

A

Abductive Thinking 68, 69
Accessing and Anchoring a
   State 189
Accessing Cues 95
AIDS 150, 151, 216, 217, 298
Allergy 129, 145, 169
Analogy *68-71*, *260*, 303,
   309, 312
Anchoring 189, 193, 199
Another Outcome *26-30*, 40,
   262, 275, 280, 281, 282,
   284, 291, 292, 304, 310, 313
Apply to Self *234-240*, *267*,
   274, 294, 307, 311, 313
Applying a Belief to Itself 234
Aristotle 9, 148, 150, 152,
   154, 159
'As If' Exercise 140
'As If' Frame 138-140, 316
Assessing Motivation for
   Change 134
Assumptions 221, 222, 229
Autonomic Nervous System
   111
Axiology 81

B

Bacteria 215
Bandler, Richard 8-9, 12, 15, 57,
   122, 206, 226, 271-288, 296
Bandura, Albert 120, 318
Bannister, Roger 114
Bateson, Gregory 68, 69, 146,
   202, 231, 232, 243,
   244, 245, 246

Behavior Level 247, 285, 286
Belief Assessment 135, 136
Belief Assessment Sheet 136
Belief Audit 164, 165, 166
Belief Chaining 197, 199,
   200, 201
Belief Chaining Procedure 199
Belief Change 176-178, 183,
   184, 192, 195, 197
Belief Change Cycle 177,
   178, 192-197
Belief Change Cycle Procedure
   192
Belief Issues Related to Change
   132
Belief Systems 110
Beliefs 80, *110-120*, 125,
   126, 131, 132, 134, 136,
   138, 142, 154, 155, 156,
   164, 165, 176, 184, 206,
   207, 211, 246, 247
Beliefs and Values Level 247
Believing 180, 193

C

Cabaret (Movie) 35
Cameron-Bandler, Leslie 38
Cancer 114, 211, 216, 223,
   228, 270, 297, 298, 311,
   312, 313
Capability Level 247
Catch-22 231
Cause 110
Cause-Effect *142-147*, 170,
   223, 284, 292
Causes *146-155*, 159

Chaining 197, 198, 199, 200, 201
Chaining Criteria 85, 86
Changing Frame Size *33-37*, 39, *261*, 274, 278, 279, 280, 282, 284, 285, 286, 288, 292, 293, 295, 304, 310, 312
Changing Logical Levels 250
Childbirth 34
Chomsky, Noam 11
Chunk Down *62-64*, 97, *258*, 274, 278, 284, 292, 293, 294, 295, 302, 309, 312
Chunk Laterally 62, 71
Chunk Up 62, *66-67*, *259*, 274, 276, 277, 278, 280, 281, 285, 287, 290, 291, 294, 303, 309, 312
Chunking 60, 61, 63, 66, 68, 69, 73, 87, 98
Chunking Down 60, 61, 63, 69, 87
Chunking Laterally 60, 68, 69, 86
Chunking Up 60, 61, 66, 67, 69, 98
Circular Argument 228, 231, 283
Collateral Energy 146
Complex Equivalence *142-144*, 170, 223, 295
Computer 'Anti-Virus' Program 218
Computer Virus 214, 215
Congruency 95
Connectives 158, 159
Consequence *127-130*, *257*, 274, 277-279, 280, 281, 283-285, 290-296, 302, 309, 312
Constraining Causes 148, 150, 154
Content Reframing 40-42
Context 22, 79, 95
Context Reframing 38, 39
Continuity 94
Core Criteria 83
Counter Example 98-102, *167-169*, *172-174*, *265*, 274, 276, 277, 278, 282, 285, 290, 292, 296, 306, 310, 313
Counter-Expectations 126
Criteria *83-89*, 98, 99, 101, 103, 104, 105, 110, 155
Criterial Equivalence *87-89*, 104-107, 129, 143, 155, 294
Criticism 43-47, 61
Critics 41, 43, 44, 46-48, 75
Currently Believe 193, 195, 196

D

Deductive Reasoning 69
Deep Structure 79, 110
Deep structure 9
Desired State 199, 200, 201
Disappointment 122, 125
Double Binds 230, 231
Dreamer 75

E

Einstein, Albert 13, 144, 147, 172
Emotions Inventory 187
Environmental Level 247
Erickson, Milton H. 27, 28, 139, 226
'Even Though' Reframe 20
Evidence Procedure 87

INDEX

Expectation 120-127, 131, 138, 206, 207, 317
Experience 14-18, 206, 207, 317
External Reference 228

F

Failure Frame 25, 211, 273, 316
Fear 130
Feedback Frame 25, 43, 63, 174, 278, 279, 294, 300, 316
Final Causes 149, 150, 151, 154
Formal Causes 149-154
Frames 22-24, 79, 288, 316
Framing 18, 22-24, 31, 79, 288, 316
Franklin, Benjamin 142
Freud, Sigmund 2, 120, 126, 241

G

General Semantics 11, 12
Generalization 63, 66, 84, 110, 207, 209, 211, 234, 292
Genetic Code 217
Goals 82
Gospel of John 236
Greek Mythology 190
Greek Philosophy 9, 10
Grinder, John 8, 9, 12, 15, 226

H

Hamlet 12
Health 132, 133, 160, 161
Heller, Joseph 231
Helplessness 116, 121
Heraclitus 10

Hierarchy of Criteria *98-106*, *266*, 286, 306, 311, 313
Hierarchy of Criteria Technique 104-106
Hitler, Adolph 123, 124, 289
Homeopathy 34
Hopelessness 116, 121
'How' Questions 46, 47, 118, 130

I

Identity 247, 250
Identity Level 247, 250, 251, 276, 285, 286, 287
Immune System 218, 219, 220, 298, 299
Inductive Reasoning 69
Inferences 221, 222
Inner Mentors 190, 191
Intention *48-49*, 62, 79, *255*, 275, 276, 277, 278, 281, 283, 284, 291, 293, 295, 301, 308, 312
Internal Representations 79
Internal State 201, 284
Internal States 184-186, 188, 203, 206, 207, 285, 317
Isomorphism 71

J

Jesus 237, 238, 289, 318
Judgment 83

K

Korzybski, Alfred 11, 12, 13

L

Language 2, 8, 9, 18
Law 55, 56
Law of Individuality 11

Law of Requisite Variety 297-299
Learning 63, 66, 68
Learning Disability 63, 66, 68
Learning II 245
Learning-To-Learn 245
Leonardo da Vinci 97
Leveraging 106
Limbic System 111
Limiting Beliefs *116-119*, 167, 170, 208, 209, 211, 212, 215, 216, 220, 223, 243, 273, 277, 288, 289, 296, 300, 301 316, 317
Linguistic Presuppositions 221, 222, 226
Linguistic Structure of Beliefs 142
Logical Levels 243, *246-249*, 250, 251
Logical Types 232, 233, 243, 244, 245, 246
Logos 9, 10
Lundy, John 114

M

Magic 2
Map and Territory 11, 56, 78, 211, 316
Mapping Key Beliefs and Expectations 131
Maslow, Abraham 113
McLuhan, Marshall 79
Meaning 78-81, 110
Medium 79
Mein Kampf 123
Mentor 137, 140, 190, 191, 193-195
Mentoring and Inner Mentors 190
Messages 79

Meta Frame *240-242, 268,* 277, 279, 280, 281, 283, 290, 292, 294, 295, 296, 307, 311, 313
'Meta' Memory 95
Meta Messages 80, 204, 243, 244
Meta Position 240
Meta Structure of Beliefs 206, 212, 317
Metaphorical Thinking 69, 71
Model of the World 16, *55-56, 263,* 277, 291, 292, 305, 310, 313
Modeling 289
Motivation 81, 82, 88, 110, 122, 134
Mozart, Wolfgang 97
Museum of Personal History 182, 193, 196

N

Native Americans 62
Natural Cycle of Belief Change 183
Natural Process of Belief Change 176
Negative Statements 45
Neuro-Linguistic Programming 8, 11
Neuro-Logical Levels 246, 247
Neurolinguistics 12
New Guinea 184
Nietzsche, Friedrich 81
NLP Presuppositions 48, 56, 127
Nominalizations 84
Non-Verbal Communication 80, 202, 203, 204
Non-Verbal Cues 188

INDEX

O

Obsessive Compulsive 128
Odysseus 190
One-Word Reframing 52, 53
Open to Believe 178, 180, 193, 195, 210
Open to Doubt 179, 181, 193, 195, 196, 210
Outcome Expectation 120-122, 130
Outcome Frame *23-24*, 43, 49, 279, 281, 282, 285, 286, 291, 293, 294, 295, 300, 316
Outcomes 26
Outframing 300

P

Pacing 107
Pain 51
Para-Messages 80
Paradox 230
Paranoia 272
Pattern 19
Perceptual Positions 55
Persuasion 102
Philo 10
Physiological Inventory 187
Placebo 121, 129
Placebo Effect 121, 129, 134
Play 243, 244
Polya, George 318
Positive Intention *40-45*, 48, 118, 201, 224, 291
Positive Reformulations of Negative Statements 45
Precipitating Causes 148, 150, 154
Presuppositions 118, 119, 213, 214, *221-227*, 229, 292

Primary Experience 16
Probability 95
Problem Frame *23-24*, 43, 49, 208, 209, 211, 273, 274, 276, 277, 279, 280, 282, 286, 287, 288, 290, 291, 293, 294, 296, 316
Problem State 199, 200
Propaganda 123, 124
Psychosis 244
Punctuation 73-75, 317

Q

Questions 45, 46, 300, 308

R

"Real Imaginary Fleas" 128, 129
Realist 75
Reality Strategy *89-97*, 129, *264*, 284, 293, 295, 305, 310, 313
Reality Strategy Exercise 93-97
Recursion 233
Redefining *48-51*, 62, 85, 201, *256*, 278, 280, 281, 282, 285, 286, 290, 295, 296, 301, 309, 312
Reframing *31-33*, 38, 40, 42, 43, 52, 53, 79, 300, 316
Reframing Critics and Criticism 43
Reinforcement 125
Remission 152, 153
Representational Systems 94, 104
Repunctuation 73
Requisite Variety 297
Russell, Bertrand 52, 232, 233, 243, 246

S

Salem Witch Trials 231
Santa Claus 182
Schizophrenia 244
Science and Sanity 11
Second Position 55, 191
Secondary Experience 16
Self Esteem 133
Self Fulfilling Prophesies 123
Self Reference 228-231, 233, 240
Self Referential Statements 230
Self-Efficacy Expectation 120-122, 130, 173
Sensory Experience 14, 15, 206
Serra, Tony 55
Six-Step Reframing 42
Sleight of Hand 6
Sleight of Mouth 2, 6, 17, 25, 154, 156, 254, 269, 270, 316
Sleight of Mouth Patterns 254-268, 269, 270, 300, 316
Sleight of Mouth Patterns Worksheet 308
Sleight of Mouth System 269, 270
Spiritual Level 247
Strengthening Belief 137, 138
Structure of Beliefs 154, 206, 316
Structure of Magic 8, 12
Structure of Meaning 78
Submodalities 88, 90, 94, 96, 104, 187, 189
Submodality Inventory 187
Surface Structure 9, 213, 289

T

Tesla, Nicola 97
Theory of Logical Types 232
Therapeutic Metaphors 71
Thought Viruses 117, *211-220*, 225, 243, 271, 272, 288, 299, 300, 318
Threshold 271
Time Frame 22
Timing 94
Trust 183, 194, 195, 196
Types of Causes 148

U

Universal Quantifiers 61
Uptime 15
Used to Believe 179, 182, 193, 196

V

Values *80-83*, 85, 87, 110, 156, 158, 206, 207, 317
Values Audit 158, 162, 163
Values Audit Worksheet 163
Variety 298
Verbal Frames for Eliciting Limiting Belief Statements 170
Verbal Framing 18, 19, 20
Verbal Prompts 170
Viral Sentence 229
Virus *214-219*, 225, 298, 299

W

Wanting to Believe 178, 179, 193, 195
Why Questions 158
Words 2, 50
Worthlessness 116

www.ingramcontent.com/pod-product-compliance
Ingram Content Group UK Ltd.
Pitfield, Milton Keynes, MK11 3LW, UK
UKHW021855140825
461856UK00006B/53